CUTTING PERFORMANCES

THEATER: THEORY/TEXT/PERFORMANCE

Series Editors: David Krasner and Rebecca Schneider

Founding Editor: Enoch Brater

Recent Titles:

The Stage Life of Props by Andrew Sofer

Playing Underground: A Critical History of the 1960s Off-Off-Broadway Movement by Stephen J. Bottoms

Arthur Miller's America: Theater and Culture in a Time of Change edited by Enoch Brater

Looking Into the Abyss: Essays on Scenography by Arnold Aronson

Avant-Garde Performance and the Limits of Criticism: Approaching the Living Theatre, Happenings/Fluxus, and the Black Arts Movement by Mike Sell

Not the Other Avant-Garde: The Transnational Foundations of Avant-Garde Performance edited by James M. Harding and John Rouse

The Purpose of Playing: Modern Acting Theories in Perspective by Robert Gordon

Staging Philosophy: Intersections of Theater, Performance, and Philosophy edited by David Krasner and David Z. Saltz

Critical Theory and Performance: Revised and Enlarged Edition edited by Janelle G. Reinelt and Joseph R. Roach

Reflections on Beckett: A Centenary Celebration edited by Anna McMullan and S. E. Wilmer

Performing Conquest: Five Centuries of Theater, History, and Identity in Tlaxcala, Mexico by Patricia A. Ybarra

The President Electric: Ronald Reagan and the Politics of Performance by Timothy Raphael

Cutting Performances: Collage Events, Feminist Artists, and the American Avant-Garde by James M. Harding

Illusive Utopia: Theater, Film, and Everyday Performance in North Korea by Suk-Young Kim

Embodying Black Experience: Stillness, Critical Memory, and the Black Body by Harvey Young

No Safe Spaces: Re-casting Race, Ethnicity, and Nationality in American Theater by Angela C. Pao

Artaud and His Doubles by Kimberly Jannarone

The Problem of the Color[blind]: Racial Transgression and the Politics of Black Performance by Brandi Wilkins Catanese

The Sarah Siddons Audio Files: Romanticism and the Lost Voice by Judith Pascoe

Paul Robeson and the Cold War Performance Complex: Race, Madness, Activism by Tony Perucci

CUTTING PERFORMANCES

Collage Events, Feminist Artists, and the American Avant-Garde

James M. Harding

THE UNIVERSITY OF MICHIGAN PRESS
Ann Arbor

First paperback edition 2012

Published in the United States of America by
The University of Michigan Press
Manufactured in the United States of America
⊗ Printed on acid-free paper

2015 2014 2013 2012 5 4 3 2

A CIP catalog record for this book is available from the British Library.

Library of Congress Cataloging-in-Publication Data

Harding, James Martin, 1958–
Cutting performances : collage events, feminist artists, and the American avant-garde / James M. Harding.
p. cm. — (Theater : theory/text/performance)
Includes bibliographical references and index.
ISBN 978-0-472-11718-5 (cloth : alk. paper)
1. Experimental theater. 2. Feminist theater. I. Title.
PN2193.E86H37 2009
792.02'2—dc22 2009033201

978-0-472-02900-6 (e-book)

ISBN: 978-0-472-03520-5 (paper : alk. paper)

for Friederike

Acknowledgments

The original conception of this book as well as its earliest drafts began during the 2001–2 academic year while I was teaching at the Institut für Theaterwissenschaft at the Freie Universität in Berlin. I want to begin by thanking the Fulbright Scholar Program for the support that it provided that year, during which I was able to complete much of the reading and initial writing for this book. I am also extremely grateful to three individuals in particular for their efforts to make that year a reality. Their support ultimately made this book possible. First and foremost, I am grateful to Erika Fischer-Lichte, who invited me to Berlin, gave me an office and a new computer, and told me to write. She challenged me as a visiting colleague and inspired me with her intellect and her inexhaustible energy as a scholar. At my home institution, the chair of my own department at that time was Bill Kemp, who went to great lengths in negotiating with our dean, Phil Hall, in his efforts to facilitate my trip to Berlin. The two of them came up with a plan that worked, and I was the beneficiary of that plan. They have both since retired. But my gratitude to them endures. The leave time that I needed in order to get this project under way would not have been possible without their efforts and goodwill.

In the scholarly and intellectual journeys that have accompanied this book, I have had the unbelievable good fortune of friendships with scholars who have generously shared their time, knowledge, insight, and criticism with me. The American Society of Theatre Research has provided much of the context for those exchanges, and its conferences have played no small role in cultivating the work that ultimately found its way into the pages of this book. Its forums have also cultivated what have become my closest intellectual and professional friendships, the very friendships that I have relied on time and again as I formulated, tested, and then reformulated the arguments that are the backbone of each of the book's individual chapters.

There are those whose goodwill and encouragement helped to facilitate this project. Then there are those without whom the core arguments in the following pages would have never taken shape. I can't begin to adequately express how profound the intellectual debt is that I owe to Cindy Rosenthal, to Mike Sell, and to John Rouse. Their critical insights echo through this book. The projects that I have had the privilege of working on with them have everything to do with what I understand the avant-garde to be and what I realize it is not. It is equally difficult for me to imagine this project without the insights I have gained from many, many hours of conversation with Jean Graham-Jones, Kimberly Jannarone, and Janelle Reinelt (who, it is worth noting, gave me feedback on the first draft of the first chapter I wrote). I have benefitted greatly from advice that Rebecca Schneider gave me as the project neared completion. I am also indebted to the advice and comments provided by my outside readers during the review process.

Looking back again to my department at the University of Mary Washington, I also know that my own students have played a significant role in the formulation of the ideas that have found their way into this book—if only because my students were willing to explore those ideas with me as I began to piece them together into arguments. I cannot imagine scholarship—this project or any other—without teaching. The two go hand in hand, and in this respect, I am grateful for the rich teaching opportunities that I have at the University of Mary Washington. Behind the scenes of those opportunities is the extremely dedicated chair of my department, Teresa Kennedy, whom I admire greatly and who semester after semester has gone out of her way to let me teach classes that would support the completion of this project. She has been a genuine friend and colleague. So too have my colleagues Marie McAllister, Mara Scanlan, Judith Parker, and Mary Rigsby—all of whom have been receptive to my questions and generous in their advice on individual points and arguments.

The most important venue for my work is, of course, the one in which it now appears: the University of Michigan Press. My sense of gratitude to the press in general is surpassed only by the specific sense of gratitude that I have for LeAnn Fields, who, simply put, is one of the champions of theater and performance studies. It is a true privilege to work with her. I am grateful to her for support and encouragement not only of this project but of my work from the earliest days of my career. I also want to thank the production staff at the University of Michigan for all of the work that they have done to put this work in print.

Finally, I want to thank my partner Friederike Eigler, the one constant throughout this entire project. It often seems a matter of convention to thank one's partner for the support that she or he has provided during the completion of a scholarly work, and by implication this suggests a kind of support that is distinct from the intellectual inquiries of scholarship itself. While in our relationship there are these kinds of moments—and they go both ways—the more significant, indeed the more fundamental, moments are those that have had a profound impact on the actual substance of what I write. Friederike's own work as a feminist scholar and literary theorist inspired me to take up a project like the one that follows, and I don't think she will ever fully realize how consistently her responses to my passing queries in conversations about theory helped me to negotiate the difficult conceptual terrain in the book that I was writing. Intellectually, there is no one to whom I am more indebted. There is no one with whom I struggle more. There is no one whom I respect more. And there is no one for whom I have deeper affection and love.

Chapter 6 is a slightly revised version of my article "The Simplest Surrealist Act: Valerie Solanas and the (Re)Assertion of Avantgarde Priorities," which was originally published in *TDR* 45.4 (2001): 142–62.

Contents

CHAPTER ONE

Toward a Feminist Historiography of American Avant-Garde Performance

Theories and Contexts

Disparate Unities: The Vanguard, the Popular, and the Erasure of Women

A little over a decade ago, Jill Dolan paused momentarily in the introductory essay that she wrote for Carol Martin's *A Sourcebook of Feminist Theatre and Performance*. In this pause, Dolan reflected on her own history as a feminist theorist and historian. Her "own history of feminism in the academy," she recalls, "is about thinking [. . . she would] be the only one," that is, about going to conferences and worrying that she would be the only feminist or worrying that she would be "the only lesbian" among feminists. This initial anxiety, she notes, ultimately gave way to a delight in discovering not only that she was not the only feminist or lesbian at the conferences she attended but also that at these conferences she "could have conversations and arguments over whatever" she perceived as her "differences."[1] In 1996 as Dolan penned these reflections, she was writing from a hard-won position within the academy that the collective efforts of feminist scholars like herself had done much to secure, and if as a point of departure I cite one related example of the continued success of those efforts—namely, the 2004 annual conference of the American Society for Theatre Research, which supported Research Groups in "Feminist Historiography" and "Queer Research"—I do so because of the pivotal role that the meeting of the Feminist Historiography Group at that conference had in my own history of feminism, in this project, and in my own subject position as its author.

My interest in Dolan's reflections rests upon a rather ironic sense of identification with her anxiousness about "being the only one" in the early years of her work as a feminist theorist and historian. I am far from blind to the larger irony of this identification, given my own position as a heterosexual male. But my more immediate concerns have to do with the disturbing implications that followed a decision to sit in on what proved to be a highly successful session of the Feminist Historiography Group at ASTR 2004—a decision that much to my dismay positioned me as the "only male" among the forty to fifty participants and observers. (One other male joined about midway through the session.) The irony here was that while Dolan's early experiences of being the "only one" heralded the emergence of new critical methodologies, my experience, I fear, signaled the gravitational pull of old critical habits and socially constructed divisions—a pull that is evident not only in theater studies but across the humanities. Whereas Dolan's experiences were part of a larger struggle by feminists to find an acknowledged place at the table, my experience suggested an ironic gendered reversal. It suggested not a struggle by men to find an acknowledged place at the table of feminist discourse but a disinclination by my male counterparts to take up the invitation that is open to them.

If that Research Group had followed something along the lines of a cultural feminist model and had been open exclusively to female scholars, perhaps there would have been little cause for my dismay. Yet the issue here was not the calculated exclusion of men in a solidarity of sisterhood but rather the apparent hesitancy of men to participate. Indeed, as an open session where I was welcomed as a colleague and friend, the meeting of the Feminist Historiography Group left me wondering how such a pronounced gender division in scholarly endeavors was even conceivable today, particularly since feminist-based scholarship arguably has done more than any other movement in the last twenty-five years to reshape understanding not only of theater studies but of virtually every discipline in the humanities. Consequently, my being "the only one," the only male, hinted at an alarming but subtle retrenchment. It suggested a gendered factional indifference fueled by a pervasive sense that feminist historiography is women's work and that the widespread institutional recognition of feminist scholarship, ironically, means men can now politically afford to overlook it without facing accusations of bias. Provocative though it may be, translating an anecdote about a particular research group into a broad characterization of the gender dynamics within the humanities may be too much of a generalization, so I want to limit the focus of this characterization to studies of the avant-garde, and in particular to studies of avant-garde performance.

At one level, Dolan provides an important justification for this focus in the same essay in which she reflects on her own history of feminism in the academy. Noting the strong interest that feminist theorists have had in "performance art" as "a resistant site of production," Dolan observes that, like performance art more generally, feminist performance art remains "culturally marginalized and 'avant-garde' in its traditions."[2] In Dolan's argument, this observation serves as a foil for a compelling plea to "feminist critics and theatremakers" to broaden their critical scope and "to generate and comment on texts written"[3] for the theatrical and literary mainstream. But before we dive too deeply into the mainstream, some consideration ought to be given to the presumptions governing the margins where Dolan positions the experimental performances of feminist artists. The need for this consideration is simple. Despite the substantial amount of scholarly attention that these performances have received, the historiographic significance that feminist art from the margins has for the very avant-garde traditions in which Dolan locates it has never been adequately theorized. Indeed, locating feminist performance art within the tradition of the avant-garde begs the question of whether the two are actually compatible, whether one compromises the other, or, to put it in more neutral terms, whether and how the association of experimental feminist art and the traditions of the avant-garde transforms our understanding of both.

Any feminist historiography of avant-garde performance has to address this question of compatibility and compromise. As has been the case with so many aspects of performance history, part of this question centers on the basic threat of erasure that has long haunted feminists in the theater more generally. Feminist theorists have frequently conceptualized the notion of "erasure" to reference the many ways in which women have found opportunities to perform only by submitting to conditions that ultimately perpetuate the structures of their own repression. In the mainstream, the terms of those opportunities have demanded a constrictive affirmation of normative assumptions about gender, sexuality, and femininity. The "desire to become part of the system that has historically excluded them," as Dolan notes in *The Feminist Spectator as Critic,* "forces some liberal feminists in theatre to acquiesce to their erasure as women."[4] In this respect, performance in the margins can legitimately be characterized as a site of enacted resistance against the compromises and acquiescence to the normative values that are demanded in the mainstream. But in at least two other respects the margins do not constitute a clear escape from erasure.

First of all, if performance in the margins has enjoyed less direct social regulation and has thus provided women with a wider range of artistic opportunities to explore their identities as women, erasure has nonetheless been the de facto by-product of the obscurity of the margins themselves, that is, of the margins functioning as a site that always vacillates between liberty and containment. To be marginalized is to be disenfranchised. To be disenfranchised is to be denied a forum, a venue, or a voice within the dominant structures of social and cultural authority. Barring some groundswell of recognition, performance in the margins may function nominally as a site of resistance, but the resistance is largely symbolic: a gesture of defiance from the already contained. However romantically or idealistically conceived, the margins are less a site of choice than of exile, and performance within the margins remains largely limited in its opportunities to become a force of significant change. There is at least a tacit acknowledgment of this limitation in Dolan's plea for feminist critics and theatermakers to look beyond the margins. So too, by contrast, does her casual association of performance in the margins with the traditions of the avant-garde acknowledge the potential cultural capital that recognition and notoriety can bring. But to be marginalized is not synonymous with being avant-garde, and the slippage in Dolan's casual association of the two highlights the second respect in which enacted resistance from within the margins—even when it becomes the object of notoriety—does not necessarily escape erasure.

For women experimental artists, the question remains open as to whether an achieved sense of avant-garde notoriety historically has counterbalanced erasure or only marked a shift in its structures. In some ideal sense, of course, the containment logic of the margins is offset by the immense cultural prestige that comes when critics designate the marginalized as avant-garde. Indeed, this prestige is influential enough that critics like Alan Woods have complained that at times "the history of . . . twentieth-century theatre, as it appears in most textbooks," seems to be little more than "the history of a series of avant-garde movements."[5] Regardless of whether one agrees with Woods' depiction, his comments underscore the cultural stock that association with the avant-garde carries (a stock that has provided the mainstream with a steady flow of ideas and innovations). The cultural value of that stock is high enough that the question of whether theater historians have given undue attention to the avant-garde is arguably less pressing than the more basic question of what is expected of those whose work vies for the designation of "avant-garde" itself, and here I am asking about the host of unspoken expectations that come in advance of any sense of the avant-garde as a nexus of radical art and radical politics.

Interestingly enough, both questions address concerns with privilege and exclusion that ultimately have a direct bearing upon feminist historiographies because women have frequently found themselves the victims of those exclusions. Woods' concern is with an undue privileging of the histories of avant-garde theater at the expense of popular theater. Yet this argument on behalf of popular theater defends a cultural form that, as Dolan notes, has a long history of accepting only those women who conform to normative cultural values and who thus participate in their own "erasure as women." We might posit a similar structure with regard to performance in the social margins. Doing so inevitably leads to questions like: what compromises are expected of women artists in order for them to gain recognition within the critical discourses that document avant-garde performance and that construct its histories? Formulated as a bit of a polemic, this latter question has both literal and rhetorical functions. There is a literal need to ask about those compromises since, for all intents and purposes, the question is nonexistent in scholarship on avant-garde performance. But rhetorically, the question obviously presumes that the compromises, while seemingly invisible, are nonetheless commonplace. Much of this book is premised upon this very presumption. Indeed, the coming chapters offer substantial evidence pointing to its accuracy, and this evidence suggests, ironically, that the erasure of women "as women" unites the vanguard with the mainstream—disrupting the implicit binary between the two—since the erasure is common to both.

Whether considered from its literal or rhetorical function, this latter question underscores the role of the critic in setting the terms by which the designation *avant-garde* is bestowed. The question positions the critic as a key bridge between the margins and the mainstream. For while their sympathies may lie with the marginalized, seldom do critics actually write in, to, or for the margins.[6] Unlike more conventional modes of performance that cater to mainstream audiences and that, historically, have regulated women into conformity with normative values because a theater's very livelihood, for instance, may depend upon its reaffirmation of the values of its patrons, the sources of erasure with regard to experimental performance are tied as much—if not more—to the terms of the histories of the avant-garde that critics write as they are to an artist's own agency. The issue here is not whether the work of women experimental artists exists but rather how critics receive that work in the histories they write.

Gender-Blind at the Cutting Edge: The Current State of Vanguard Studies

While accounts of experimental performances by marginalized women artists are not particularly difficult to find, what has motivated me, perhaps more than anything else, to write this book is the rather stunning absence of critical assessments that explore how the experimental work of women artists challenges dominant scholarly assumptions about the American avant-garde. Roughly four scholarly trends circle this lacuna. First there are pathbreaking studies like Charlotte Canning's *Feminist Theaters in the U.S.A.,* which—while devoting considerable attention to experimental women's theaters and to the work of women artists associated with avant-garde theaters like the Open Theatre and the San Francisco Mime Troupe—is concerned with a historically based notion of a feminist theater rather than with a notion of the avant-garde or with how the intersection of feminist theater and avant-garde theater changes our understanding of the avant-garde.[7] Second, there are equally important works like Yolanda Broyles-Gonzalez's *El Teatro Campesino: Theater in the Chicano Movement* (1994) or Rebecca Schneider's *The Explicit Body in Performance* (1997), which either critique the patriarchal structures governing vanguard troupes like El Teatro Campesino or position postmodern experimental performances by women in opposition to a more generalized notion of the avant-garde whose embrace of racist and sexist ideologies they reject. Then there are studies like Sarah Bay-Cheng's *Mama Dada: Gertrude Stein's Avant-Garde Theatre* (2004) or Cindy Rosenthal's "Ellen Stewart: La Mama of Us All,"[8] both of which are more concerned with the work of individual artists rather than with a more general notion of the avant-garde. Finally, at the opposite end of the spectrum, there are the works that frame their projects as studies of the avant-garde and that have little or no concern with feminist theater and performance

At best, these latter studies tend to consider how the work of experimental women artists might fit into an already established notion of the avant-garde rather than how they might transform understanding of the avant-garde as such. I position my own work as a response to this lacuna.

At the same time, I am fully conscious that a number of decisions that have accompanied the formulation of my response will delight some and disappoint others, particularly with regard to the book's methodology. In my individual chapters, I spend very little time, for example, exploring strategies for reading into existent feminist theory the work of the artists whom I discuss. Instead, early in this project I look to feminist theorists and historians for models that can be derived from their scholarly praxis and their treatment of specific instances of theater history. What, I implicitly ask, can Sue-Ellen Case's work on Hrotsvit von Gandersheim or Elin Diamond's work on Bertolt Brecht, for instance, provide by way of scholarly example for a project that seeks to redress the nonfeminist treatment of the histories of avant-garde performance? How might the example of their work as feminist theater historians provide paradigms for the treatment of experimental feminist artists in ways that will position the work of those artists not so much within the current of extant feminist theory as against the current of extant theories and histories of avant-garde performance? In this respect, I am less interested in feminist theory more generally than I am in experimental feminist artists whose feminism is manifested in the particulars of their performative praxis and whose praxis has the potential to change the course of current theories of the avant-garde.

The book is thus intended as a provocation, both in the sense of challenging existing scholarly paradigms and in the sense of prompting what I hope will be a new direction for scholarship on avant-garde performance. At the most basic level the goal of this study is a fundamental rethinking of the American avant-garde along gendered lines. Although the path of this study involves ferreting out the grossly underacknowledged sexism with which women artists moving in avant-garde circles have had to contend from the earliest days of New York Dada on up to the present moment, my objective lies beyond a simple cataloging of examples of sexism. I am interested in pressing hard against the entrenched assumptions of existing critical discourse. The type of rethinking that this book pursues thus aims at overturning the most basic discursive categories of value and identification that mediate—indeed define—what critics recognize and celebrate as avant-garde. In this respect, the aims of the book extend well beyond the realms of theater and performance and have a wide cultural understanding of the avant-garde in their sights.

My goal is to cultivate a critical awareness of how, with regard to questions of gender and with regard to the work of women artists, the present critical discourse about the avant-garde has long been caught in a Faustian bargain. That discourse provides critical insight by blinding us to the patriarchal assumptions that it takes for granted and reinforces. Breaking the trap of the bargain that the current discourse on the avant-garde entails necessitates more than moving it from the shadows into the spotlight. It requires new theoretical terms and new (or revised) historical categories: it requires, in short, a substantial shift in the critical discourse not just about the avant-garde but about what we designate as avant-garde. Thus, I look to the women artists discussed in this book not so much because they need to be added to the ranks of the avant-garde but rather because their work, when taken seriously, lays the foundation for a radically different discourse about what constitutes American avant-garde performance. This objective is fraught with irony because it ultimately seeks to redress the anachronisms of a dominant scholarly discourse that, while ostensibly about the vanguard, has long since fallen behind with regard to some of the most significant theoretical and historiographical currents in scholarship. With regard to questions of gender, studies of the vanguard have decisively remained in the rearguard.

In their general neglect of the performances of women artists or in their casual incorporation of women artists into long-standing truisms about the traditions of American experimental performance, the most recent trends in scholarship on the avant-garde continue what is perhaps the most consistent pattern in studies of avant-garde performance: a tendency to give women artists what is at best a nominal but not a decisive or defining position in its history and aesthetics. This tendency is so pronounced that one is tempted to suggest that the almost requisite refrain about the military origins of the term *avant-garde,* which seems to accompany every new study, carries an implicit argument by analogy: one in which women in the avant-garde, like women in the military, are—unfairly—always suspect and second class and are only taken seriously insofar as they play a man's game. Crass though this analogy may be, it is consistent with the broad privileging of male artists in existent histories of the avant-garde. A review of some of the most recent scholarship on the avant-garde by scholars like Günter Berghaus, Arnold Aronson, and Mike Sell illustrates this very point. I have a great degree of respect for the work of each of these scholars, but I single them out here in order to underscore the critical vacuum in which studies of the avant-garde continue to function vis-à-vis the feminist theories that have radically transformed the rest of our profession. It is no small irony, I would suggest, that studies of the vanguard have devolved into a bastion of patriarchal discourse.

Of these three scholars, Berghaus is, on the face of it, the most removed since rather than offering a study of American avant-garde performance, his *Theatre, Performance, and the Historical Avant-Garde*[9] focuses on what critics have long characterized as the historical European avant-garde. Providing a meticulous overview of the primary documents associated with the most widely recognized European avant-garde movements in the twentieth century, Berghaus displays an admirable command of the material that critics generally consider to be foundational to very notion of an avant-garde.[10] Although a number of scholars have recently questioned this Eurocentric genealogy,[11] it has had a profound influence on how critics have understood the subsequent traditions of American avant-garde performance. Indeed, this influence has everything to do with why Berghaus's work is so important to this present study. For while at some level, the impact of the European avant-garde on the arts in the United States is the result of the migration of ideas that coincided with the flight of artists and intellectuals to the United States from an increasingly fascist Europe in the 1930s and 1940s, that impact is also the product of a selective and largely unchallenged male-centered construction of the history of ideas and aesthetics associated with the avant-garde. Berghaus's work does little to disrupt that constructed history of avant-garde performance, which, with the linear notions of history that it assumes, has long served as a backdrop for a common tendency among scholars to position the European avant-garde as the progenitor (i.e., father) of the performance aesthetics of the American avant-garde—a tendency that Berghaus himself furthers in *Avant-Garde Performance: Live Events and Electronic Technologies*,[12] the book he published concurrently with *Theatre, Performance, and the Historical Avant-Garde.*

There is much in the way of overlap in these two books, particularly in their opening sections,[13] and that overlap underscores the seamless trajectory that Berghaus projects from a presumably established and stable historical European avant-garde tradition to a postwar American avant-garde and its related performance art corollaries. Both of these books are quite informative, but the problem in the history that Berghaus constructs with them is that both books reaffirm an uncontested image of a European avant-garde tradition that is not only undertheorized but that also implicitly serves as the intellectual and artistic foundation for a subsequently posited tradition of American avant-garde performance. In this respect, the books reinforce the linear and positivistic historiography that has been a mainstay in studies of avant-garde performance for the last three decades.

The absence of theory as well as the avoidance of substantial scholarly debate throughout both books strikes at the heart of Berghaus's work as a project on the avant-garde. Undercutting Berghaus's often encyclopedic cataloging of historical detail or "facts" is a pronounced disinclination to conceptualize the "facts" of the avant-garde's history as contested territory, that is, as the substance of conflict, controversy, and debate. As Paul Mann emphasizes throughout *The Theory-Death of the Avant-Garde,*[14] the history of the avant-garde is a history of controversy regarding its definition and, consequently, its trajectory. For Berghaus, by contrast, the history of the avant-garde is a process of gradual evolution rather than a messy sequence of often irreconcilable conflicts. There is no demand in his history that we be partisan, that we take issues with previous interpretations, or, above all, that we resist the temptation to sweep aside the conflicts in favor of the construction of a stable avant-garde trajectory or tradition. Yet the stability of that tradition is built upon a series of exclusions that produce a selective, indeed biased, set of aesthetic criteria against which historians measure the work of subsequent experimental artists and decide whether it qualifies as avant-garde.

Immediate examples of the conflicts that Berghaus's studies elide include those that emerge from Naomi Sawelson-Gorse's volume *Women in Dada.*[15] Not only does the collection of essays in that volume document the major unacknowledged contributions that women like Emmy Hennings, Sophie Tauber, and Suzanne Duchamp made to the historical avant-garde, but as a whole Sawelson-Gorse's volume radically challenges the underlying historiographical assumptions governing the trajectory of the avant-garde that Berghaus posits in his books. The issue with regard to *Women in Dada,* however, is not merely the gesture of a recovery it attempts in what Tracy Davis more generally calls an "indispensable first step of feminist scholarship."[16] Beyond that recovery are the conceptual consequences it brings, the historiographical reverberations of which *Women in Dada* can only begin to explore because they are so far reaching. Placing the categories of gender and sexuality as crucial sites of contestation in the very definition and trajectory of the historical European avant-garde, Sawelson-Gorse exposes a process of containment and exclusion that carefully regulates the constructed stability not only of the male-centered tradition that Berghaus champions but also of the very terms by which critics have understood that tradition to function.

If the gestures of recovery in *Women in Dada* destabilize the received history of the European avant-garde by documenting the contributions that women have made to an avant-garde tradition in which critics (primarily male critics) have failed to give them a defining role, so too does that instability raise fundamental questions regarding the genealogy that critics have long posited between the historical European and the American avant-gardes. To take that genealogy for granted allows the gendered bias of the former to cultivate a comparable bias in the measure of the latter. In fact, the specter of that bias even seeps into works like Arnold Aronson's *American Avant-Garde Theatre,* despite Aronson's having taken significant steps not only toward an understanding of the emergence of the American avant-garde within a much broader and distinctly American cultural and historical context but also toward an understanding that positions Gertrude Stein (along with John Cage) as one of the two "pillars" of the American avant-garde tradition.[17]

Arguably the most influential work on American avant-garde theater in the past decade, Aronson's *American Avant-Garde Theatre* provides an insightful look at some of the most widely celebrated moments in the history of postwar U.S. experimental theater as it surveys Off Broadway, the happenings, and performance art; groups like the Living Theatre and the Wooster Group; and artists like Cage, Smith, Wilson, Foreman, and Reza Abdoh. Yet at a conceptual level—particularly with regard to the underlying historiographical assumptions of his study—there is little to distinguish Aronson's book from the male-centered narratives that have dominated studies of the avant-garde for over forty years, and in this respect, it is well worth asking whose image of the avant-garde Aronson's history privileges and reinforces.

The milestones cited in Aronson's history are important but familiar ones. But though his accounts may be more detailed than what other scholars have offered, they do not fall far from previous studies like Christopher Innes's *Holy Theatre* (1981)[18] and RoseLee Goldberg's *Performance* (1979),[19] or from the image of the avant-garde that took shape in the sixties and seventies in classic essays like Michael Kirby's "The New Theatre" (1965).[20] Most of all what Aronson's book has in common with these earlier works (the same is true, by the way, of Berghaus' two books) is its appeal to a market for descriptive narrative histories of theater that are unproblematized by theory and that display no sense of obligation to engage scholars who challenge the tidy positivistic narratives that are commonplace in histories of the avant-garde. Not only does that appeal allow for a genealogy that assumes precisely the kind of stable European avant-garde tradition that works like *Women in Dada* challenge, but it also extends similar assumptions into the historiography of American avant-garde performance.

Positioning the first appearance of American avant-garde theater "with the production of Erik Satie's *Ruse of the Medusa* at Black Mountain College in 1948,"[21] Aronson argues that postwar America was the site of "a new avant-garde theatre" that emerged from a melting pot of ideas from Cage, Stein, Artaud, and "a dash of Brecht," as well as ideas from other artists exiled by "the ravages of Nazism and World War II" who provided a direct link between American experimental performance and the aesthetics of "symbolism, expressionism, futurism, surrealism, and especially Dada."[22] If this genealogy tacitly overlooks the gendered construction of the historical European avant-garde traditions that, according to Aronson, inspired the American avant-garde, so too do the positivistic underpinnings of its discourse mask the tenuousness of the history of American avant-garde theater that Aronson's book ultimately constructs. Ironically, Aronson acknowledges that tenuousness while simultaneously downplaying its significance.

In his preface, Aronson acknowledges a wide array of women artists whose work he does not discuss in his book because he wants to focus on those he believes "broke new ground or had the greatest impact on the evolution of the avant-garde." Another critic "constructing a different narrative," he notes, "might make other choices."[23] But where would those other choices lead? What narrative history of the avant-garde could a different critic possibly construct if Aronson's own choices, as he claims, focus on those who were innovators rather than imitators and on those whose work was influential rather than historically insignificant? This question is all the more salient if we are talking about something called "the avant-garde" rather than an avant-garde. The sleight of hand here is Aronson's notion that there is "the avant-garde" rather than a variety of avant-garde communities, trajectories, or traditions where the sense of breaking new ground is always a relative variable subject to context rather than categorical absolutes.

Another critic constructing a different narrative would have to begin by challenging the implied universals in Aronson's discourse, particularly with regard to his notions of impact and evolution. Like the notion of breaking new ground, these too are contextual notions and specific to which avant-garde community a critic choices to privilege at another's expense. The sad history is that in scholarship on the avant-garde, time and again those choices incline toward argumentation that positions male artists as the standard-bearers who provide the precedent after which women artists are measured. Aronson's work follows this inclination. Both in terms of its focus and its methodologies, his history of American avant-garde theater ultimately reaffirms the kind of positivistic discourse that has long sustained patriarchal prerogatives and that in most other areas of theater and performance studies has lost its critical viability.

Granted, some may question this line of argumentation, given that Aronson places Gertrude Stein in such a prominent position in the early part of his historical narrative. But the issue here is not whether Stein's work makes its way into the histories of the American avant-garde, but rather how it is positioned within those histories. For all the prominence that Aronson nominally gives to Stein, her work and ideas do little to reshape the notion of the avant-garde that he ultimately endorses in his book. In this respect, it is not a matter of coincidence that the book closes with an echo of Richard Schechner's well-known assertion that the avant-garde has devolved into little more than a style.[24] For the importance that Aronson assigns to Stein's work has to do with the stylistic inspiration that notions like "landscape drama" and the "continuous present" provided for the early Living Theatre and for Richard Foreman's aesthetics[25] rather than with the radical epistemologies or subtle political aesthetics of her work more generally. In no way does the importance that he assigns to her address in substance the way in which the epistemologies or political aesthetics of her work might reshape the conceptual terms by which critics understand the avant-garde, particularly with regard to categories of gender and sexuality.

Von Gandersheim among the Vanguard: Precedent, Criticism, and the Avant-Garde

What critical strategies might offer a consequential weighing of the epistemological and political aesthetic implications of Stein's work for a feminist historiography of the American avant-garde? One answer to this question lies in the conceptual models of reception that feminist scholars have developed in other areas of theater and performance history. What I would like to suggest here is that the broad notions of a feminist theater historiography articulated by scholars like Sue-Ellen Case are relevant not only because they help us to place the history of the avant-garde within a larger framework of a more general feminist theater history, but also because those notions provide a model for understanding the particulars of the history of the avant-garde itself. Going back to one of Case's most influential early essays in feminist theater historiography, I thus would like to suggest a strategic conceptual parallel and to urge a consideration of Stein's work in its relation to the history of the American avant-garde that follows the conceptual model that Case urges scholars to adopt in their assessment of the work of Hrotsvit von Gandersheim in its relation to theater history more generally.

Although the issue here centers on what historians of avant-garde performance might learn from the feminist reception and theorizing of Hrotsvit von Gandersheim's work vis-à-vis the accepted assumptions of theater history, it is worth noting that in many respects Stein's work actually echoes that of her counterpart from the tenth century. Like Stein, Hrotsvit was a playwright. Indeed she was "the first known woman playwright of written texts," and similar to Stein's notion of the continuous present, Hrotsvit emphasized a notion of "contiguity rather than linear development"in her dramas.[26] But most important of all, Hrotsvit's dramas, which, as Sue-Ellen Case notes, offered "a feminist revision of the misogynistic images of women in the plays of the Roman playwright Terence,"[27] fell prey to prejudicial stage practices that thwarted their theatrical production and thus curtailed the opportunity for them to exercise influence. While in the long run of theater history this thwarted opportunity for influence may have affected how scholars have conceptualized the place of playwrights like Gertrude Stein in the general history of theater and drama, I want to shift the focus of my own discussion away from the broad history of theater and concentrate it instead on the American experimental arts in the twentieth century. In doing so, I want to suggest that the existing assessment of Stein and comparable experimental women artists has resulted in a thwarting of their influence on how we conceptualize the history of American avant-garde performance.

But understanding this suggestion necessitates a return to Case's assessment of Hrotsvit. It was Case who first theorized that the prejudice her work encountered not only suppressed "the importance of the first woman playwright" but also produced "a reciprocal depression of values" that shaped critical perception and that led to theater histories in which "both the pioneer of the tradition and those who follow receive only minor regard."[28] The effects of this suppression, Case argues, reach all the way into the present:

> On the one hand, contemporary women's plays are more likely to be excluded from the canon because they appear not to have any precedent and do not follow a discernible tradition of development, and, on the other, the position of the pioneer continues to be ignored because there is no discernible tradition of development which springs from her initial model.[29]

Obviously, one would be hard pressed to suggest that Stein has only received minor regard. But the issue that Case raises with the example of Hrotsvit is not merely whether a subsequent artist receives recognition. Equally important is the perspective from which that recognition comes and the values that it preserves or cultivates.

Certainly, the critical reception of Stein's work within accounts of the avant-garde has provided no excavation of the tradition or values that might link the common concerns of Hrotsvit and Stein or that might do so in a way that would radically question the placement of men at the center of uniform notions of the evolution of the theater and of the avant-garde.[30] While the significance of such an excavation would be in the radical transformation of the avant-garde's so-called break with history into a break with history as we know it, the point here has less to do with establishing a countertradition that would link Hrotsvit and Stein than it does with recognizing that at the conceptual levels that govern critical reception Stein's fate has not been unlike that of Hrotsvit. Indeed, the reception of Stein's work has hardly led toward a conception of the avant-garde that is shaped by women artists, the substance of whose work challenges the misogynistic images of women in culture more generally, the repression of their art, or the silencing of their political voices.

If the suppression of Hrotsvit contributed to the emergence of "dramatic standards" that shared the "partiarchal biases . . . of the culture at large"[31] and if the historical effects of that suppression are as far-reaching as Case suggests, there is good reason to ask whether similar biases have regulated Stein's critical reception in histories of the avant-garde. There is reason to ask whether that reception has skewed her position in the very history where she ostensibly figures so prominently. What I am suggesting is a reception that has selectively highlighted her stylistic innovations while erasing what she has most in common with Hrotsvit, namely a "strong voice"[32]—the kind of strong feminine voice that, as I will be arguing in the third chapter, is particularly evident in works like *The Mother of Us All.* In substance, that voice positions categories of gender and sexuality not only at the center of stylistic innovation but also at the center of a feminist political aesthetic in which the "critique of the 'dominant male discourse'" and the assertion of a feminist discourse in its stead are recognized not merely as elements of a feminist historiography or of a feminist epistemology but also as crucial components of an American avant-garde aesthetic.[33] Pivotal in this regard is the question not of what Stein's work accomplishes in some abstract sense but rather of the practical realities of how critics have received her work or the work of other women artists into the constructed canon of the American avant-garde.

To some extent, this latter question seeks a dialogue with the basic thesis of Mike Sell's highly provocative *Avant-Garde Performance and the Limits of Criticism* (2005). Sell deserves substantial credit not only for his departure from the positivistic models that have long dominated studies of the avant-garde but also for his concerted effort to shift debate about the avant-garde from issues of form and style into a highly theorized analysis of the avant-garde's political and historical contexts. Arguably, however, the real significance of this shift lies in the sensitivity that Sell displays for the strained relations between the political aesthetics of the avant-garde and the institution of cultural criticism, particularly as it is practiced in the academy. Building on Peter Bürger's critique of the institutional conditions of art, Sell questions the historical limits of criticism as an institution as well:

> If, as Peter Bürger has demonstrated, the historical avant-gardes were the first to recognize and thematize the institutional conditions of art, the avant-gardes of the 1960s thematized institutions that Bürger himself fails to recognize: his own institutions, the institutions of criticism, scholarship, and pedagogy.[34]

Much of this questioning of the limits of criticism—a questioning central to Sell's entire project—derives from a sympathetic reading of the hostility that avant-garde communities frequently display toward institutions of higher learning. "Even if scholars, critics and teachers serve as a critical force within liberal democracy," Sell argues, "they were and are, in the end, no true friend of the avant-garde."[35]

While such categorical pronouncements are certainly debatable,[36] Sell is not alone in his questioning of the limits of criticism. Indeed, feminist theorists and historians will recognize an ironically familiar structure in his skeptical attitude toward the institutions of criticism, scholarship, and pedagogy—all of which historically have contributed to "a discourse that," as Charlotte Canning noted in the early 1990s, "feminists, at best distrust and, at worst, reject outright."[37] It is a troubling comment on the state of scholarship on the avant-garde more generally that only now theorists like Sell are examining the limits of criticism. Not only have feminists long questioned the institutions that, according to Sell, have been no friend of the avant-garde, but previous feminist theory has much to add to what Sell only begins. Indeed, reading the avant garde with an attentiveness to questions of gender highlights a needed revision of Sell's key assertion. Rather than merely suggesting that the academy has been no friend of the avant-garde—a suggestion that implicitly grants a privileged objective status to the avant-garde and inclines toward a conception of the avant-garde *avant le lettre*—it would be more appropriate to note the biased institutional structures that always already mediate the concept of the avant-garde as such. It's not that the academy has been "no true friend of the avant-garde." The avant-garde as historically and currently conceptualized by scholars, critics and teachers is "no true friend" of women.

The issue here has less to do with what Sell calls the avant-garde's "long acquaintance with misogyny"[38] than it does with how the institutional discourse of cultural criticism has framed our understanding of the avant-garde itself. Indeed, if we are to speak of the limits of criticism, then a good place to begin is with the recognition that the "long acquaintance with misogyny" to which Sell refers is sound evidence of a critical tradition that selectively champions the work of artists whose aesthetics threaten patriarchy least. While there certainly is a misogynistic tradition in the avant-garde, it is not the only tradition. It is not the only avant-garde. It just happens to be the one with which critics have the longest acquaintance because it is the one that they have consistently privileged. But how might one counter the weight of that tradition and the lure of its discourse?

One trend that suggests a strategy for countering that tradition has been the feminist reception of the work of Bertolt Brecht—who, as is well known, had his own acquaintance with misogyny and who, as Elin Diamond notes in *Unmasking Mimesis,* "exhibits a typical Marxian blindness toward gender relations."[39] Of the many ways that the feminist reception of Brecht might be important to a feminist historiography of the avant-garde, this reception is perhaps most significant because the reading of Brecht by feminist theorists like Diamond demonstrates a keen sensibility for not throwing the baby out with the bathwater. In their discerning gestures toward a rehabilitation of Brechtian theory for feminist criticism, such readings suggest a viable alternative to two potentially debilitating responses to the avant-garde that come from opposite ends of the critical spectrum: first, they avoid categorical dismissals of the avant-garde on the grounds that it is irretrievably bound to a misogynistic tradition; and second, they avoid references to the avant-garde's "long acquaintance with misogyny" that sidestep the necessity of critically engaging the institutional and historiographical structures of that acquaintance.[40]

Coincidentally, Diamond's efforts to highlight the radical potential of Brecht's work for feminist theory takes as its point of departure a short anecdote about a drive that Gertrude Stein and Alice Toklas took in the 1930s. In this anecdote Stein frustrates Toklas by refusing simply to admire a configuration of clouds, choosing instead to read them as "scrambled eggs," a choice that she justifies by telling Toklas: "I'm reading the signs. I love to read the signs."[41] Beneath the apparent idiosyncracy of Stein's insistence is the realization that in advance of our recognizing clouds to be clouds, those things in the sky are perhaps the quintessential example of free-floating signifiers: clouds only by convention, institution, and ideology. They are a cumulus of potential signs blown into particular significance by the chance conventions governing signification.

For Diamond, this anecdote about resistance to established conventions of perception serves as an analogy for her own resistance to the established institutions of interpreting Brecht. It offers her a pretext for proposing an intertextual reading of Brechtian theory and feminist theory that, she argues, can provoke "a recovery of the radical potential of the Brechtian critique and a discovery, for feminist theory, of the specificity of theater."[42] Rather than merely dismissing Brecht as yet another male playwright who "created conventionally gendered plays and too many saintly mothers,"[43] she argues that established institutions of criticism have clouded the feminist potential in Brecht's theories. This argument marks the beginning of one of the most important lines of feminist thought in theater studies in the last decade and a half. It also establishes a precedent for studies of the avant-garde: as Stein reads clouds into eggs, as Diamond reads Brechtian theory into feminist thought, so too would I suggest a shaving of the conventional understanding of the vanguard back to the level of the sign in a gesture of recovery that is premised upon a recalibration of the radical potential of the avant-garde's critical edge—a recovery that is initiated by and for feminist theory. That recalibration necessitates one additional consideration of Diamond's feminist reading of Brechtian theory.

Diamond's movement toward a gestic feminist criticism departs from the traditional and segues into a very different modern and postmodern canon: one populated by figures like Aphra Behn, Caryl Churchill, Adrienne Kennedy, Peggy Shaw, Robbie McCauley, and Deb Margolin. In no uncertain terms, the significance of her recovery of the radical potential of the Brechtian critique thus is measured by the new historiographical terrain that it navigates—a navigation facilitated by the previously unacknowledged significance and value that it illuminates. Following the precedent set by Diamond, I would suggest that movement toward a feminist historiography of the avant-garde would thus seem to pivot on two basic but related inquiries.

To what extent, it behooves scholars to ask first of all, do the historians of the avant-garde subscribe to an institutional discourse that is "based on norms and values" that ultimately perpetuate "patriarchal interests"?[44] And here one begins to move into territory beyond those same traditional points of reference that historians of the avant-garde have taken for granted for the last forty years. It is not enough to claim, as Sell does, that "the avant-garde functions as a force that reshapes the very way we think about and produce history."[45] Of equal importance to that first question concerning how we "think about" or "produce history" is the second question concerning whose history one ultimately produces or reproduces. This is the question of whose work scholars ultimately discuss, to what end, and in whose interest? While a full-scale feminist critique of the accepted canon of avant-garde theater and performance would certainly yield important results—and is a project that has not yet been undertaken in a systematic way—a feminist historiography of avant-garde performance necessitates a radical shift in focus from a male-dominated canon to the experimental work of women artists if it is to excavate a set of norms and values that does not serve patriarchal interests.

Basic though these two questions might seem, the answers they require have to reach well beyond a mere identification and discussion of women avant-garde artists. If they are to critically engage the institutional and historiographical structures that shape our understanding of the avant-garde, those answers cannot simply add the names of women to the list of those belonging to the avant-garde canon. Neither can they characterize women avant-garde artists as comprising "a separate community, a separate culture, with its own customs, its own epistemology, and . . . its own [distinct] aesthetic."[46] If the former approach measures the work of women artists against standards and values to which they do not contribute and which they do not threaten, the latter ultimately ghettoizes them safely within a conceptual vacuum (i.e., a separate sphere) that does not actually exist. In the final analysis, both serve patriarchal interests. Both are avenues of containment. The necessary answers, I would suggest, are those that lie somewhere between these two approaches. They are those that add women to the ranks of the avant-garde as workers add paint remover to pieces of furniture in order to strip it down to its underlying base so as to make it new. They are those that see the epistemologies and aesthetics in the work of women avant-garde artists not as elements of a separate culture or community but rather as a source of radical engagement capable not only of "exploding the canon" of the avant-garde but of "questioning [the] underlying assumptions" of the avant-garde as scholars have heretofore conceptualized it as a "field of study."[47]

Feminist Historiographies and Collage Aesthetics

A feminist historiography of avant-garde performance thus requires a skillful negotiation. While it needs to focus on the work of experimental women artists, it cannot compartmentalize their work, partitioning it off from their male counterparts. In short, it needs to consider the work of experimental women artists not in a vacuum but as a vanguard that engages and challenges the world around it—a world largely dominated by a climate of male social, cultural, and aesthetic privilege. It must challenge what Carolee Schneemann, in a moment of bitting sarcasm, called the "Art Stud Club."[48] Humorous though that moment of sarcasm might be as a passing remark, I would suggest that Schneemann's comment lays claim to the cultural community whose regulatory practices it ridicules. Her comment demands entry by challenging the terms of admittance. On a small scale, that comment thereby exemplifies the kind of critical engagement with the culture of male privilege that a feminist historiography of avant-garde performance must also follow.

Schneemann's comment serves as a reminder that the path toward a feminist critique of the canon of avant-garde theater and performance begins not only with feminist scholarship that carefully rethinks the prejudicial reception of individual works or the biased construction of specific artistic movements. It also begins with experimental women artists like Schneemann who, in their own performance work, have ventured down this critical path on their own. In fact, it is precisely through enacted feminist critiques of their male counterparts that experimental women artists like Schneemann have resisted attempts to relegate them to a separate and contained community of women. Throughout this book, I will suggest that such moments of resistance have positioned the work of artists like Schneemann as dissident voices within a larger mixed community of avant garde artists a community whose gendered hierarchies the performative enactment of a feminist critique not only challenges but whose very makeup as a community that enactment also redefines (or at least potentially redefines depending upon the type of reception it receives among scholars of the avant-garde).

Although invoking an image of dissident voices within a larger artistic community meshes well with the dissonant aesthetics of collage that are central to the considerations of this book, this invocation also draws attention to the multiple notions of community that had currency in the 1960s when artists like Schneemann, Ono, and Solanas performed the works that I discuss in the pages that follow. I will take up the issue of community (and collaboration) again in the final section of the book, but here I do want to pause momentarily to note that the notions of community with which I identify Schneemann and the other women artists examined in this book played out against the backdrop of an emergent experimental theater scene in the 1960s that located its center of gravity in more visible manifestations of community—specifically, in alternative communities that were grounded in collective theatrical practice. Theater historians like Karen Malpede, Margaret Croyden, and later Charlotte Canning have all argued that in the United States much of the politically viable and ultimately feminist experimental theater of the 1960s pivoted on an embrace of collaboration and "creative communities."[49] When it came to feminist political agendas, those communities, far from relying on inspired individual voices of defiance, developed an artistic dynamic not unlike the political traditions of collective bargaining. What I mean here is simply that there is strength in numbers, and frequently the creative communities that emerged from the experimental theater scene in the 1960s coalesced as collective political artistic forces. They provided individual members with much-needed artistic and political support, and they were able to set up alternative spaces with which the established theater community ultimately had to reckon.

Arguably a sense of the strength of these collectives surfaces in Schneemann's own work some thirty years later in a comment as fleeting as her earlier reference to the "Art Stud Club." On February 14, 1997, Schneemann participated in a soiree/performance entitled *Arensberg Salon at St. Duchamp* that was orchestrated by the cultural historian Steven Watson. Each participant assumed the identity of one of the wide circle of artists, writers, and intellectuals who frequented the home of Walter and Louise Arensberg in the early part of the twentieth century, and in a rich moment not merely of role playing but of identification Schneemann assumed the identity of one of her predecessors, the Baroness Elsa von Freytag-Loringhoven (whose work I discuss in the next chapter). Schneemann spent a good part of her performance reciting fragments from the Baroness's poetry, but what was most noteworthy was her introduction of herself as the Baroness. Rather than stating who she was, Schneemann performed the Baroness speaking from beyond the grave, recounting her own lonely and isolated "death by asphyxiation" in a decrepit Parisian flat.[50] Given the deference to poetic expression that marked the rest of her performance, it is hard not to read Schneemann's opening reference to "asphyxiation" as a metaphor for the consequences of the artistic isolation to which, in the absence of community, the Baroness literally succumbed.

At the same time, however, Schneemann's appearance as the Baroness suggests the possibility of unconventional notions of community through moments of inspiration and identification beyond the confines of space and time. In a very literal way Schneemann's performance constructed a sense of unity with the one artist who is most plausibly her predecessor, and in doing so Schneemann glanced both backward and forward in the search for a community constructed in legacy: backward in a gesture of acknowledgment of a kindred spirit and forward in an inviting gesture of comradery to like-minded artists to come. Whether these gestures were as effective as the collaborative artistic endeavors of the "creative communities" cataloged by feminist historians like Canning is, to my mind, less important than recognizing that the successes of the latter do not preclude the legitimacy of the former. The two coexist, I would suggest, as distinct avant-garde traditions: the legacy of experimental feminist theater that Canning explores,[51] and the legacy of experimental feminist solo performance that is largely the focus of this book.

One thing that becomes evident from that focus is that Schneemann was not unique in her gestures toward a sense of community or comradery constructed in a shared legacy. Gertrude Stein arguably pursued a comparable course in her depiction of the suffragette Susan B. Anthony in *The Mother of Us All*—a depiction that, as I note in my chapter on Stein, critics have frequently argued was constructed in such a manner that it invites direct comparisons between Anthony's plight as a feminist activist and Stein's plight as a woman artist. Neither is Schneemann alone in the dissident, feminist voice that emerges in her work's position in relation to her male contemporaries. That voice—which, in a variety of forms, she shares with each of the other experimental women artists I discuss throughout this book—is also woven into an aesthetic that I argue is common among them as well: an aesthetic that is grounded in the radical juxtapositions of collage.

Widely viewed as the twentieth century's "single most revolutionary formal innovation in artistic representation," collage involves a highly self-conscious or metacritical technique of radical juxtaposition.[52] Its signature gesture is that of disrupting conventional meanings by an act of recontextualization that juxtaposes seemingly incongruent objects, images, ideas, or performative acts within a conceptual aesthetic construct. At its most basic level, collage technique fosters the chance associations and "new possibilities of signification" that result, as Marjorie Perloff has noted, from "the transfer of [objects,] words and images" as well as specific acts, gestures and behaviors "from their original sources to the collage construction."[53] Though often associated with the graphic arts, the germinal techniques of twentieth-century collage in the West are identifiable across the disciplines.[54] Indeed, the techniques of collage have had a particularly strong resonance in the history of experimental theater and drama, taking a wide variety of forms in everything from the structural experimentations with nonlinear narrative that epitomize the work of artists like Gertrude Stein to the chance operations that mark the work of the happening artists who followed John Cage.

The historical significance of collage as an aesthetic strategy has as much to do with raising fundamental questions, in an openly self-reflective manner, regarding representation and its limitations as it does with the production of new associations and meanings. As mode of artistic expression, it thus possesses amazing potential for structured feminist dissent and resistance to the hierarchies of male privilege. It gives space to dissidence as part of an aesthetics of dissonance and as part of the counter-hierarchies of parataxis—as part, in short, of the aesthetics constituted in the radical juxtapositions of collage. It also has profound implications for how critics do history. In this respect, the most striking similarity among the women artists whose work I discuss in the pages that follow is a recurrent and innovative variation of the aesthetics of collage that enacts a feminist critique of the patriarchal norms and values that critics subtly preserve in the frequently celebrated avant-garde aesthetics of their male counterparts. At one level, then, exploring the variation of collage aesthetics that connects artists like Elsa von Freytag-Loringhoven, Gertrude Stein, Yoko Ono, Carolee Schneemann, and Valerie Solanas is a calculated gesture intended not only to contest "the hegemony of male artists"[55] but also to destabilize the aesthetic values that sustain that hegemony.

The links connecting the work of these women situates them at a peculiar but highly significant historiographic juncture with regard to avant-garde performance. Their use of collage aesthetics positions performance at the intersection of two competing definitions of the "cutting edge"—definitions that presume different models of history because, first and foremost, the term *cutting edge* belongs to the discourse of historiography. Historically, the term has functioned as a synonym for the avant-garde's presumed position at the vanguard of artistic experimentation, and it has thus suggested not only a forward-looking aesthetic but also a forward-moving, linear development that presumably is teleological in its bearing. Yet this suggestion is as ideologically charged as it is sorely underexamined. A construct of academic convenience, the term *cutting edge* as it has conventionally been used is a historical category: mediating, shaping, indeed filtering scholarly perceptions of history. It has functioned more as a tool for the critic than as an adequate description of the myriad trajectories of the avant-gardes. Inasmuch as it has encouraged scholars to conceptualize the history of the avant-garde as a traceable evolution in artistic innovation, this popularly disseminated definition of the term tends to dull "the cutting edge" into a blunt instrument: for narrating a story about the gradual refining of artistic techniques and style; for expunging the heterogenous; and, I would argue, for obfuscating the constructed hegemony of male artists. Vying against this first definition of the "cutting edge" are the edges openly cut and spliced together in collage's candid acknowledgment of the constructedness of its images. That candid acknowledgment is rich in historiographic implications, and it thus offers a profound alternative to the model of history implied in the popular and conventional understanding of the term *cutting edge,* particularly with respect to how that popular model has contributed to the suppression of the work of experimental women artists in the avant-garde.

In contrast to the conventional definition of the term, this second definition of the "cutting edge"—the definition provoked by the feminist variation of collage aesthetics—offers a subversive and yet immensely malleable alternative to the linear models of history that have consistently privileged the work of male avant-gardists. In its calculated embrace not only of the jarring edges left by cutting but also of the radical juxtaposition of those edges, collage raises fundamental questions, in an openly self-reflective manner, regarding representation and its limitations. Critics have especially argued that the provisional unity that a collage imposes on its heterogenous elements—a unity where the seams of construction are tenuous and never entirely hidden—ultimately undermines the authority of signification in society's dominant systems of representation and logic. This subversion extends to systems of historical representation as well. In belying the unity of their own construction, the seams of collage highlight the constructed unity of linear historical narratives—narratives like those that are implied in the conventional understanding of the term *cutting edge.*[56]

The value that this aspect of collage has for a feminist historiography of avant-garde performance is significant. Not only is the emergence of collage aesthetics a part of the actual history of the avant-garde, but at a conceptual level collage aesthetics offers new ways to think about history that potentially enable us to see what the extant histories of the avant-garde have silenced. And here the logic is not merely that of juxtaposition but of the radical dynamic that begins to emerge as a consequence of the juxtaposition. With respect to referentiality, the clashing juxtapositions of collage frequently illuminate that which the conventional tools of representation and the assumptions governing the logic of linear thought both elide. Calling attention to that which remains unaccounted for in conventional representation and logic, the radical juxtapositions of collage thus reenfranchise the vanquished amid tense unreconciled dialectical oppositions. Unreconciled though they may be, the different points of opposition in those juxtapositions remain engaged with these other elements of the collage, and it is in that engagement that we find the model for a feminist historiography for avant-garde performance.

More important, ultimately, than the juxtaposition of the work of women experimental artists with the work of their male counterparts is how the work of the former engages the work of the latter amid the juxtaposition itself. If that engagement is not disruptive, if it does not give space to an otherwise disenfranchised aesthetic of the avant-garde, if it does not change the categories by which we designate and identify the avant-garde as such, then the juxtaposition has accomplished little more than resurrecting the old routine of measuring the work of women against values and standards that they had little to no part in establishing. The desire to avoid this latter prospect has everything to do with the selection of the women artists whose work I discuss in this book. Not only can we observe powerfully innovative variations of collage aesthetics in their work—variations that provisionally unite them within a larger shared project of a feminist rethinking of collage—but those variations are interesting and significant because they directly engage and disrupt the aesthetics propagated in the work of their male counterparts, whether that engagement is manifested in Elsa von Freytag-Loringhoven's intimidating interactions with William Carlos Williams, in Gertrude Stein's rethinking of political discourse in *The Mother of Us All,* in Carolee Schneemann's staged provocations at the Dialectics of Liberation Congress, in Yoko Ono's critical "unmaking" of action-collage technique in *Cut Piece,* or in Valerie Solanas's highly theatricalized attempted murder of Andy Warhol. Together the work of these artists lays out the beginning of a radically different discursive terrain for conceptualizing American avant-garde performance.

Engendering a Feminist Discourse for Avant-Garde Performance

Some rough sense of the structure of this discursive terrain surfaces at various moments in feminist scholarship tangentially related to studies of the avant-garde. Probably the most important work in this regard is Rebecca Schneider's *Explicit Body in Performance,* which, while primarily concerned with feminist postmodern performance, not only "wrestles with the historical Euro-American avant-garde" but also articulates the most compelling critique of its gendered and racist underpinnings to date.[57] As compelling as I find Schneider's arguments—and they have influenced my own thinking in more ways than I can express—they tend to position feminist performance as an antinomy to the avant-garde as a whole (or what she calls the "ghost of the avant-garde")[58] rather than positioning it in such a way as to wrestle us into new discursive paradigms for conceptualizing the avant-garde, its precedents, and its histories. Part of this positioning results, I think, from the obvious fact that Schneider's project concerns the general feminist implications of the explicit body in performance rather than a rehabilitation of scholarly notions of the avant-garde. Nonetheless, at least two of the recurrent themes that she finds in "thirty years of feminist explicit body performance from its earliest manifestations in the 1960s" have immediate and substantial relevance to the categories I want to posit for a feminist historiography of avant-garde performance. First and foremost, I would suggest an almost direct correspondence between what I call the "disruptive engagements" of the feminist adaptations of collage aesthetics and what Schneider identifies as the way that "feminist explicit body work talks back to precedent terms of avant-garde transgression."[59] Both interrogate and challenge popular cultural understandings—whether those understandings concern who ultimately gets to regulate the supposedly proper use of the term *avant-garde* or "who gets to mark" what is or is not "appropriately transgressive."[60]

Despite significant instances of overlap, not all feminist explicit body works vie for avant-garde status. Neither do all feminist avant-garde events employ the explicit body. Still there is much, for example, in Schneider's notion of "the body of the artist as stage"[61] that is crucial to the articulation of a feminist historiography of avant-garde performance. Of particular importance in this regard is the fact that by conceptualizing the body as stage, Schneider avoids a naive sense of immediacy and authenticity. There is no sense here of nakedness as essence. Neither is there any sense of the unproblematized notions of radical actuality or unmediated reality that are so often taken for granted in the aesthetics attributed to the avant-garde or that are so often passed over in the critical rush to celebrate the avant-garde's blurring of art and life. For the purposes of the arguments in this book, however, Schneider's focus on the body as stage is only one example of the larger questioning of the avant-garde's embrace of immediacy that must go hand and hand with a rehabilitation of scholarly notions of the avant-garde along feminist lines. *Indeed, the feminist discourse for avant-garde performance only begins when the curtain has fallen on the myth of immediacy.*

Schneider is not the first feminist theorist to question notions of immediacy, and thus it may come as no surprise that building upon the implications of her notion of the body as stage involves a bit of backward glance. Interestingly enough, that glance does a lot to put long-standing assumptions about American avant-garde performance in a feminist perspective. In a now classic statement of feminist performance theory from the mid-1980s, for example, Sue-Ellen Case and Jeanie K. Forte challenged those assumptions and their unproblematized notions of "real life":

> The eruption of Happenings, The Living Theater [*sic*], The Performance Group and the extension of performance into Conceptual Art destroyed the formalist frame of aesthetic closure and fused the conventions of art with those of real life. The frame of art could be extended to include daily life—the documentation of daily life could create a frame for art. Thus, the 60s challenged the borders of art and life, but the sense of the documentary, which allowed for the exchange of meaning between the two, rested upon an unchallenged assumption about the way meaning was generated. This documentary sense assumed a stable system of representation. The actor/activist could represent (or refer to) real life without questioning the legitimacy or perspective of representation itself.[62]

It is perhaps indicative of the rancorous resistance to feminist performance theory in theater studies (indeed across the disciplines) during the 1980s that scholars of avant-garde performance have given little or no consideration to Case and Forte's trenchant critique of the assumptions that, two decades later, continue to shape histories of American avant-garde performance. Those assumptions, as Case and Forte note, are tainted with complicity in abetting discursive ideologies that institutionalize social repression along race, class, and gender lines. Implicit in Case and Forte's argument is thus a call for a sociopolitical performance aesthetic: capable, first of all, of teasing out the repressive ideologies that seethe beneath the notions of "real life" in the aesthetics of the avant-garde; and capable also of challenging the systems of representation that sustain those problematic notions. In answering that call, one need not turn from the tradition of the avant-garde itself, only from the tradition as we know it.

Inasmuch as the radical juxtapositions of collage exemplify an aesthetic that raises fundamental questions regarding representation and its limitations, the adaptation of collage for feminist performance would seem to answer Case and Forte's more general call at the same time that it radically shifts the theoretical discourse on the avant-garde in gender-conscious directions. In many respects, this is the very point that I argue throughout my book. But the more important argument is that the appropriation of collage aesthetics for feminist performance only answers Case and Forte's call in its modified adaptations of collage, that is, in its enactment of an immanent critique of collage aesthetics. For if collage challenges systems of representation, so too does it—particularly in the spheres of performance—rely on problematic notions like that of *found objects* for much of its substance. While at one level those *found objects* bridge the experimental and the everyday, the work of artists like von Freytag-Loringhoven, Ono, and Schneemann repeatedly demonstrates that such objects tend to be shaded with repressive gendered sensibilities rather than being bathed in the light of neutrality or immediacy. In short, where historians of the avant-garde have repeatedly found clouds, the women experimental artists discussed in this book show us scrambled eggs.

Above all, the adaption of collage aesthetics for feminist performance—or at least the variation of collage aesthetics by the artists discussed in the following pages—suggests the need for a number of categorical shifts in the discourse with which we designate works as "avant-garde." While much of the logic behind these shifts is developed in the chapters that follow, I want to conclude this introduction with a rough map of what those shifts are. As a kind of bearing for that map, it is worth looking to the final chapter of the book and its discussions of Valerie Solanas. But the reason for looking to the end as a point of departure has less to do with establishing a linear trajectory for my own arguments than it does with recognizing that the "real life" in the blurring of art and life equation of the avant-garde was far from a facile notion. As Mike Sell has duly noted in *Avant-Garde Performance and the Limits of Criticism,* the American avant-garde's blurring of art and life almost always involved an acute and highly critical consciousness of how embedded "real life" was in commodity fetishism and the logic of late capitalism. As an avant-gardist, Solanas shares that consciousness, and yet the militant anticapitalist rhetoric of her *SCUM Manifesto,* for example, draws clear lines linking the structures of capitalism and the structures of patriarchy. One cannot redress the repressiveness of the former, she argues, without simultaneously redressing the repressiveness of the latter. In her arguments, capitalism and patriarchy are not related social structures; they are two sides of the same coin.

In substance, Solanas's argument is traceable to largely ignored political-aesthetic precedents in Berlin Dada, but within its own historical context the argument is significant not because it adds a new category of gender to the discussion of the avant-garde but rather because it recalibrates a signature trope of American avant-gardism (e.g., a fervent anticapitalism) along gendered lines. Following this line of thought, I would suggest the first in a series of precepts for a feminist historiography of avant-garde performance: *an anticapitalist aesthetic becomes a trope of the avant-garde only to the extent that it is simultaneously antipatriarchal, only to the extent that the two are indistinguishable.* While the equation of anticapitalist and antipatriarchal sentiment in Solanas's work surfaces initially from within the explicit articulations of her manifesto, comparable equations are widespread in the work of the artists discussed in this book. They appear frequently, for example, in the precedent-setting performance practices of New York Dada's arguably most provocative yet least acknowledged figure, the Baroness Elsa von Freytag-Loringhoven. Indeed, it is legitimately tempting to characterize the Baroness (rather than Gertrude Stein) as the American avant-garde's Hrotsvit von Gandersheim. At numerous levels, the precedents set in the Baroness's work call for a substantial revision of the standards and values by which we confer the designation *avant-garde,* but one of the most understated yet far-reaching in implications from those precedents is the subtle alternative metaphor that her work offers to Antonin Artaud's celebrated association of radical theatrical practice with the visceral ravages of the plague.

Some four decades before the English translation of *The Theatre and Its Double,* the Baroness stirred up controversy by summoning up the specter of a different kind of plague: the specter of syphilis in the socially constructed image of the syphilitic woman. In contrast to the seemingly indiscriminate character of Artaud's metaphor for a radical theatricality, the Baroness appropriated an illness as metaphor that is as visceral as Artaud's subsequent appropriation of the plague but never loses sight of its socially (en)gendered moorings. While referencing a plague in its own right, the specter of syphilis does not succumb to what is arguably the most problematic yet least discussed sleight of hand in the rhetoric of Artaud's image of the theater as plague, namely its implied argument by analogy: its unacknowledged suggestion that the metaphor of the biologically indiscriminate character of contagion (i.e., the plague) can overwrite the always already socially discriminate character of theater and performance in the public sphere.[63] The specter of syphilis, by contrast, carries no rhetorical pretensions to being indiscriminate. Although anyone is vulnerable to infection, syphilitic contagion is embedded in the social, material, and gendered realities of sexual politics, and as a metaphor for a radical, visceral theatricality, the specter of syphilis is always simultaneously a metaphor for the gendered hierarchies governing sexual politics in the public and covert spaces of society. As a second precept for a feminist historiography of avant-garde performance, I would suggest a direct alternative to Artaud's image of the theater as plague, an alternative that, while preserving the visceral quality of his argument, does not elide the material realities of gender: *similar to Solanas's later blurring of anticapitalist and antipatriarchal sentiment, the Baroness's metaphorical use of syphilis offers a key strategy for a feminist avant-garde aesthetic precisely because it links radical theatricality with a recognition of the risk-laden economics of sexual politics and gender construction.*

Beyond the revision of these two categories, much of the shift in the values and standards associated with the avant-garde focuses on a feminist revision of what falls generally under the rubric of the Duchamp-Cage aesthetic, and it is here that the feminist revision of collage is evident. Much of that revision centers on a radical rethinking of the notion of *found objects,* which is closely tied to collage aesthetics since found objects frequently find their way into collage compositions. As a nonpainterly or nonrepresentational object, the found object is also conceptually linked to the notions of immediacy (what Case and Forte call the documentary) that critics associate with some of the most celebrated trajectories in American avant-garde performance. Indeed, the concept of found objects and its variants *found sounds, found behaviors,* and *found actions* play a decisive role in how critics have conceptualized the Duchamp-Cage aesthetic and the experimental performance traditions that this aesthetic inspired. A feminist rethinking of the notion of found objects, on the other hand, touches upon a central tenet of how critics identify and assess a work's value as avant-garde. It also exposes the extent to which, in the arena of gender politics, the question of who does the finding is as important as the object found. A third precept for a feminist historiography of avant-garde performance involves a fundamental rethinking of found objects and the aesthetic immediacy that they presuppose: *found objects posses neither neutrality nor immediacy but become elements within an avant-garde aesthetic only to the extent that the illusion of their neutrality or immediacy is exposed as a guise for regulating gender and sexuality at the most basic levels of quotidian experience.*

At the center of that rethinking is a challenge to the presumed neutrality and immediacy of all objects large and small—even of the detritus "found" in the city streets. Once again, von Freytag-Loringhoven emerges as the precedent-setting figure in this regard and not merely because of her tense personal interactions with Duchamp, interactions about which she was often highly critical. As one of Greenwich Village's most eccentric residents, the Baroness was her own walking collage, having frequently constructed her attire out of tin cans, old spoons, and whatever else was available in the large collection of items that she had recovered from the New York City streets and amassed in her apartment. But the responses both to her clothing and to her found object–filled apartment tell us more about the regulation of gender roles than about a baseline aesthetic neutrality that a found object presumably provides. As I mention in the next chapter of this book, Kurt Schwitters received critical acclaim, for example, when he filled his Cologne apartment with found objects; the Baroness, by contrast, was denounced as a dirty housekeeper.

If the Baroness took found objects into social spaces that dispelled the illusion of their immediacy and that exposed their unacknowledged role as conduits for the regulation of gender, subsequent performance artists like Yoko Ono and Carolee Schneemann developed aesthetic strategies that take decisive steps toward establishing clear alternatives to the values and standards that critics have distilled from their embrace of the Duchamp-Cage aesthetic. Nowhere is that process of distillation clearer, I argue in my chapter on Ono's *Cut Piece,* than in Michael Kirby's highly influential notion of *nonmatrixed performance,* the concept that he posited in the late 1960s to account for the found behaviors and found actions included in the aesthetics of the happenings and Fluxus events. The mechanisms of Ono's *Cut Piece,* I argue, not only challenge the unproblematized reaffirmation of "the documentary" in the concept of nonmatrixed performance but also the unproblematized embrace of the audience/spectators more generally within the experimental modes of performance that Kirby calls "the new theatre." Thus, as an alternative to Kirby's notion of nonmatrixed performance, I want to suggest a fourth precept for a feminist historiography of avant-garde performance—one that, based upon Ono's work, I will characterize as *submatrixed performance.* As a theoretical concept, submatrixed performance identifies avant-garde gestures in their doubled trajectory: *submatrixed performance departs from the fabricated narrative contexts of conventional text-based theater while at the same time underscoring the always already ideologically mediated social contexts of performance itself—and here that mediation refers specifically to the regulation of gender, sexuality, and race.* The complement to this argument is, I maintain, at play in the performance that Carolee Schneemann orchestrated in 1967 at the Dialectics of Liberation Congress wherein she displayed an amazingly savvy ability—an ability evident in almost all of her work—to resist the lure of merely incorporating found behaviors into her performance and focused instead on what I want to characterize as *found restrictive behaviors.* As a fifth precept for a feminist historiography of avant-garde performance, I want to suggest that *found behaviors are avant-garde only inasmuch as their exploration exposes the extent to which they regulate gender and sexuality at a level that goes generally unnoticed or that even runs contrary to official discourse.* Schneemann's performance at the Dialectics of Liberation Congress was thus avant-garde because it inconveniently exposed how the Congress's promise of a discourse of liberation was belied by a rigid adherence to patriarchal hierarchies. With specific regard to Ono and Schneemann, then, I am suggesting the need to measure a work's avant-garde status either by the extent to which it underscores sociosexual or sociopolitical *submatrixes* that regulate sexuality, gender, and race, or by the extent to which it displays a keen sensibility for provoking into play the *found restrictive behaviors* that sustain those submatrixes.

Finally, my book seeks to locate American avant-garde performance in the conceptual spaces that exist between what Gertrude Stein characterizes in *The Mother of Us All* as an unwelcome vitiating absorption into the repressive mainstream and what Valerie Solanas characterizes in *The SCUM Manifesto* as a kind of permanent outlaw status. By underscoring those in-between spaces, what I am suggesting as a final precept for a feminist historiography of American avant-garde performance is a *deliberative liminality: one that measures the avant-garde status of a work according to the extent to which its seeks not to negotiate the terms of its surrender, resignation, or absorption, but rather the extent to which it negotiates a revision in the authority of the terms that exile it and make it outlaw.* This is perhaps the most utopian of the categories that I am proposing, but at the same time it is the most necessary. For it is the one category that ensures a constant renegotiation of what scholars and historians deem avant-garde. It is the one category that presupposes interlocutors with whom one can and must negotiate. It is the one category that does not supplant one theory of the avant-garde with another but rather that ultimately situates multiple theories of the avant-garde in the tense dialectic of radical juxtaposition. It is the one category that moves us from a history of the avant-garde into a serious consideration of the messy, frequently irreconcilable, but rich and concurrent histories of American avant-garde performance.

There is no pretense here about the exhaustiveness of the precepts I have proposed. They are little more than a beginning, and I would be the first to characterize them as more provisional than prescriptive. I am less interested in their permanence than I am in the rough orientation that they provide. While that orientation certainly points toward an historical terrain of avant-garde performance that has remained too little surveyed for too long, what I hope for with this book is that in its own small way it disrupts the possibility of business as usual in subsequent studies of avant-garde performance. This issue here is not merely that of positioning gender as an established category within the basic definitions of the avant-garde. Rather it is that of repeatedly exploring how issues of gender radically alter the way scholars conceptualize the avant-garde as such.

CHAPTER TWO

Nude Descending Bleecker Street

Baroness Elsa von Freytag-Loringhoven and Performing Gender in New York Dada

Baroness Elsa von Freytag-Loringhoven, once proclaimed by her New York contemporaries to be "the first American dada" if not "the Original Dada," was fifty-three years old when she died in 1927.[1] She had spent the last three years of her life in a kind of self-imposed obscurity in Berlin, where, after a tumultuous decade and a half in the United States, she had returned hoping "to find ease and the leisure to write."[2] The move proved to be disastrous. Precipitated initially by a disgust with American language and culture—a disgust that had motivated her departure only after it had first served as a wellspring for a wide variety of Dada expressions and performances—her plans for a renewed life in Germany fell prey to disillusionment and to "the grim fight for survival in postwar Berlin."[3] Though she had struggled through the late teens and early twenties in New York, where she had been stranded penniless after her husband had committed suicide in France while trying to return to Germany at the outbreak of World War I, nothing had prepared her for bleak economic crises of the Weimar Republic. While she had been able to support herself in New York posing for other artists, in Berlin she had been reduced to hawking newspapers for currency rendered worthless in the rampant inflation of postwar Germany. As she told Djuna Barnes in an undated letter from that time, a letter that unmistakably included an implicit plea for help: "I am poor and deserted . . . my country is slowly wearing me to rags—body and spirit. . . . many ants can kill the strongest, proudest life if it is fettered to ant heap—as I am to life in Germany—to life—to terrible poverty and its obligations—one may perish on a formality—winter approaching—rain, hail—cold,—I on the streets—freezing."[4]

The final images that history has provided us of Elsa von Freytag-Loringhoven are an ironic conclusion to the responses prompted by her implicit pleas for help. They are that of an impoverished bilingual poet, sculpturer, and proto-performance artist accidentally asphyxiating from gas in a Paris apartment while she slept. When she died in mid-December 1927, she had only been in Paris a few months, having arrived around May earlier that year at the behest of friends like Djuna Barnes who had pooled their resources and procured an apartment for the Baroness in order to rescue her from the abject poverty and desperation into which she had fallen since leaving New York and returning to Berlin in April 1923. In the obituary that Djuna Barnes wrote for her friend, she described the accidental death of the Baroness as "a stupid joke" and as an "unfitting end" for a person who "was, as a woman, amply appreciated by those who had loved her in youth" but whose acumen and artistic talent were "never appropriately appreciated."[5]

One can puzzle long over an assertion that an artist has not been "appropriately appreciated," and it is certainly puzzling that Barnes would on the one hand make this assertion and then on the other never follow though on her plans either to publish a volume of the Baroness's poetry (poetry that Barnes had in her possession) or even to publish the Baroness's autobiographical writings (writings that Barnes herself had commissioned). Although it is certainly plausible that publishing more of the Baroness's writings would have helped to solidify the limited reputation that von Freytag-Loringhoven had already gained through the circulation of her work in the literary magazine the *Little Review,* my mention of this puzzling side of Barnes's involvement with von Freytag-Loringhoven is not intended to exaggerate the importance of a disservice done by someone who in so many other respects had shown genuine support for the Baroness when it really mattered to her. I mention this peculiar side of Barnes's relationship with the Baroness more as a point of departure and as a way of focusing my own discussion on the question of what an appropriate appreciation of Elsa von Freytag-Loringhoven would entail, especially since at the time of Barnes's obituary the list of the Baroness's admirers would have been the envy of almost any English-speaking artist of her era. Not only did Margaret Anderson, the editor of the *Little Review,* proclaim that von Freytag-Loringhoven was "the only figure of our generation who deserves the epithet extraordinary,"[6] but when all was said and done, the chorus of voices that at various moments and in various forms had paid tribute to the Baroness included the likes of none other than William Carlos Williams, Marcel Duchamp, Man Ray, Djuna Barnes, Ezra Pound, and Wallace Stevens—not to mention the critics who praised her poetry, graphic art, and unpredictable antics and who heralded her as everything from "the first Dadaist in New York"[7] to "the Mother of Dada" itself.[8]

At the most practical level, the call in Barnes's obituary for an adequate appreciation of the Baroness's work is complicated first of all by the fact that the scope of her artistic endeavors included the literary, plastic, and performing arts and second by the fact that in all of these areas von Freytag-Loringhoven's work transgressed the boundaries separating the individual arts. Yet whether one attempts a piecemeal assessment of the Baroness's work along disciplinary lines or a collective interdisciplinary assessment, the one area where her contributions have never received the critical appreciation they deserve is within the realm of performance, and while an assessment of her experimental performance practices would stand on its own, such an assessment is doubly merited because the performance aesthetic governing those practices not only figured as a driving force in all of her work but in her practice of everyday life as well. Indeed, it is only when her performative transformation of everyday experience is taken into account that the full scope of von Freytag-Loringhoven's work emerges and that the radical social challenge that that work poses begins to take shape. In this respect, an "adequate" appreciation of the performative aesthetic underlying von Freytag-Loringhoven's work, appearing as that aesthetic did at a defining movement in the American avant-garde, has much to tell us about how we conceptualize the history of American experimental performance—especially since that aesthetic, as yet, has received no defining recognition in the history of American avant-garde performance as we know it.

Von Freytag-Loringhoven's performance aesthetic bears an important but critical affinity with the performative undercurrents associated with the use of *found objects* in collage, assemblages, and environments. It is thus worth contextualizing them within the aesthetic currents that they not only helped to initiate but that some four decades later were also the subject of a bitter polemic penned by the art historian Michael Fried. That now legendary polemic was remarkable as a quixotic attempt to wrestle painting from the whims of its beholders and to secure it once again within the autonomous integrity of the traditional frame. In an astute but bitter recognition of what were arguably the most important experimental performative developments in American twentieth-century art, Fried attacked what, in his infamous 1967 essay "Art and Objecthood," he identified as "literalist art," a term he offered as an alternative to minimalism.[9] His criticism focused specifically on artistic expressions that, in their penchant for incorporating preexisting objects and forms into works of art, vacillated between painting and sculpture. In that vacillation, Fried argued, literalist art produced a kind of theatrical situation that was "at war" not only with painting and sculpture as such but also with art in general.[10] Ironically, Fried's attempt to discredit literalist art by associating it with theatricality acknowledged what would prove to be one of the most dynamic aesthetic developments of his era, developments epitomized in happenings and newly emerging forms of performance art.

However inadvertently insightful Fried's essay might have been regarding American experimental art in the mid-1960s, his defense of tradition was marred by a significant oversight. The literalist trends that he identified with Robert Morris and Donald Judd, though innovative in their own rights, were hardly new. Those trends emerged from a tradition that in 1967 was already half a century old and that had its roots in the antipictorial substances of collage and in the related Dada aesthetics of found objects. In pointing out this oversight, I am less interested in Fried's selective sense of tradition than in the wider relevance of his association of literalist art with performance, particularly with what, whether he acknowledged them or not, were the earliest forms of experimental performance associated with the iconoclastic gestures of Dada. Indeed, there is an unmistakable echo of Dada's anticultural agenda at the core of Fried's association of literalist art with theater. "The literalist espousal of objecthood," he argues, "amounts to nothing other than a plea for a new genre of theatre; and theatre is now the negation of art."[11] A more precise positioning of Dada performance in its relation to mainstream culture would be difficult to find, both with regard to the graphic arts and with regard to theater itself. The rub is in this latter aspect. The flip side of Fried's diatribe against literalist art follows the path of his antitheatrical bias, and that path segues directly into Dada. The "espousal of objecthood," at least among the Dadaists, chafed not only against institutionalized notions of painting and sculpture but against the established institutions of theater as well.

Such inverted appropriations of Fried's polemic against literalist art, I would argue, point to a shared aesthetic space where the physical substances of collage and the aesthetically recontextualized articles known as found objects overlap at the crossroads of a redefinition of conventional theater. Across the spectrum of Dada we can find numerous examples of this redefinition, but within the short explosion of Dada activity in New York City in the late teens and early twenties, no one pushed the redefinition of theater further than the Baroness Elsa von Freytag-Loringhoven. Nor was anyone even close to her in her ability to effectively associate that redefinition with a concomitant radical rethinking of conventional notions of masculinity and femininity. In this respect, von Freytag-Loringhoven is more than merely a vastly underrated figure in the cultural histories of the period; she is a figure whose profound importance within the history of American avant-garde performance has never really been addressed. The nature of that importance is not in her limited influence but rather in the alternative precedents that she set and in the ways that those precedents redefine the germinal terms that have been used to characterize American experimental performance for well over three decades. We can only speculate about whether the Baroness's limited influence is the result of the vehement resistance to conventional notions of gender and sexuality that characterizes her performance aesthetics, but one thing that a closer examination of her work can substantiate: the contours of her aesthetics were structured in a critical resistance to the governing patriarchal assumptions that the first American avant-garde, however critical it might have been of society in other respects, nonetheless carried over from the American social mainstream. That resistance poses a significant problem for scholars who would make room for von Freytag-Loringhoven within the existing annals of the American avant-garde.

Simply put, her work, like that of the majority of the women artists discussed in this book, revolts against such simple, neutralizing accommodations.[12] Unlike other women avant-garde artists, however, the Baroness's work is of singular importance because of the unique historical context in which it unfolded. The Baroness's unconventional poetry, her readymade assemblages and her defiant, experimental performances took hold amid the fertile ground of New York's fledgling Dada movement—a movement that embraced and identified itself with the provocations and scandalous antics that had already made von Freytag-Loringhoven a notorious figure within New York's bohemian subculture before the term *Dada* had made its way into the vocabulary of the American intellectual and artistic elite. On its own, the Baroness's work thus offers us a performance theory and practice that would merit our attention. But within the larger narrative contexts of American avant-garde history—where, if not altogether forgotten, von Freytag-Loringhoven is portrayed as a minor figure—her work has gradually accumulated new and added significance with each passing generation. Indeed, in its openly critical attitude toward her male avant-garde contemporaries, the Baroness's work strikes at the accepted pillars of American avant-garde history, belying some of its most enduring myths, and, as a consequence, critically reverberates, domino-like, through that history's constructed patrilineal tradition.

Since the Baroness had no immediately identifiable connection with theatrical institutions and since her dramatic fragment "Chimera" has never been published, her absence from the historiographical landscape of American experimental performance is at one level not surprising. Yet the earliest accounts that we have of von Freytag-Loringhoven—when, for example, she first entered the offices of the *Little Review* bedecked with found objects like the tea balls hanging from her breasts and the spoons and feathers attached to the "black velvet tam o'shanter" that she used as a hat—suggest she arrived on the New York artistic scene with a full-blown performance aesthetic that was as evident in her outrageous costumes as it was in her use of the title she obtained not from birth but from marriage.[13] Indeed, at one level, her costumes would appear to be critically tied to the life in the theater that impoverished circumstances originally denied her in her formative years. We now know for instance that, when still very young and in living in Berlin with her aunt, von Freytag-Loringhoven unsuccessfully attempted "a career as an actress," finding work only "as a 'living statue' in a travelling tableau, and next as a chorus girl."[14] Despite some formal training in drama, the Baroness's career in the theater ultimately ended with her inability to purchase a wardrobe.

The extent to which those early disappointments played a significant role in the flamboyantly constructed costumes that von Freytag-Loringhoven paraded through the streets of New York is anyone's guess. But it is certainly worth noting that, in the construction of her costumes out of found objects, the Baroness effected a kind of living collage that erased the boundaries between life and art and that in a very literal sense foreshadowed Fried's association of literalist art with a redefinition of theater. On this note we need only consider that von Freytag-Loringhoven was willing, for example, first to boycott an invitation to a performance by the opera singer Marguerite D'Alvarez and then to disrupt the subsequent reception with her own counterperformance. Arriving dramatically and fashionably late at the reception, von Freytag-Loringhoven shocked everyone into a stunned silence when she entered wearing "a blue-green dress and a peacock fan," a coal bucket on her head with spoons dangling from it as well as a pink "canceled postage stamp" on the side of her face—which was otherwise powdered in yellow and accentuated with black painted lips.[15] When D'Alvarez, who was clearly provoked by this upstaging, attempted to regain control by explaining that her own work in the opera was art devoted to humanity, the Baroness trumped her again by crudely stating that she "wouldn't lift a leg for humanity" and by then mesmerizing everyone for the next hour with an impromptu explanation of why her anticostume was beautiful.[16]

Allusions like her crude reference to a male dog marking out its territory were typical of a defiance of gendered expectations that characterized not only her irreverent statements but also the costumes with which she scandalized her community. That defiance was evident even in the smallest details. While many stereotypically may have assumed a natural affinity between a woman and a kitchen spoon, for example, no one conceptualized that affinity in terms of an ornamental headdress, and thus the Baroness's costume—which was so successfully ruffled the expectations of New York's high society operagoers—nettled conventional notions of both theater and gender. Indeed, the overlapping of a redefinition of theater with a rejection of the prescriptive theatricality of conventional notions of gender and sexuality permeates von Freytag-Loringhoven's work, both in terms of theory and in terms of performative practice.

From Poetry to Practice: Performance Theory between the Institutions of Theater and Marriage

Inasmuch as the Baroness can be said to have worked out a theory of performance, that theory took shape in the poetry that frequently graced the pages of the *Little Review,* a small but important literary magazine whose editors, Jane Heap and Margaret Anderson, became some of the Baroness's most loyal defenders. A rather unconventional platform for her theoretical explorations of performance, the journal gave von Freytag-Loringhoven substantial poetic liberty, and in the journal's pages the Baroness's poetically charged theoretical explorations of performance coincided with her constant efforts to combine art and life in all of her activities. The pivotal piece in this regard is the Baroness's 1921 poem "Thee

I Call 'Hamlet of Wedding-Ring': A Criticism of William Carlos William's [*sic*] 'Kora in Hell' and why . . .," which was published in two installments since von Freytag-Loringhoven rejected the editors' suggestions for shortening it.[17]

Performative in its own right, von Freytag-Loringhoven's "Thee I Call 'Hamlet of Wedding-Ring'" blurs the boundaries between poetry, literary criticism, and aesthetics and develops a theory of performance contradicting what it implies are the assumptions that unite the institutions of conventional bourgeois theater and the institutions that regulate the social construction of gender and sexuality. At the core of this theory is a challenge to the prescriptive authority that literary dramatic texts have traditionally exercised over performance, an authority to which von Freytag-Loringhoven likens the prescriptive conceptions of gender and sexuality that regulate activity in the public sphere. Support for this analogy is evident in the very title of von Freytag-Loringhoven's poem, which parodies the language of Shakespeare and thus mocks the accepted pinnacles of dramatic literary expression by reducing Hamlet's introspective meditations to a metaphor for the paralyzing effect that social institutions like marriage have (as the poem subsequently explains) on one's ability to defy the restrictive roles that social convention foists upon men and women. The implied argument here is that deference to the social conventions associated with gender and sexuality, like deference to the authority of a literary dramatic text, ultimately contains men and women within a vicious cycle of narrowly defined performative behavior.

Where the title of the poem is subtle and indirect, the content of the poem is unsparing in its mockery of what is perhaps the quintessential example of high dramatic literature. That mockery culminates in an hilarious equation of "Hamlet of Wedding-Ring" with an intoxicated and sentimental "male brute" whose blubbering von Freytag-Loringhoven uses to discredit Shakespearean drama and the institutions of marriage and to characterize them both as a distortion of reality:

> True to formula—male brute intoxicated bemoans world—(into that he never stepped)—his existence—all existence!
> Example:—Hamlet of Wedding-Ring:
> "WhatshallforFlosh—agh? eckshishtensch—eck—eck—eck—shish—damn!—
> life damn! wife damn! art damhc!!! Hellshotashhell—."[18]

While transposing Hamlet's metaphysical reflections into a slurred reference to a toilet ("WhatshallforFlosh" read as "What is all for flush?") typifies the irreverence that critics have long associated with the avant-garde's often playful disdain for the cultural institutions of literature and established theater, the critical weight of von Freytag-Loringhoven's parody falls on the subsequent coinage "eckshishtensch," and on its concise dismissive synopsis not only of Shakespearean metaphysics but also of the social institutions with which she associates them. Like the preceding phrase "WhatshallforFlosh—agh?" "eckshichtensch" is basically a phonetic transcription of slurred pronunciation, but within that slurred pronunciation is the suggestion that literary and social values—spanning the gamut from Shakespearean theater to the rituals of marriage—amount to little more than a drunkard's distortion of "existence."

Crucial to the parallels that von Freytag-Loringhoven draws between the prescriptive authority of a literary dramatic text and the prescriptive enforcement of conventional notions of gender and sexuality is an understanding of those latter, social conventions as a system in which masculinity and femininity derive their meanings and significance not from an essential reality but rather from their constructed performative relationship to each other as binary opposites.[19] Indeed, she portrays this gendered binary not as a reflection of masculinity or femininity per se but rather as a basic failure to come to terms with the complex lived realities seething beneath conventional constructions of gender.[20] Male brutality and ultimately feminine sentimentality are, she argues, two sides of the same "brazen cloak of inexperience," covering and obscuring a fear of life and serving as a kind of diversion from a deeper fear: a fear "to go get—live merry—die trying."[21]

Indispensable to the critical force of this admonishment "to go get" is the theory of performance that coincides with von Freytag-Loringhoven's break with conventional notions of theater and that ultimately allows her to challenge mainstream notions of gender and sexuality without simply exchanging one set of essentialist notions with another. Telling in this regard is the fact that von Freytag-Loringhoven advocates a mode of performance that, at one point, she associates with the loosely scripted traditions of the circus that encourage spontaneity, improvisation, and virtuosity. Against the prescriptive authority of literary texts, which von Freytag-Loringhoven criticizes for being "without point" and for being unable "to point,"[22] von Freytag-Loringhoven lifts up a "value for value:

daring for treasure—valour for deed."[23] She praises "Performance—action—work: breathless—highest tension," and, almost two decades before Antonin Artaud would call for an "affective athleticism," she embraces the circus "Clown—sauntering leisurely—aimlessly—taut in muscle—brain—*to purpose—carries point.*"[24]

In many respects, references such as this one to the circus rescue von Freytag-Loringhoven from the cult of authenticity that so often haunts the critical aesthetics of modernism. For, while moving us away from logocentrism, von Freytag-Loringhoven's references to the circus locate human experience not in notions of the essential but in the performative. In fact, such references provide us crucial insight into the most important dimensions of the overlapping assumptions that she recognizes in the established institutions regulating theater and the established conventions governing gender and sexuality. For in simultaneously challenging the prescriptive authority of dramatic literature and of socially contrived notions of masculinity and femininity, von Freytag-Loringhoven establishes a link between art and life that she then appropriates in an inverted form. Subtly associated with the improvisatory virtuosity of the circus, that inversion equates the blurring of art and life with the unscripted performance of gender and sexuality. At one level the inversion enacts one of the great avant-garde goals of the early twentieth century. But combining a challenge to conventional text-based theater and conventional prescriptive notions of gender gives the blurring of art and life a tenor that was virtually unheard of in early avant-garde circles and that presages much of the experimental feminist art that would emerge as the later part of the twentieth century unfolded.

The personal investment that von Freytag-Loringhoven has in this inversion is evident in the subtext running throughout her poem. Billed in the subtitle as "Criticism of William Carlos William's [*sic*] 'Kora in Hell' and why . . .," the poem is directed as much against Williams personally as it is against the conventional notions of masculinity and femininity perpetuated in his work. Yet even the ad hominem attacks on Williams serve a dual function: the contradiction between his radically experimental art, on the one hand, and his commitment to the structure and privileges of conventional bourgeois marriage, on the other, assume a larger significance for von Freytag-Loringhoven and become emblematic of the general tacit support of patriarchal values within the dominant currents of the early American avant-garde. Von Freytag-Loringhoven encountered these contradictions firsthand in her dealings with Williams on a personal level, and like her poetic criticism of his literary work, her personal interactions with him were never far from her vigilant resistance to a separation of art and life.

Reperforming the Domestic Space

> And here it may be helpful to remember that *collage,* literally a pasting, is also a slang expression for two people living (pasted) together—that is to say an illicit sexual union—and that the past participle "colle" means "faked" or "pretended."[25]

Charged with complicated sexual politics, von Freytag-Loringhoven's unconventional relationship with William Carlos Williams segues from the more theoretical aspects of her poem into the practical aspects of her experimental performances. Unfortunately, von Freytag-Loringhoven did little to document the specifics of her interactions with Williams, and thus we must in part rely on Williams's own recollections. This may be more helpful than it first appears. Though there are numerous accounts of von Freytag-Loringhoven's eccentric activities in Greenwich Village in the late teens and early twenties, Williams's accounts of his interactions with her, though not the most lengthy and though somewhat begrudging in expressed appreciation, contain what may very well be the best traces that we have of an active performance aesthetic functioning beneath the more colorful accounts of her costumed antics in the Village.

When one reads Williams's account of their interactions, four significant events tend to stand out in his narrative. First there was their initial encounter when Williams, impressed by von Freytag-Loringhoven's assemblage *Portrait of Marcel Duchamp,* was so keen to make her acquaintance that on the day of her release from the Tombs (where she had been detained for stealing an umbrella), he rushed to meet her and "took her to breakfast."[26] In a later description of this meeting, Williams recalled that "she talked and he listened till their heads melted together and went up in a vermillion balloon through the ceiling drawing Europe and America after them."[27] More rendezvous and conversation followed, which took a decisively sexual turn when Williams presented the Baroness with a basket of very ripe peaches. Von Freytag-Loringhoven understood the peaches as gesture toward seduction: "Not just peaches," she told Margaret Anderson (editor of the *Little Review*), "they were ripe peaches. Are American men really so naive as that?"[28] This then led to their second major encounter: a meeting in which, as Williams recalls, von Freytag-Loringhoven "had an intimate talk with me and advised me that what I needed to make me great was to contract syphilis from her and so free my mind for serious art."[29] Around this same time, a third encounter occurred that was site specific: Williams paid a visit to her flat, a dirty "subbasement apartment on West Eighteenth Street," which was full of junk and "rubbage [*sic*] found in the streets" and which Williams described as part of "the most unspeakably filthy tenement in the city."[30] There, Williams saw two of the Baroness's small dogs going "at it on her dirty bed" and von Freytag-Loringhoven apparently unsuccessfully came on to him again.[31]

Their fourth encounter began as seductive ruse and ended as one of the most legendary altercations of the period. Williams, who was a medical doctor and married, recalls that von Freytag-Loringhoven "had had some little squirt of an accomplice" lure him out on an emergency house call so that she could steal him away for an evening of sex—a ruse that made light of both Williams's professional and private life. Williams was completely surprised by the setup, later explaining, "I was taken aback, as may easily be imagined, and non-plused besides, because—she was a woman." A woman indeed! When Williams resisted her advances, she "hauled off and hit" him on the neck. He was shocked enough that he went home, bought a punching bag, began training, and several months later when she made advances again, he hit her in the mouth and "had her arrested."[32] Surprising in this last encounter is the extent to which later accounts of Williams' assault have deferred to his portrayal of it as a justifiable retaliation for the earlier altercation. Despite the amount of time that had passed and despite the fact that a woman lay on the ground, having taken a fist in the face, the police intervened on Williams' behalf—as if to make clear once and for all that women who are forward enough to pursue their own sexual desires need to be disciplined both in the private and public spheres. Despite his clear conflict of interest in this matter, no one has ever seriously questioned Williams' account. One thing, however, is clear, and it has criminal implication to which the police turned a blind eye. Whereas the Baroness surprised him with a spontaneous outburst, he later responded with a premeditated assault.

Although these amateurish boxing rounds easily parody the macho posturing of figures like Arthur Cravan, the more important aspects of the encounters between von Freytag-Loringhoven and Williams have to do with von Freytag-Loringhoven's sexual forwardness and with the threat of syphilis that Williams associated with her erotic advances. Since Williams himself is the source of our knowledge of von Freytag-Loringhoven's desire to liberate him with syphilitic infection, it is unclear whether von Freytag-Loringhoven made the proposal to give Williams syphilis before or after she had published "Thee I Call 'Hamlet of Wedding-Ring.'" But the significance of the proposal, which critics have understood as an overzealous response to the love letter that Williams apparently sent to von Freytag-Loringhoven, is if not directly tied to, then at the very least illuminated by, the theories of performance articulated in her poem.[33]

One of the main reasons for suggesting this connection is that the specter of syphilis appears to have been a performative construct created by von Freytag-Loringhoven. Irene Gammel notes that though the Baroness had been successfully treated for syphilis twenty-five years earlier when she was working as a chorus girl in Leipzig and Halle, "there is no medical evidence" suggesting that she "was ill or infectious with the disease."[34] So despite Williams' claim—"I could not go to bed with her. Disease has no attraction for me"—medical evidence, as well as the testimony of her friends, indicates that von Freytag-Loringhoven did not actually have syphilis at all.[35] Indeed, one would be hard pressed to explain Williams's anxiety about contracting syphilis from the Baroness as being founded on anything more than a conventional framing of her proposal within the stereotypical association of promiscuous women, first of all, with the spread of a disease that we now know historically to have been propagated largely by men[36] and, second, with a collapse of an accepted social order that largely relegated women to domestic roles. Ironically enough, these same stereotypes overlapped with the threat that, according to the dictates of bourgeois morality, theater posed to society at large as the presumably seditious, home-wrecking site of licentiousness behavior and radical ideas—a threat often conceptualized as being of epidemic proportions.

This overlap has everything to do with a blurring of the image of syphilis with von Freytag-Lovinghoven's notion of the performative. Inasmuch as the advanced stages of syphilis actually do attack and destroy the mind, the threat that the disease presents provides an apt parallel for the disruptive social implications posed by performative gestures in which von Freytag-Loringhoven assertively defied conventional gender roles. The issue is not so much whether her promiscuity was a threat to public health but whether her radical sexuality was a threat to the accepted ideological order of the body politic. And in this respect, von Freytag-Loringhoven's proposal to Williams exemplifies a radically subversive appropriation and inversion of the stereotypical image of the syphilitic woman.

That image, inasmuch as it is implicitly connected with a freeing of the mind for "serious art," is positioned in an irreconcilable, hostile, and threatening relation to the underlying assumptions governing the notions of art and order that Williams, despite his avant-garde affiliations, maintains for example in "Kora in Hell." Consider, from "Kora in Hell," his depiction of the consolations of art:

> A man watches his wife clean house. He is filled with knowledge by his wife's exertions. This is incomprehensible to her. Knowing she will never understand his excitement he consoles himself with the thought of art.[37]

One doesn't have to delve too deeply to grasp the problematic side of Williams' characterization of art as a source of consolation for his wife's inability to comprehend his excitement about her performing the role of a domestic servant. From a historical standpoint, however, the characterization is important because it illuminates the limits of social experimentation that artists like Williams were willing to tolerate and that artists like von Freytag-Loringhoven emphatically opposed. We will return momentarily to this image of domestic tidiness and to the manner in which the Baroness's "unspeakably filthy" West Eighteenth Street apartment desperately needs a critical examination that illuminates its role as an counterdomestic installation or performance site where the blurring of art and life challenges the social order at a degree not even achieved even by Kurt Schwitters's celebrated *Merzbau.* But for the moment, it is worth pausing to consider the far-reaching implications of von Freytag-Loringhoven's representation of herself as a disruptive syphilitic woman.

The stakes here would seem to be pretty high. For if, at a conceptual level, the threat of syphilis functioned as a model for the theories structuring not only the course of the Baroness's own activities and of what she considered "serious art" but also specifically the course of what amounted to her radically subversive blending of life and art, then her passing proposal to William Carlos Williams offers us a glimpse at a notion of performance whose implications rival Antonin Artaud's use of the plague as a metaphor for a theater "that attacks not bodies but customs," and that like "poison," once "injected into the social body, disintegrates it."[38] The comparison of von Freytag-Loringhoven's use of syphilis to Artuad's use of the plague is hardly contrived, but it is specified in an emphasis on issues of gender and sexuality that are easily lost in Artaud's broad challenge to "all sorts of national or international conventions."[39] In this regard, it is important to remember that historically syphilis was a plague in its own right, coming from America and sweeping across Europe a little more than two hundred years before the 1720 plague of Marseille that Artaud describes in the opening chapter of *The Theater and Its Double.*

Even after it had been brought under control, syphilis retained its association with the plague, and by the nineteenth century that association had jelled in the popular consciousness into a pivotal element in a constructed ideological battle between all the social anarchy, on the one hand, that Artaud himself associates with the plague and the hallowed institutions of marriage and the family, on the other, that supposedly sustain the social order. In the case of syphilis, the threatening specter of anarchy was ideologically tied to moral arguments that both warned against sexual activity beyond the sanctioned auspices of marriage and that reinforced an idealized image of domestic women as chaste and devoid of sexual desire. Indeed, by the early twentieth century, the specter of syphilis was considered to be a threat not only to the patriarchal structures of the family, but, true to the spirit of anarchy, it was considered to be a threat to the state as well.

During the First World War, the syphilitic woman was even considered to be unpatriotic since she ultimately hampered the production of healthy soldiers for the trenches.[40] Probably, the best evidence of this attitude is to be found in the pamphlet "When You Go Home—Take this Book With You" that was published in 1918 by the War Department's Commission on Training Camp Activities and that was distributed to new recruits. The pamphlet specifically claimed that "most loose women have clap or syphilis. Many have both." It warned that "a man who goes with any loose woman, no matter what she may say, or how she may look, runs the risk of getting clap or syphilis," and in its closing admonishments, the pamphlet asserted, "Every man should know that going with loose women not only exposes him to disease or other injury, but unfits him for his highest duties as [a] citizen, husband, and father."

"Self-interest, decency, patriotism, regard for others who may suffer from his acts," it concluded, "all demand of a man an effort to attain clean manhood."[41]

At one level, then, von Freytag-Loringhoven's invitation to a perilous intercourse and a conscious procreative exposure to infection amounts to a blurring of seduction with sedition, and as a performative gesture directed against one of the central contemporary figures of the early American avant-garde the proposal is its own tour de force. Cultivating a kind of critical revolt from within—a revolt consistent with von Freytag-Loringhoven's critical attitude toward Duchamp and Tzara as well—her seditious come-on presents us with a performative gesture from the earliest, formative years of the American avant-garde that, more than merely challenging the sexual economies of bourgeois domesticity, positioned that challenge as the cornerstone of an authentically subversive avant-garde. Not only did the gesture identify the traditional bourgeois family as the repressive linchpin in the social mainstream, but it also illuminated a perpetuation of the underlying presumptions of that same conventional social order in the tacit support of male privilege among New York's avant-garde elite.

The implications of this gendered blurring of performance and plague in an invitation to syphilitic infection are by no means limited to the immediate historical context of New York in the early 1920s. Nor are those implications limited to the single gesture of the Baroness's proposition. In fact, the proposition figures into a larger complex of performance activities that lead us directly back to the Baroness's West Eighteenth Street apartment—the apartment that Williams found to be so appallingly filthy. In that apartment, von Freytag-Loringhoven's daily activities took place within constructed surroundings that defied some of the most basic expectations associated with the gendered division of labor. Her apartment is of particular importance to us here because it was packed with found objects, that is, debris from the streets that not only were used for her assemblages and costumes but transformed her apartment into a collage environment that was as disturbing as it was effective in blurring the boundaries between art and life. Offering a kind of sanctuary to the discarded objects of city life (a gesture worthy of consideration on its own), the Baroness simultaneously transformed those same objects and her apartment into the material substances of an antidomesticated space, which mediated the performative dimensions of her daily activities. Some sense of just how radical that transformation was is evident if one considers it in light of Barbara Haskell's explanation of the problematic reception that Robert Rauschenberg encountered four decades later when he began incorporating discarded objects into his art: This, Haskell notes, was not the kind of stuff that people wanted in their homes.[42] True enough, but it was the kind of stuff that von Freytag-Loringhoven arguably recognized to be only truly subversive when it was in the home.

That critics have never considered the aesthetic significance of this proto-loft where von Freytag-Loringhoven combined her artistic work and daily life is indicative of a bias that skews the accepted, conceptual history of American avant-garde performance. In its most general terms, this bias, ironically, has produced a genealogy of the American avant-garde that circumvents American Dada and looks to European Dada for precedents instead. While the work of von Freytag-Loringhoven is perhaps most adversely affected by this circumvention (since the most pronounced performative expressions of American Dada originate with her), the issue here is not so much who receives recognition but rather how scholarly recognition fashions the critical discourse that frames our understanding of subsequent developments in American experimental performance. Telling in this respect is Michael Kirby's highly influential introduction to his 1965 anthology *Happenings* (arguably the urtext of American avant-garde performance history).[43] In this introduction, Kirby posits a critical genealogy for the happenings that links them specifically to the work of Kurt Schwitters and the early European dadaists.[44] At one level, Kirby's discussions of Schwitters and Dada are evidence of the profound impact that the publication of Robert Motherwell's *Dada Painters and Poets* (1951) had on shaping the framework that we continue to use to conceptualize our understanding not only of the happenings but also of the American avant-garde in general.[45] But regardless of its sources, Kirby's focus on Schwitters produces a critical discourse for discussing the American avant-garde that unconsciously reproduces the very notions of male privilege that are incompatible with the governing aesthetic of von Freytag-Loringhoven's work.[46]

That privilege is most immediately evident in the precedent that Kirby argues was set by Schwitters's *Merzbau,* which bears a stunning similarity to von Freytag-Loringhoven's apartment. Just as the Baroness's apartment was teeming with the rubbish and junk that she had hauled in from the streets, so too, as Georges Hugnet noted, was Schwitters's home full of "heaps of wooden junk, tufts of horsehair, old rags [and] broken and unrecognizable objects."[47] But whereas Schwitters, through this predilection for detritus, is recognized for "apparently succeed[ing] in evoking the impossible,"[48] von Freytag-Loringhoven is implicitly characterized as a wretch for living in an "unspeakably filthy tenement."[49] Even positive accounts of her work have not evinced the conceptual wherewithal to recognize the critical and aesthetic implications of her having introjected a random chaotic collection of found objects into precisely that space, the domestic space, which she as a woman was expected to maintain in an orderly, tidy fashion.

In terms of precedent, the implications of the Baroness's disruption of domestic sanitary sanctity reverberate well beyond the contrast between von Freytag-Loringhoven and Schwitters, and they suggest the need to rethink along gendered lines what Barbara Haskell has called the "aesthetics of junk" that emerged from beneath the shadows of abstract expressionism and that, for example, pepper Allan Kaprow's 1966 book *Assemblage, Environments, & Happenings.* That key documentation of the happenings is divided by section titles like "Specters from Refuse," "Out of Gutters and Garbage Cans," and "Debris and Debris."[50] While such references and the concomitant use of "soiled and untidy artifacts of the street" in the performative expressions of happenings artists like Allan Kaprow, Jim Dine, and Claus Oldenburg may very well indicate, as Barbara Haskell has noted, a departure from the "subjective abstraction" of abstract expressionism and while they may "mark a shift . . . toward a more objective, unmediated relationship with the environment" and toward the "vernacular realism" of the happenings, those same titles and the vernacular realism to which they refer perpetuate a gendered performative discourse illuminated in the precedent set by von Freytag-Loringhoven's junk-filled dwelling.[51] There is in the histories of the avant-garde a telling contrast between the disregard for the Baroness's cluttered apartment and the critical delight with the messiness of Schwitters's *Merzbau,* of Duchamp's *dust breeding,* of Dine's *The House* or even of Oldenburg's *Snapshots from the City.* Indeed, that contrast tells us much about how conventional our understanding of the early American avant-garde is when it comes to questions of gender. For the message heretofore is unmistakable: boys who play with junk and dirt are creative and innovative, while girls who play with junk are derelict and dirty.

In a more practical sense the message is that male artists may embrace "soiled and untidy artifacts of the streets"[52] while tacitly reaffirming the domestic division of labor, and in this respect that embrace simultaneously reaffirms the most conventional domestic traditions of bourgeois society. Not only are those same traditions reaffirmed in the disregard of von Freytag-Loringhoven's disruption of the domestic space, but that disregard also silences a vital tradition within the history of American experimental performance, one that begins with von Freytag-Loringhoven and is present in Stein's *Mother of Us All* and that becomes a pivotal element in the Fluxus events of figures like Yoko Ono and Alison Knowles, who, apparently unaware of von Freytag-Loringhoven's radical challenge to the conventional domestic space, began questioning domestic sanctity in Fluxus works like *Kitchen Piece* (Ono) and *Salad Piece* (Knowles). Yet without any significant attempts to trace that tradition, a major current in the American avant-garde remains buried and obscure.

Three Episodes from a History of Erasure

> How you know I write that poem?
> I am not entirely without imagination, said Jane.
> My real name is another thing. I write it out for you.
> She sat down and with extreme ceremony, the peasant buttons
> ringing like bells, wrote "Baroness Elsa von Freytag von
> Loringhoven"[53]

Given the critical antagonism that so often characterized Dada's attitudes toward the institutions of mainstream culture, some have argued that the Baroness's obscure position within the extant chronicles of American avant-garde performance history is its own ironic success.[54] Yet whatever lighthearted homage to von Freytag-Loringhoven such arguments may intend, they are arguably grounded in a conceptual model of avant-garde practice that provides ideological cover for the crassest mishandling of the Baroness's work, and I am thinking here of a model that lends tacit approval to an appropriation and ultimate distortion of her work at material, intellectual, and performative levels. Nowhere are the ideological underpinnings of that model more evident than in the adverse relationship that von Freytag-Loringhoven's work has with presumably fundamental principles of avant-garde practice like those posited by Peter Bürger in his short book *Theory of the Avant-Garde,* and indeed, suggestions that the Baroness's obscurity is somehow tied to a conscious Dada strategy arguably derive from Bürger's contention that Duchamp's readymades exemplify the avant-garde's more general "radical negation of the category of individual creation," or, in other words, that they exemplify a basic rejection of the bourgeois category of the artist as producer, a rejection that Bürger suggests is typical across the spectrum of avant-garde practice.[55] Not only is it debatable whether Bürger's arguments accurately characterize Duchamp's work, but to attempt to fit von Freytag-Loringhoven into a model derived from Bürger's arguments distracts us from a more pressing issue that the Baroness's case highlights.

Rather than a characterization of the Baroness's obscurity as an ironic affirmation of the Dadaist rejection of the notion of the artist as producer, what is really needed is some critical reflection on the extent to which the "negation of the category of individual creation" is, in fact, a kind of ruse that is not nearly as radical as Bürger suggests and that discourages a closer examination of how women artists like von Freytag-Loringhoven have been pushed into obscurity by an often crass appropriation (indeed, if not a conscious seizure) of their work—an appropriation that reconfigures their political aesthetics and that in the specific instance of von Freytag-Loringhoven neutralizes her criticism of the very attitudes that, ironically, led to the appropriation of her work in the first place. To give this examination a more pointed articulation: we need, in short, to be vigilant in asking basic critical questions like who gains the most and who loses the most when the "radical negation of the category of individual creation" is posited as a fundamental paradigm of the avant-garde. In an environment where the work of women artists was vulnerable to a kind of subtle piracy, the answer is that women ended up on the losing end.

There is no better illustration of this latter point than in the simple contrast between Duchamp's supposed negation of individual creation and the misattribution of von Freytag-Loringhoven's work to other artists. Indeed, this latter mishandling of the Baroness's work is more instructive than one might first imagine. For as a point of contrast, it illuminates just how provisional the Dadaist "negation of the category of individual creation" actually was, and that illumination, in turn, returns us to fundamental questions of performance, authority, and privilege.

Significant in this regard, first of all, is a small readymade assemblage with the lofty title *God* that is part of the Arensberg collection at the Philadelphia Museum of Art and that stands just outside of the entrance to the Duchamp collection where Duchamp's *Fountain* (or rather a delightfully ironic reproduction of Duchamp's *Fountain*) is on display. Long attributed to Morton Schamberg—and, in fact, the display case at the museum still officially attributes the piece to him—this small assemblage was constructed out of an inverted plumbing trap placed in a miter box shortly after Duchamp's *Fountain* was rejected from the Independents exhibition in 1917.[56] Spearheaded by the research of Francis Naumann, however, a substantial consensus of historians now attributes the work to von Freytag-Loringhoven.[57] There are strong stylistic justifications for crediting this piece to her, which we need not rehearse here since Naumann does an eloquent job of presenting them in his book *New York Dada, 1915–1923*. More important for our purposes are the piece's political aesthetics, which are so consistent with the critical rethinking of gender and sexuality in von Freytag-Loringhoven's other work that it is difficult to imagine Schamberg being responsible for the piece.

As we will see momentarily, those aesthetics are tied to a notion of the performative that critically engages the derogatory attitudes toward women assumed in works like Duchamp's *Fountain.* But pushing toward a critical exploration of the performative dimensions of *God* also moves us in a direction that belies the assumption that avant-garde expression negates the category of the artist as creator. This is as true of Duchamp's *Fountain* as it is of von Freytag-Loringhoven's *God,* and, specifically as it pertains to Duchamp's *Fountain,* the question with regard to individual creation pivots on a slippage between Duchamp and the signature "R. Mutt," which he inscribed across what became the bottom side of the urinal once he had inverted it. However one finally interprets the significance of the signature "R. Mutt,"[58] two aspects of that signature remain constant and are of fundamental importance to understanding the larger significance of the misattribution of von Freytag-Loringhoven's work to other artists. First of all, with this signature, Duchamp assumed the role of a character—a character that he created—even if the enactment of that role was literally as fleeting as Roland Barthes tells us the role of the author is: the author who is only an author in the tangible act of writing itself. Second, when all the theorizing is done, even Peter Bürger ultimately attributes *Fountain* to Duchamp (as Duchamp's contemporaries also quickly did). The negation that Bürger posits theoretically pales in the actual attribution of *Fountain* to Duchamp.

While Bürger claims that Duchamp's *Fountain* radically negates "the category of individual creation,"[59] his actual attribution of the piece to Duchamp ultimately reaffirms the artist as creator. Yet what obscures that reaffirmation is a surprisingly conservative antitheatrical bias that, conceptually, Bürger shares with the art critic Michael Fried. In their definitions of art and antiart, neither acknowledges the gesture as a source of creative production. Yet if anything supersedes the "negation of individual creation" in *Fountain,* it is the Duchampian gesture, which is at its most rudimentary level a performative gesture. Not only does this performative gesture underscore how utterly divorced Bürger's theories of the avant-garde are from any theoretical understanding of the performative dimensions of avant-garde practice, it also constitutes its own specific instance of individual creation, one that by Duchamp's own accounting largely pivots on the specific rapport that he develops with his audience. Although the Duchamp in that rapport is admittedly no less a creative construct than R. Mutt, taking Duchamp out of the R. Mutt equation of *Fountain* would substantially alter the gesture's aesthetics. At the very least, a recognition of the performative underpinnings of Duchamp's *Fountain* highlights that it is imperative for theater historians and performance theorists to radically rethink the paradigms that Bürger provides us for understanding the avant-garde, and in this respect, it is important to remember that the performative gesture in Duchamp's *Fountain* is by no means unique to Duchampian aesthetics.

The aesthetic, indeed the political, force of the constructed role of the artist as creator is no less a factor in von Freytag-Loringhoven's work than in Duchamp's, and the misattribution of the Baroness's work to other artists like Shamberg, which has significantly contributed to her obscurity, has also short-circuited a fuller exploration of what for lack of a better term we might call the von Freytag-Loringhovenian gesture. That gesture and its performative dimensions are evident in the readymade assemblage *God;* so too is the dissident, aesthetic rapport that the gesture builds in relation to von Freytag-Loringhoven's contemporaries in the first American avant-garde.[60] Far from paying homage to Duchamp, whom the Baroness once described as having come "to this *country*—protected—carried by fame to use its plumbing fixtures—[and] mechanical comforts," the assemblage of plumbing trap and miter box is arguably positioned not as an echo of the aesthetics of Duchamp's readymades as critics have often suggested (especially those who would attribute the work to Shamberg) but rather as an intensely critical, indeed hostile, retort to the latent misogyny in Duchamp's *Fountain.*[61]

Amplifying the performative dimensions of that retort is the implicitly enacted threat of dismemberment suggested by the severed and twisted phallic plumbing trap still held in the clutches of the miter box. Evoking the specter of the *vagina dentata* (the Indian myth of the fanged vagina that so concisely symbolizes the stereotypical projections emanating from male anxieties about female power), the miter box poses a threat that, on a symbolic level, the Baroness did not hesitate to perform as a *fait accompli.* Francis Naumann recalls, for example, that von Freytag-Loringhoven carried a plaster penis with her, which she delighted in showing "to all the 'old maids.'"[62] As shockingly indecorous as that plaster penis might have been, von Freytag-Loringhoven's possession of it goes a long way toward establishing her authority as the artistic force behind the assemblage *God,* and, combined, the assemblage and the plaster penis offer an early example of the Baroness consciously seizing the symbols of male anxiety in a performative gesture that recast them as crucial elements in a radical rethinking of gender and sexuality. In this respect, von Freytag-Loringhoven's assemblage pivots on a disturbingly provocative gesture that foreshadows her later inverted appropriation of the stereotypical image of the syphilitic woman.

Just how provocative a riposte this gesture was within the avant-garde itself only becomes apparent when contrasted with the sexual connotations of Duchamp's *Fountain.* Although those sexual connotations are well known, they are worth recalling briefly. By presenting the porcelain urinal in a rotated position, Duchamp not only separated the urinal from "its utilitarian context" but "the hole at the base [of the urinal] scurrilously evokes . . . [a woman's] vulva" as well.[63] However typical this gesture may be of the blurring of gender that scholars like Amelia Jones have traced throughout Duchamp's work,[64] it also reminds us to be cautious in assuming that a blurring of gender is necessarily a signal of progressive sexual politics. For if the association of the womb with a urinal blurs the boundaries between masculinity and femininity, it does so while simultaneously preserving a constructed, fetished debasement of women. Whether directed specifically at Duchamp's *Fountain* or merely at the misogynistic attitudes that Duchamp's readymade perpetuates, von Freytag-Loringhoven's assemblage answers the derogatory representation of women as a pissoir with a gesture that wittily equates masculinity with a trap (a plumbing trap), or that, more precisely, equates the kind of masculinity that pivots on a degradation of women with a trap—a trap for both women and men. Getting out of that trap, the piece implies, necessitates radical action: dismemberment of the offending male member (the phallic "Cast Iron Lover").[65]

Von Freytag-Loringhoven's critical inversion of the cultural symbols of male anxiety was a recurrent strategy in her aesthetics that consistently positioned the Baroness as a voice of profound dissent within the ranks of the avant-garde, and in this respect the critical tension that her assemblage *God* builds in relation to Duchamp's *Fountain* is more typical than one might first imagine, and it is typical both with respect to questions of aesthetics and with respect to questions of attribution. At its most basic level, that tension endured in von Freytag-Loringhoven's aesthetics because the misogynistic underpinnings of Duchamp's *Fountain* were by no means unique to that particular piece or to Duchamp himself. This last observation may be so obvious that we could easily fail to ponder its implications long enough to recognize what is perhaps the most important lesson that *Fountain* offers us about the sexual politics of the American avant-garde: namely, that a blurring of gender is not necessarily synonymous with progressive sexual politics and may in fact cloak a regressive reaffirmation of the most conservative sexist attitudes.

In many respects, the unfolding of this regressive sexual political undercurrent in the performative practices of the early American avant-garde produced two histories of Dada: the former indigenous, unofficial, and chaotic; the later imported, official, and programmatic. If the fate of Elsa von Freytag-Loringhoven as a Dadaist is any indication of the consequences of fitting the former into the latter, then the official arrival of Dada on the New York scene was its own small disaster. That arrival initiated a process that substantially erased the dynamics of dissent that characterized the work of the one person whom her contemporaries identified as "the first Dadaist in New York."[66] and, more precisely, whose performative practices were in a very literal sense Dada *avant le lettre.* Ironically, while offering a platform for the Baroness's iconoclastic artistic expression, official Dada also had an homogenizing effect. It appropriated von Freytag-Loringhoven's general outrageous irreverence while filtering out her acerbic assault on conventional notions of male privilege. Arguably that process inclined toward an image that was epitomized in Duchamp's alter ego Rrose Sélavy (the constructed persona in whom Duchamp, as we will see momentarily, repeated the sexual politics of *Fountain,* blurring the boundaries of gender while nonetheless perpetuating the most conventional of images of women). Moreover, that process was indisputably fueled in part by a callous disregard of von Freytag-Loringhoven's intellectual property, a disregard that, not surprisingly, was not present in the handling of the work or performances of her male counterparts. The two major instances of this disregard were directly tied to her experiences with Man Ray and the official arrival of Dada in New York.

As an official movement, Dada in New York was short-lived enough that Marcel Duchamp and Man Ray only managed to put together a single issue of the journal that they appropriately entitled *New York Dada.* While the journal's appearance in April 1921 might suggest a belated arrival of Dada on the American shores, the journal did less to initiate a Dadaist movement in New York than it did to provide a specific characterization of work already under way by artists whose predilections were provocative and iconoclastic enough that they needed little guidance or inspiration from impresarios like Tristan Tzara (who extended his permission to use the word *Dada* in a letter printed in the journal). That the final page of the journal bore two portraits of Elsa von Freytag-Loringhoven underscored precisely this point. The characterization *Dada* followed the Baroness's activities rather than inspiring them. As Hart Crane noted in a letter to a friend shortly after the journal appeared: "I like the way the discovery has suddenly been made that she [the Baroness] has all along been, unconsciously, a Dadaist. I cannot figure out just what Dadaism is beyond an insane jumble of the four winds, the six senses, and plum pudding. But if the Baroness is to be a keystone for it—then I think I can possibly know when it is coming and avoid it."[67] Crane's reaction to the Baroness was by no means unique. Wallace Stevens, for example, "was afraid to venture below Fourteenth Street for fear of running into her."[68] Yet as humorous as Crane's reaction might have been to the Baroness's inclusion in *New York Dada,* he perceptively identified von Freytag-Loringhoven as no less a polarizing figure than the Dada movement proved to be as a cultural phenomenon, and the only real fault in the analogy Crane drew between Dada and the Baroness was his failure to recognize the extent to which the Baroness continued to be a polarizing figure not just as part of the general Dadaist assault on culture but within the official Dada movement itself.

With regard to this latter polarization, it is safe to say that if the journal *New York Dada* offered the Baroness a new conceptual venue for her work, then the rewards of having "all along been, unconsciously, a Dadaist" proved to be mixed. For inasmuch as the journal heightened the Baroness's profile by prominently situating her within the ranks of an official Dada program, so too did the journal ultimately participate in a neutralizing appropriation of her authority as an artist—an appropriation that is disturbingly typical of the handling of her work by her male contemporaries. Seething beneath that appropriation is an unofficial, largely unacknowledged manifestation of American Dada that possessed its own unique dynamic and that in the case of von Freytag-Loringhoven had a specifically proto-feminist bent. As we shall see momentarily, that manifestation is, in its broadest terms, evident in the contrasting modes of performance that characterize Duchamp's masquerade as Rrose Sélavy and von Freytag-Loringhoven's costumed provocations in the streets of Greenwich Village. But on a more immediate level, the dynamics of that manifestation and its appropriation were evident even in the layout of the journal *New York Dada.*

The Baroness's prominent position within the journal was in no small part the result of being the only other person besides Duchamp whose photograph adorned the pages of the single issue of *New York Dada.* The two portraits of von Freytag-Loringhoven in the upper left-hand corner of the closing page gave her a billing comparable to that of Duchamp, who appeared in drag as Rrose Sélavy on the front cover.[69] It is worth noting that Duchamp wore a feathered hat in that photo, which closely resembled the constructed headdress proudly displayed by von Freytag-Loringhoven in the first of her two portraits, and since Man Ray contributed the photos of von Freytag-Loringhoven and Duchamp, it is hard to imagine that this similarity was merely a matter of coincidence—even though scholars have never really taken note of it. Indeed, the similarity is strong enough that one might venture the speculation that this famous instance of Duchampian drag was in fact inspired by von Freytag-Loringhoven, and if true, the speculation would necessitate a complete rethinking of Duchamp's use of Rrose Sélavy in his work.

The other similarity between the cover and the final page of the journal was that both included inverted print. Duchamp appeared "against a background mesh of minute, inverted, typed letters, repeatedly spelling out the words 'new york dada april 1921' "[70] and only the Baroness's name separated her portraits from an inverted poem on the back page that was entitled "Yours with Devotion / trumpets and drums" and that almost certainly was penned by von Freytag-Loringhoven. Unfortunately, the layout of the journal left this poem unattributed even though the authorship of other works, like Tristan Tzara's contribution, was duly noted. Despite the fact that the poem appeared (upside down) next to the Baroness's name and that stylistically the poem resembles the Baroness's other work in both form and content, critics have attributed the poem to Marsden Hartley.[71] While initially one might cite this lack of authorial clarity as another instance of the negation of the artist as individual creator, the failure to attribute "Yours with Devotion" to von Freytag-Loringhoven had an effect reminiscent of the attribution of the assemblage *God* to Schamberg rather than to the Baroness. Indeed, the misattribution of "Yours with Devotion" neutralized what is probably the clearest symbolic indication we have of the Baroness's polarizing significance in the official New York Dada program. The inverted position of "Yours with Devotion" has a lot to do with that status. Gaining a proper perspective on the poem necessitated an inversion of the entire journal, which in turn rendered legible the otherwise inverted phrase "new york dada april 1921." In terms of visual rhetoric, this inversion implicitly equated an understanding of the Baroness's work with an understanding of the dynamics of New York Dada itself—provided of course that one understood that the poem belonged to von Freytag-Loringhoven. Assuming the authorship of the poem was clear, the inverted placement of the poem also implied that gaining a proper perspective on the Baroness's work would turn the work of Duchamp, Ray, Stieglitz, and Tzara upside-down.

Whether this depiction was intentional or not, one could hardly have conceived of a better characterization of von Freytag-Loringhoven's complex polarizing relation to the first American avant-garde. We might debate about whether subsequent generations have been in a better position to assess the Baroness's contributions to the early days of the period once described by Robert Hughes as "the days of antic weirdness."[72] But the suggestion that the work of the Baroness might offer us a perspective that would turn the American avant-garde on its head obviously pivots on whether she receives credit for her contributions in the first place. Denial of that credit affected her in virtually all aspects of her work. Not only were her readymade assemblages and poetry susceptible to appropriation and misattribution, but even her performances were vulnerable to a kind of casual piracy that, at one level, is so obvious that we would be hard pressed to explain the tacit scholarly acceptance of it as anything other than the crudest example of institutionalized sexism. Among the most important examples of this piracy is an explicit performance piece in which (a half a century before the work of Carolee Schneemann, Karen Finley, and Annie Sprinkle) the Baroness's pubic hair was shaved in a critically symbolic gesture that took aim at the likes of Marcel Duchamp and Tristan Tzara. While at some immediate level the performance was identifiable as a critical inversion of the latent misogyny in the whiskers that Duchamp painted on the *Mona Lisa* in *LHOOQ*,[73] in a much broader sense von Freytag-Loringhoven's gesture indicted the official

Dada movement. As Robert Reiss has noted: "The death of Dada in America was announced by the shearing of the hair upon the womb of the Baroness, a woman who was called the 'mother of Dada.'"[74] Yet as provocative as this performance may have been, especially in the Baroness's use of her body as the site of performance, the history of its reception is a tale of the most conventional crass assertions of male authority and control over the female body. It is a tale, in short, that runs counter to numerous subsequent examples of women who like von Freytag-Loringhoven in this proto-feminist piece have performed the explicit body to assert authority over their own bodies.

At any number of levels the reception of that performance is indicative of the precarious but critical position that von Freytag-Loringhoven's work occupied in the male-dominated milieu of the New York avant-garde in the 1920s, and, in this regard, Man Ray's careless handling of the Baroness's poetry in the journal *New York Dada* was consistent with his handling of the Baroness's performance. Indeed, our knowledge of that performance is in a very literal sense framed by the male gaze of Ray's botched attempt to record it in celluloid. Initially intended as a film for Marcel Duchamp, the negative of the performance was destroyed when May Ray accidentally ruined it in the developing process. A sole surviving frame of that film in which the Baroness stood nude in a position that resembled the letter "A" became part of the word America in a postcard sent to Tzara letting him know that Dada was dead in America because it could not "live in New York." Because Ray filmed von Freytag-Loringhoven's performance and because it was Ray who actually sent the postcard to Tzara, this radically experimental use of the body as the site of performance has historically been attributed to him and not to von Freytag-Loringhoven. Some small sense of the peculiarity of that attribution can be garnered simply by recalling that critics consistently discuss Man Ray's photos of Duchamp in drag in terms of a Duchampian performative aesthetic. Within that aesthetic Ray as photographer is justifiably considered to have played a secondary technical role because at a conceptual level Rrose Sélavy belonged to Duchamp. So too, on a conceptual level, were both the performance behind the photo and the pronouncements regarding the death of Dada in the postcard sent to Tzara indebted to von Freytag-Loringhoven, even though this debt and its larger critical implications have been completely eclipsed by the exaggerated credit that Ray has received for what was largely his technical assistance in the postcard and the performance behind it.

Not only did von Freytag-Loringhoven consciously positioned her own aesthetic in direct opposition to the death by absorption into mainstream American values that she admonished Duchamp and others against, but this admonishment constitutes one of the most acerbic and important aspects of von Freytag-Loringhoven's aesthetics, particularly with regard to her polemical position within the ranks of the early American avant-garde. Indeed, in her poetry she had specifically connected Duchamp and Tzara with a death of Dada that resulted from their having compromised on the extent to which they (like Williams Carlos Williams) were willing to extend its artistic principles into the social sphere. Her poem "Love—Chemical Relationship," for example, which begins with the identifications "Un enfant Francais: Marcel (A Futurist) / Ein Deutsches Kind: Else (A Future Futurist),"[75] specifically cites the "Death" of "Marcel," which results from a stagnancy that, in letters to Margaret Anderson, von Freytag-Loringhoven attributed to Duchamp having accommodated himself to "the shallowness of American society."[76] In the poem "Mefk Maru Mustir Daas,"[77] which she also dedicated to Duchamp and which appeared shortly after "Love—Chemical Relationship," she likens Duchamp's willingness to accommodate himself to American shallowness to becoming "the prey of mice," the consequence of which she describes as a slow death.

The Baroness harbored comparable if not harsher sentiments regarding Tzara,[78] whose manliness she taunted as she implicitly called him a fool in the tone poem "Klink—Hratzvenga (Deathwail)":

> Klink—Hratzvenga
> (Deathwail)
> Narin—Tzarissamanili
> (He is dead!)[79]

Playing hard and fast with a shortened feminized version of the German word for fool ("Narin" and *Narr*) and with a distilled German taunt suggesting that Tzara was a wimp ("Tzarissamanili" as *Tzara ist ein Mannili*), the poem implied that Tzara was unable to cultivate a viable notion of masculinity and then rhetorically linked that inability with the death of Dada that her poem personifies in him. Not only did this notion of the death of Dada extend throughout her Dada poetry and her unpublished philosophical writings, but it also surfaced in other performative provocations like the theft of a "crêpe from the door of a house of morning," which she then used as a dress to accentuate the shocking effect of having shaved her head and "lacquered it in high vermilion."[80]

While these performative gestures are interesting in their own right as Dada antics and spectacles, the point is that with their implicit critique of figures like Duchamp and Tzara they subtly set the terms for an aesthetic that like Baroness's critique of Williams Carlos Williams is critically at odds with the dominant aesthetic currents traditionally associated with the avant-garde in the early 1920s. Not only was that aesthetic lost in the credit that May Ray received for what might easily constitute the Baroness's most radically explicit performance, it articulated a critique of patriarchal society that while belonging to the germinal expressions of the American avant-garde is missing from the foundational discourse of American experimental performance history. The lacuna created by that absence has become all the more gaping in recent years as critics like Amelia Jones have argued that Duchamp's use of Rrose Sélavy marked a radical departure from conventional notions of gender in the performative practices of the early American avant-garde.[81] Just how guarded and conventional Duchamp's notions of gender were in contrast with the performance aesthetics practiced by von Freytag-Loringhoven is easily obscured by the deep personal affection that the Baroness felt for Duchamp as a person.

A confusion of that affection for an affinity in their notions of gendered performance arguably mars the parallel that Jones would draw between von Freytag-Loringhoven and Duchamp. Indeed, that parallel substantially diminishes the radical dimensions of Freytag-Loringhoven's performances as actual acts of provocation that had political consequences and as conceptual gestures that exposed the conventional notions of femininity reinforced by the image of Rrose Sélavy. Some sense of this diminishment is evident in the comparison that Jones makes between von Freytag-Loringhoven and Duchamp in an article published shortly after her book on Duchamp appeared. Here she argues that "the Baroness Elsa von Freytag-Loringhoven's bizarre, sexually ambiguous self-performances in the streets of New York and Duchamp's masquerade as a woman ('Rrose Sélavy') in the well known series of photographs are dramatic *performances* of Dada," both of which in their "confusion of gender and overt sexualizations of the artist/viewer relationship challenged post-Enlightenment subjectivity."[82]

What is amazing about this comparison is how blithely Jones skips over the differing terrains of the performances that she equates—and the differences are rather profound. The Baroness took her performances to the streets, where the blurring of art and life was manifested in a direct confrontation with the body politic. In this respect, her performances resonated with at least implicit if not self-conscious sexual-political agitation. Parading through Greenwich Village in sexually explosive attire that often scantily clad her body with detritus found in the streets, her actions were provocative enough that she was repeatedly subjected to police restraint. As Margaret Anderson recalls:

> Tired of conventional dressing, she [the Baroness] began creating costumes which resulted in her arrest whenever she appeared upon the streets. Tired of official restraint, she leaped from patrol wagons with such agility that policemen let her go in admiration.[83]

At a time when Duchamp's readymades were pressing the question "What is art?" von Freytag-Loringhoven was clothing herself in found objects and marching off into social spaces where her performances pressed not just the question "Where is art permissible?" but also "Where is art by women permissible?" and "To what extent may a woman assert control over the relation of her body to the practices of art?" Indeed, von Freytag-Loringhoven's repeated confrontation with the authorities and the personal risks that those confrontations meant to her as a woman cast a glaring light on the emperor's new clothes, and exposed how safe and contained Duchamp really was in the security of May Ray's studio where he twice put on a woman's hat and coat while Man Ray photographed him.

Since those portraits stopped at the shoulders, there is no reason to believe that Duchamp didn't keep his pants on. Indeed, that probability carries a tremendous amount of symbolic weight, especially if, as Jones suggests, the image portrayed in the portraits coincides with the "contemporary visual codes signifying the [proper and] fashionable bourgeois female."[84] In this respect, the portraits of Duchamp as Rrose Sélavy lend themselves as much to a fundamentally conservative reaffirmation of male projections of femininity as they do to any challenge to post-Enlightenment subjectivity. They easily function not as a challenge but as a dramatic illustration of a patriarchal authoring of women, an illustration that can be substantiated with immediate and tangible examples of how von Freytag-Loringhoven's work has been received (or perhaps could have received) in contrast to Duchamp's.

The long-range implications of that contrast are difficult if not impossible to calculate. For it is one thing to recover the work of an artist at a scholarly level and to use that act of recovery as the basis for rewriting cultural or performance history, and it is another thing to recognize in that act of recovery the numerous historical junctures where an unhindered or unmanipulated visibility of von Freytag-Loringhoven's work might have substantially altered the performative practices of artists from subsequent generations. In the final analysis, the act of recovery constitutes a reconstructed history of precedent; recognition of what was hindered, on the other hand, constitutes a history of the privilege of influence. Though the importance of reconstructing the history of precedent is that it dispels the illusion that influence is merely a product of artistic innovation and merit, lingering unanswerable questions haunt the performance legacy that von Freytag-Loringhoven left behind. What impact would her revisioning of the domestic space have had on the shape of works like Carolee Schneemann's *Eye/Body,* or what impact would the shaving of her pubic hair and its implicit critique of gendered tropes of Dada have had on the significance we attribute to neo-Dada Fluxus events like Shigeko Kubota's *Vagina Painting?* What emerges from the aesthetic affinities between feminist artists like von Freytag-Loringhoven and feminist artists like Schneeman, Ono, Kubota, Finley, and Spinkle (to name merely a few) is a sense of persistence that repeatedly and inexhaustibly reconstitutes and renews itself despite social historical currents that have obstructed a linear momentum.

CHAPTER THREE

Avant-Garde Performance, Collage Aesthetics, and Feminist Historiographies in Gertrude Stein's *The Mother of Us All*

One of the most persistent characteristics in the critical reception of twentieth-century collage, especially the reception of its extension beyond the graphic arts into literature and the performing arts, is the widespread tendency to equate a formalistic grasp of collage techniques with a comprehension of collage aesthetics. Yet some sense that the stakes in collage aesthetics go well beyond a focus on technique is evident at least as far back as Max Ernst's famous 1936 assertion: "Si c'est la plume qui fait le plumage, ce n'est pas la colle qui fait le collage" (While the feather may make the plume, it's not the paste that makes the collage).[1] Delightfully open-ended, Ernst's assertion provokes speculation; indeed, it arguably demands a critical examination capable of probing beneath the paste into the underpinning aesthetic assumptions of collage before the pasting begins. In this respect, Ernst's assertion pushes us toward still uncharted conceptual terrain—where the aesthetics of collage precede conscious commitment to any one of the arts and where the history of collage, consequently, can no longer be characterized as a successive (and hence linear) adaptation in the literary and performing arts of techniques first forged in the graphic arts.[2] The liminal spaces of this predisciplinary or fundamentally interdisciplinary aesthetic terrain are the site of some of the most important metacritical reflections fashioned in the twentieth century. Consistent with the defiantly interdisciplinary predilections of the avant-garde, those metacritical reflections resonated well beyond a consideration of the technical particulars of avant-garde expression and simultaneously gave voice to larger epistemological concerns. The avant-garde's self-conscious reflections on how it produced its meanings, thus, emerged hand and hand with an identifiable, working epistemology that queried the production of meaning more generally.

Clearly, the dynamics of that epistemology vary from case to case, but in the confluent, liminal spaces between the literary and performing arts—which are the particular focus of this chapter—the coupling of epistemological and metacritical reflections in avant-garde expression is perhaps nowhere more profoundly exemplified than in the historiographical concerns underlying Gertrude Stein's implicit embrace of collage aesthetics in *The Mother of Us All* (1946).[3] Stein's libretto *The Mother of Us All* provides an unconventional historical narrative that generally focuses on the life of Susan B. Anthony as a committed suffragette and advocate for women's rights. Accompanying this narrative are a number of minor fictional narratives dealing with courtship, weddings, and reflections on the meaning of marriage for women—all of which play against the backdrop of actual historical figures populating the stage and engaging in political debate. Among those historical figures are the piece's two acting narrators, Virgil T. and Gertrude S., who are modeled after Virgil Thomson and Gertrude Stein herself and who count among the libretto's more than twenty-five characters. Most of the fictional characters are trivial in significance, whereas those like Anthony and her companion Anne (Anna Howard Shaw) enjoy significant positions within the annals of history.

In *The Mother of Us All,* Susan B. Anthony moves among prominent American presidents and politicians, who are folded into the narrative without regard to the temporal restrictions of chronological history. The most significant of these is Daniel Webster, the Massachusetts state senator and later secretary of state from the first half of the nineteenth century, with whom Susan B. debates in the second scene in what is arguably the pivotal moment of the first act—a debate constructed out of actual speeches given by Webster and Anthony. With respect to history, it is not a matter of coincidence that in the opening scene of Stein's libretto, which precedes this debate, Susan B. is pasting clippings into a scrapbook (a kind of domestic version of collage). Gertrude Stein, as we shall see momentarily, undertakes a similar endeavor with her use of historical documents.

If the first act highlights Susan B.'s political struggles as a feminist activist, the second act casts a dark shadow across her eventual successes, leaving open the question of whether her efforts have accomplished more than creating a space within a political order that those efforts sought to overturn. The second act thus begins with Susan B. reluctantly breaking away from housework to give a political speech—a speech that ultimately is so successful that she fears a backlash that would prove detrimental to the cause of woman's suffrage. The scene then changes and the narrative picks up years later when Susan B., now dead, is being celebrated and a monument has been erected in her honor. As characters surround the statue, Susan B.'s voice can be heard reflecting not just on her life's work but also on the question of whether that work has effected real change or been absorbed into a political order that has for all intents and purposes remained intact. In simplest terms, this line of questioning coincides with what one might posit as the question looming over the reception of Stein's work within the extant histories of the avant-garde, a question whose implicit answers are linked in Stein's libretto with the scrapbook collage of history she constructs.

Indeed, I want to argue that the underlying epistemologies of her libretto pivot on this implicit embrace of collage and thus on how the aesthetics of collage reconfigure the ways in which we conceptualize and know history. Knowledge in this particular instance is historical knowledge, and the reconfiguration of historical knowledge in *The Mother of Us All* is important not only because of its more general epistemological implications but also because Stein's libretto appeared on the cusp of what critics have long argued to be the defining period of American avant-garde performance. Situated midway between RoseLee Goldberg's claim that American avant-garde performance became "an activity in its own right"[4] in 1945 and Arnold Aronson's claim that "American avant-garde theatre . . . made its first appearance with a production of Erik Satie's *Ruse of the Medusa* at Black Mountain College in 1948,"[5] *The Mother of Us All* radically challenged the structures of historical knowledge, and thus, I would argue, also offered a germinal conceptual model for understanding the history of the avant-garde that was then unfolding in the United States. That conceptual model not only characterized the logic of avant-garde performance both in its relation to history and in its relation to historiography, but can also be read as having subtly displayed a knowledge of the emerging history of the avant-garde—knowledge self-conscious enough to critically challenge its patriarchal assumptions.

At a conceptual level, then, the collage aesthetics at play in *The Mother of Us All* facilitate two related trajectories in the work's thematic structures. On the one hand, they initiate a process of reconceptualizing historiography that overlaps with the avant-garde's long-standing antagonism toward history and tradition. At the same time, the content of her libretto, specifically its focus on Susan B. Anthony's fight to obtain a viable political voice for women, channeled the avant-garde's more general antagonism toward history into a self-conscious and highly critical meditation on the gendered construction of the avant-garde's own history. At its most basic thematic level, *The Mother of Us All* questions the patriarchal underpinnings of that history. But the issue here (and in fact, this issue is the driving force behind my entire book) is not merely a challenge that demands a more prominent position for women experimental artists within the existing, accepted histories of American avant-garde performance—something one might conceivably achieve by offering up *The Mother of Us All* as an alternative to Aronson's citation of the 1948 production of Satie's *Ruse of the Medusa* as the beginning of American avant-garde theater. The challenge presented by *The Mother of Us All* is not merely "to recover data about women and fill in the 'female blanks' of [experimental performance] history."[6] On the contrary, in that Stein's implicit embrace of collage aesthetics in *The Mother of Us All* combined feminist activism with a restructuring of historical knowledge, the piece arguably links the call for an adequate assessment of women within the avant-garde with a requisite, radical reconceptualization of the conceptual structures of the avant-garde's historiography. Indeed, if one can speak of a major issue reverberating beyond the frame of Stein's libretto, it is that the former can only be achieved by simultaneously pursuing the latter.

Specifically with regard to that reconceptualization, *The Mother of Us All* plays what I want to argue is a dual role within the history of American avant-garde performance. At a crucial moment in the history of American experimental art—when the critical reception of abstract expressionism, for example, was defining the terms that would dominate our notions of experimental performance well beyond the sixties[7]—not only did Stein's libretto posit the aesthetics of collage as the foundation for a feminist historiography of experimental performance, but the libretto's own structural use of collage techniques further cultivated what was becoming a recurrent metacritical strategy of feminist expression within the performative avant-garde itself. In both respects, *The Mother of Us All* broke conceptual paths that theater and cultural historians have not followed. One might speculate about whether the feminist edge in Stein's libretto alienated critics who might have built upon the conceptual paths that *The Mother of Us All* offered. Such speculations certainly raise important questions, for example, about the underlying assumptions in Michael Kirby's privileging of the action paintings of abstract expressionism over the theory and practice of collage when he defines "the new theatre" and performative practices associated with the happenings.[8] But the fact remains that a half a century after Stein finished what, because of her untimely death, turned out to be her last completed work, the recorded history of American experimental performance has neither built upon the theoretical foundation for a feminist historiography that Stein provided in *The Mother of Us All* nor offered a systematic analysis of the fundamental role that collage aesthetics has played for women experimental artists like Stein in an ongoing critical feminist engagement with the basic concepts of the avant-garde.

In light of the historical narratives of American experimental performance that critics have produced since Stein's death, the significance of her libretto has arguably only increased and so too has its potential for radically altering our understanding of the history of American avant-garde. Exploring the performative dimensions of collage aesthetics, both as a mode of feminist expression and as a historiographical model for the history of the American avant-garde is, broadly speaking, the basic project of this book. Stein's libretto serves as one of a number of different points of departure in this exploration because the specific variation of collage aesthetics that it employs provides the conceptual tools necessary for rethinking the history of American avant-garde performance along feminist lines.

In *The Mother of Us All,* this rethinking is directly tied to a highly self-conscious staging of a crisis in representation that, seen through a variety of paratactical juxtapositions, illuminates the inability of the written word to provide a reliable sense of objective referentiality, and thus my study begins with a consideration of how Stein's libretto challenges the representational stability of both literary and historical texts and blurs the distinction between the two within a self-reflective mediation on the limited referential capabilities of the written word. Important in this regard is the sense in which Stein's libretto, in a profound moment of self-reflective deconstruction, erases the illusion of textual authority and elevates the status of performance both in its relation to artistic expression and in its relation to historical events.[9] In this respect, *The Mother of Us All,* I want to suggest, argues that the events of history have more in common with the events of theater than either has in common with the texts to which we habitually refer when discussing both. Delimited both as an authority for subjugating theatrical performance and as a tool for representing objective (historical) reality—both of which the libretto implicitly posits as always already more than a text can convey—the written word is positioned in *The Mother of Us All* as one element among many over which it possesses no sovereign control. The relation of the written word to performance is thus also structured in Stein's libretto by the radical nonhierarchical juxtapositions that are the signature gestures of collage and that position performance on an autonomous and equal footing with writing itself.

At the historical level, it is this particular aspect of performance (as always already more than the dramatic text) that is of interest to me, especially with regard to the implications that this aspect of performance has for a feminist historiography. For in practical terms, the elements of performance that are least accounted for within the discursive economies that Stein's libretto utilizes are those that the rhetoric of her libretto suggests are most consistently associated with the elided experiences of women. The contrast between text and performance in *The Mother of Us All* thus offers us an important strategy for illuminating the subtle ways in which women are silenced in history. As I will demonstrate momentarily, this strategy pivots on a literary-theatrical dynamic that results from Stein's having constructed her libretto out of a seemingly indiscriminate collage of literary texts and historical documents. Not only does that collage challenge the referential authority of historical documents, but the challenge itself is complimented by a mode of performance that, in its critical relation to Stein's own literary dramatic text, specifically illuminates the limited ability of historical documents to account for feminine experience.[10] The result of this strategy is not only a feminist reconceptualization of historiography but also a feminist recalibration of the avant-garde's privileging of performance over text. Indeed, the historical and the histrionic converge in the feminist currents of Stein's notion of performance, and this convergence has direct bearing on the historiography of the avant-garde itself.

Inasmuch as the history of the avant-garde can partially be traced in the rise of performance as an autonomous sphere of radical experimentation—and even, as a sphere where radical experimentation and radical politics coalesce—the implicit association of experimental performance with feminist activism in *The Mother of Us All* advocates a very different historiography of avant-garde performance than we have seen heretofore. But even with the decisively feminist orientation of Stein's notion of performance, it would be a mistake to assume that *The Mother of Us All* is grounded in a call for a separate and distinct history for women experimental artists.[11] For just as the aesthetics of collage arguably provide the conceptual framework for understanding the juxtaposition of text and performance in *The Mother of Us All*, so too do they provide the conceptual framework for understanding the unreconciled currents of history that Stein's libretto would have us juxtapose in the historiography of the American avant-garde. Simply put, the stakes laid out in *The Mother of Us All* are not geared toward supplanting one historical narrative with another. Rather they are geared toward a strategy that, drawing upon the radical juxtapositions of collage, accommodates a diversity of seemingly irreconcilable aesthetic tendencies while simultaneously calling attention to the constructed nature of the history that the libretto offers.

History as Literature

If the underlying collage aesthetics of *The Mother of Us All* suggests a strategy for a feminist rethinking of the historiography of American experimental performance, that strategy, I would argue, begins with the blurring of literature and history in the composition of Stein's libretto. Important in this regard is the broad questioning that this blurring generates with regard to our general epistemological assumptions about the objective nature of historical knowledge. Since that knowledge is largely based upon historical texts and documents, it too falls under the deconstructive purview of collage aesthetics and of the more fundamental challenge that collage poses not merely to our basic presumptions about the representational capabilities of literature but of language more generally. Since that challenge makes no distinction between literary texts and historical documents and since Stein's libretto is constructed out of both, a fundamental link unites her libretto's self-conscious metacritical literary expressions with the implied historiographical concerns of her text. Both, in short, are joined by a decisive and important challenge to logocentrism, and inasmuch as the collage aesthetics of *The Mother of Us All* queries the accepted foundations of literary expression, so too does it simultaneously query the accepted foundations of historical knowledge.

Much of the force of that query results from the absence in Stein's libretto of any identifiable signs that would indicate qualitative differences between Stein's own production of text and the incorporation of existing historical documents into her work. Incorporated fragments from historical documents like those from Susan B. Anthony's first public speech in 1849 and those from Daniel Webster's most famous speech in the Senate in 1830 are virtually indistinguishable from Stein's own writing, and only the painstaking detective work of scholars like Jane Palatini Bowers has cataloged Stein's tendency in her libretto to blend historical documents (like those mentioned above) with her own literary fabrications.[12]

At the very least, the unqualified juxtaposition of historical documents and literary texts in Stein's libretto, a juxtaposition based upon the aesthetics of collage, suggests that in specific contexts, the substances of history and of literature can be reduced to a comparable status, especially since what we generally understand as the substance of history is derived in large part from privileged documents—and here "privilege" specifically refers to the questionable assumption that historical documents, unlike literary texts, offer us unproblematic instances of objective referentiality. It is precisely on this point that an understanding of those juxtapositions within the conceptual structures of collage aesthetics is particularly helpful. For in its ability to expose a seemingly inexhaustible multiplicity of often contradictory significations attached to countless varieties of everyday objects, collage radically questions whether objective referentiality is even possible with found objects, let alone with textual artifacts. Stein's juxtaposition of historical and literary texts in her libretto is thus not so much the creation of a rarified context in which two modes of textual expression are reduced to a similar status as it is an acknowledgment of the unstable representations and slippages affecting all texts.[13]

Although the aesthetics of collage may be a novel source for the conclusion that historiography bears a close affinity to literary practice, the conclusion itself is a widely accepted perspective among critical theorists today. Much of that acceptance owes a significant debt to the work of Hayden White who in germinal theoretical essays like "The Historical Text as Literary Artifact" (1974)[14] reminded us, first of all, that the substance of our historical narratives is largely textual and based upon documents and manuscripts rather than events themselves; and second, that where there are texts, interpretations, not facts, ultimately prevail. Far from providing a direct link to an earlier objective reality, the representations of historical contexts are always already and always primarily instances of textual exegesis. Establishing a historical context for any work of art is thus an interpretive act, that is, a construction that is subject to all the aesthetic, political, and cultural presuppositions of the literary critic and historian. As White so astutely observed, "These contexts of the texts that literary scholars study, are themselves products of the fictive capabilities of the historians who have studied those contexts."[15]

The lure of White's work can be found in the liberating and astonishingly flexible historiography that he posits. Since that historiography pivots on an equation of the writing of history with the writing of literature, it has amazing potential not only for illuminating how we do history but also for theorizing the work of writers like Stein who appropriate the substance of history (those unruly historical texts) for the production of literature. But the problem is that though Stein and White arguably share a recognition of the literary underpinnings of historiography and of the constructed nature of the histories we take for granted, they have radically different if not altogether irreconcilable conceptions of literature. Indeed, the more carefully one examines White's arguments in "The Historical Text as Literary Artifact" the more apparent it becomes not only how out of sync Stein is with White's sense of literature but also how entangled White's arguments are in a kind of dialectical bind, which seemingly posits a liberating conception of history while simultaneously building that conception on a reassertion of an excessively restrictive and conventional notion of literature that runs counter to the aesthetics of modernism and that is firmly grounded in the established categories of "emplotment" and storytelling.[16] Although White certainly has helped scholars to recognize the primacy of texts where previously they had assumed the prevalence of fact, he paves the bridge between the writing of literature and the writing of history with the mainstream linear notions of narrative that Gertrude Stein resisted throughout her career and that *The Mother of Us All* implicitly equates with a silencing of women.

Certainly, Stein was not alone in her resistance to the notions of literature later (re)perpetuated by White—although her libretto is unique in its channeling of that resistance into what lends itself to a feminist metacritique of the very experimental traditions that she ultimately profoundly influenced. But enough works of twentieth-century literature defy White's restrictive characterization that one can only speculate about the motivations behind his disregard of the experimental modes of literary expression that dominated the period of modernism and gave rise to the avant-garde. This disregard is especially puzzling given the fact that some eight years prior to publishing "The Historical Text as Literary Artifact," White had taken a very different line in an essay entitled "The

Burden of History" (1966). Here he admonished historians to follow the lead of avant-garde novelists and poets and "to conceive of the possibility of using . . . surrealistic, and (perhaps) even actionist modes of representation" in the writing of history.[17] Though he ultimately left his comments undeveloped, the irony of White's call for experimental modes of representation in the writing of history is that while he would later admonish us to openly acknowledge the centrality of texts to the substance of what we call history and while he would argue, furthermore, for the need to recognize those historical texts as literary artifacts, he does so after having encouraged us to adopt a historiography that, in many respects, moves in an antithetical direction.

Consider White's allusion to surrealist representation. Not only did the avant-garde expressions of the surrealists (especially their early Dada-inspired expressions) pivot on a radical break with tradition and history; they also voiced anticultural sentiments that were frequently manifested in an emphatic rejection of literature. Indeed, to get a sense of how antithetical White's call for a surrealistic historiography is to his own later project, both with regard to the call's commitment to history and with regard to its commitment to the literary artifactual underpinnings of that history, one need only think of the example of Antonin Artaud, the surrealist poet and visionary of the theater who emphatically called for "No More Masterpieces" and who, as Susan Sontag has argued, envisaged "nothing less than a complete repudiation of the modern Western theater, with its cult of masterpieces [and] its primary emphasis on the written text (the word)."[18]

At one level, then, White's call for an experimental historiography implicitly rejects the privileged status of texts, and it would move the focus of history toward the unrecorded realms of histrionics, performance, and action. In this respect, White's ephemeral flirtation with "the possibility of using . . . surrealistic, and (perhaps) even actionist modes of representation" in the writing of history might be dismissed as a literary historian's provocative and fanciful interdisciplinary musings were it not for his recognition that novelists and poets—in short, modernist writers like Gertrude Stein—have engaged in the type of historiographical models that he only passingly entertains. With Stein in particular—at least the Stein writing *The Mother of Us All*—experimenting with the boundaries of literature goes hand in hand with an exploration of alternative historiographies, and here alternative refers specifically to an exploration of the slippage between the historical and the histrionic and thus moves toward a performance-based revision of historiography.

One small but exceptionally important example of the performance-based historiography emerging from Stein's subversion of literary genre is tied to the short fragmentary narrative "Interlude" that Stein includes between the final scene of the first act and the beginning of the second act of *The Mother of Us All.* The significance of that narrative, to which Stein appropriately gives the fragmentary title "Susan B. A Short Story" (i.e., a fragmentary title for a fragmentary narrative) has as much to do with the destabilizing effect that its inclusion has on accepted notions of genre as it does with underscoring the chasm separating the textual production of meaning and the performative production of meaning. The effect of including this "Short Story" as an "Interlude" in a dramatic script is thus not only to challenge our conventional preconceptions about literature and narrative, but also, as a consequence, to challenge the implicit historiography in White's equation of the writing of history with the writing of literature. First and foremost, the inclusion of this fragmentary "Interlude" clashes markedly with the integrity of the libretto as a drama as well as with the narrative as a mode of communication. On a microcosmic level, the clash is echoed in the short story's repeated use of parataxis, that nonlinear, countersyntactical deployment of words and phrases that Stein so masterfully perfected as a tool for teasing out meanings eclipsed by conventional usage. Likewise, the abrupt, unexpected shift from dramatic dialogue to fictional narrative yields a paratactical effect, accentuating while simultaneously subverting the delimiting boundaries separating the genres of drama and fiction.

This seemingly simple paratactical juxtaposition of literary styles is fraught with implications for equating the writing of history with the writing of literature. For in emphasizing the liminal space between the genres of drama and fiction, *The Mother of Us All* suggests that established forms of literary expression (as is also the case with the conventional usages of language) consistently suppress a wide range of inchoate but significant meanings. More importantly, this suggestion carries with it a similar indictment of any historiography that, while seeming to radicalize our notion of history with the assertion that historical texts are literary artifacts, adheres nonetheless to a conventional notion of literature. The point is that Stein, inasmuch as her libretto equates the writing of history with the writing of literature, is not content with blurring the conventional boundaries between fact and fiction. In the juxtaposition of dramatic and narrative forms, *The Mother of Us All* thus calls not only for a new mode of literary expression; it demands a radically new way of doing history as well.

Performance

If the parataxis and juxtapositions of *The Mother of Us All* are indicative of Stein's conceptual preferences, then it is not too hard to speculate about the methodology she has in mind for doing that history. As Marjorie Perloff has noted, parataxis is "the basic structural principle" of collage.[19] The methodological underpinnings of Stein's historiography thus originate in an aesthetic with which Stein, because of her deeply perceptive and early interest in modern art, had been familiar since Picasso and Braque constructed the first modern graphic collages at the beginning of the twentieth century, collages akin to those Stein herself developed in the literary arts. In this respect, the equation of the writing of history with the writing of literature in *The Mother of Us All* pivots on an already destabilized notion of literature as a whole, one that simultaneously defies the constructed boundaries of genre even as it also transgresses the boundaries separating the various arts and disciplines. Just as collage undermines the distinction between the graphic and plastic arts, so too do works like *The Mother of Us All* consciously revolt against disciplinary boundaries. Skirting the fence between literature and history is certainly one example of that revolt. But in a manner wholly consistent with the aesthetics of collage, the juxtaposition of literature and history in *The Mother of Us All* is complicated by other equally provocative juxtapositions that destabilize the primacy of literature itself because they result from the "questioning of referentiality [that is] inherent in collage" more generally.[20]

In the fine arts that questioning took a number of different but often parallel forms. This is certainly the case with the larger context of Stein's libretto, specifically its performative context. For there are direct parallels that can be drawn between the mode of performance presumed by *The Mother of Us All* and the questioning of referentiality that is implied, for example, by the use of found objects in works like Juan Gris's *La Lavabo.* The "first collage to be exhibited publically," *La Lavabo* confronted Gris's contemporaries with what they could only describe as an "antipictorial" gesture.[21] That gesture amounted to a bold illumination of the problematic limitations of representational painting. *La Lavabo*'s use of objects like the famous piece of mirror pasted to its canvas—objects, in short, that defied painterly representation—established collage as an aesthetic context that potentially gave a voice to objects elided by the accepted modes of artistic expression. A tool of representation itself, the mirror fragment in Gris's collage offered a cogent metacritical reflection that profoundly questioned referentiality vis-à-vis a presentation of that which painterly representation unavoidably leaves out.

With regard to questions of representation and immediacy, this "antipictorial" gesture is, at one level, typical of avant-garde gestures across the spectrum of the arts. But in the specific work of Stein, it finds one of its most important parallels in a basic equation of the immediacy of found objects with the immediacy of performance, and here that sense of immediacy conceptualizes performative acts with a complexity that is every bit as rich as the piece of mirror that Gris pasted onto *La Lavabo.*[22] Indeed, a sense of performance as a presentation of a semiotic field that written texts inevitably compromise sustains the antiliterary sentiments that permeate *The Mother of Us All* and that shape its historiographical concerns. In this respect, the most provocative aspect of the collage of juxtapositions employed in Stein's libretto is the one most closely aligned with a twofold strategy recurrent in modern theater: the first of these strategies involves a rejection of the traditionally subservient role that performance played in relation to the literary dramatic text (e.g., the role of representing the literary text); the second strategy follows the first by reconceptualizing the relation of text and performance, setting the two on equal terms and depicting their relation as a radical juxtaposition of two autonomous art forms.[23] As is the case with the paratactical compositions of collage, the juxtaposition of text and performance on a nonhierarchical plane yields a mutually disruptive albeit richly suggestive dynamic.

The subtleties of that dynamic fall well within the parameters of collage aesthetics, especially with regard to the three-dimensionality that pushed collages beyond the painter's frame.[24] Just as collage ultimately brought painting into three dimensional spaces, so too does Stein's incorporation of a short story into her drama ultimately bring a fictional literary narrative into the three-dimensional spaces of performance where its productions of meaning are radically altered and the limitations of textual representation are exposed. The consequence of this shift in locality and medium is, among other things, an implied transformation of negation into knowledge, an epistemological transformation that occurs in the transition from reading to recitation or, more simply put, in the transition from page to stage. Consider, for example, the exchange between Susan B. and Alice about midway through the short story. In response to Alice's suggestion "let us think about everything," the short story attributes the following to Susan B.: "No, said Susan B. no, no no, I know, I know said Susan B. no, said Susan B. No."[25] On the page, Susan B.'s response playfully fluctuates between the homonyms "no" and "know," with the emphasis decidedly on the negative, an emphasis that is lost on the stage, where even a skillful recitation may or may not succeed in clearly distinguishing the occurrences of "no" from "know."

At one level, the slippage between these two homonyms is typical of Stein's playful manipulations of language throughout all of her writings. But in the performative context *of The Mother of Us All*, the distinction between negation and knowledge pivots on a distinction between text and performance. For on a textual level, Susan B.'s response to Alice's suggestion "let us think about everything" is that she does not want to think about everything. The answer is an emphatic negation, an emphatic "No." On the level of performance, however, this negation is subject to a fundamental inversion. In response to Alice's suggestion "let us think about everything," Susan B.'s reply easily functions as a corrective that substantially ups the ante. Not satisfied with thinking about everything, Susan B.'s corrective demands knowledge; she demands to "know," and the knowledge she demands, unlike the negation associated with the text, is knowledge that is affirmed here in action and performance, not in literature. At the very least, in that knowledge there is no inherent connection between actual deeds and the representation of actions in the written word. The written word is thus equated with negation, and performance is equated with a knowledge that, while not absolute, is nonetheless capable of illuminating compromises and exclusions perpetuated in the written word. The challenge that this illumination issues extends to historical documents as well. In its implications, Stein's libretto thus casts a wide epistemological net for the basic tensions that Diannah Pladott has argued characterize the libretto's dramatic and performance texts. Pladott is correct in her assertion that "it is impossible . . . [in *The Mother of Us All*] to connect words to actual deeds and thus to reconstruct a represented action—what the speakers enact on stage—as a correlation of their words."[26] But this impossibility is not limited to the stage. It is in fact an impossibility that the libretto suggests is indicative of the narratives of history in their relation to actual events.

That suggestion is borne out in the closing lines of the libretto. Rhetorically, the slippage between negation and knowledge tarnishes the authority of the text with a hue of blindness and exclusion, casting it in constructed opposition to knowledge itself. The shadow of this negative hew extends across the rest of Stein's piece, culminating in the closing lines of the libretto, where, in front of "The Congressional Hall" amid a celebration of the codification of Susan B. Anthony's agenda into law, the disembodied voice of an absent and deceased Anthony weighs the gravity of immediacy, presence, and action against the significance of the historical textual document that is the celebrated fruit of her activism and labor.

As if to inculcate an abstract sense of the ephemerality of performance and action and of the impossibility of accurate representation, Anthony ironically begins repeating variations of the line "We cannot retrace our steps, retrace our steps."[27] This refrain, in turn, leads to a subtle if ambivalent disavowal of the legislative document ostensibly giving women the voice that Anthony has sought on their behalf, and the disavowal itself is positioned in a pronounced opposition between the legislative document and the actions of Anthony's life, that is, in an opposition between text and performance.[28] As Anthony tells the audience: "I was a martyr all my life not to what I won but to what was done."[29] While this disavowal reiterates the libretto's fundamental challenge to the primacy of text over performance, it also questions whether adequate assessment of Anthony's life can be obtained vis-à-vis a privileged historical document. Just as the juxtaposition of text and performance earlier destabilized conventional notions of literature, here in the closing section of the libretto, that same juxtaposition destabilizes our conceptions of history.

The challenge to our accepted notions of history takes the form of a question that Anthony poses directly to the audience in the closing lines of the opera. Subtly returning to the distinction between knowledge and negation (i.e., "know" vs. "no"), Anthony queries the audience about the source and extent of its understanding of who she is or was:

> Do you know because I tell you so, or do
> You know, do you know.
> (Silence)
> My long life, my long life.[30]

Given the disavowal of the historical text associated with Anthony's labor and given that disavowal's implicit, concomitant rejection of objective historical knowledge, the audience would be hard pressed to answer anything other than "No, we do not know Anthony's long life." At one level, the logic governing the ending of *The Mother of Us All* might very well suggest that the real question posed here is whether knowing Anthony's life is even possible or, similarly, whether the writing of history is possible. Indeed, at that same level, the ending of *The Mother of Us All* could be written off as an aesthetic articulation of an intriguing but stubbornly extreme if not solipsistic form of relativism. Yet such a response would overlook the underlying epistemology in the subtle allusion that Anthony's question makes back to the libretto's earlier distinction between knowledge and negation. More importantly, it would overlook the fact that the work's nonhierarchical juxtaposition of text and performance had among its different effects the transformation of negation into knowledge (i.e., "no" performed as "know"). Somewhere in the three-dimensional spaces of the collage event, which that juxtaposition creates, knowledge is possible.

The beginning of that knowledge is the negation not of knowledge per se but of knowledge as we know it; it is the negation not of literature per se but of literature as we know it; and finally, it is the negation not of history per se but of history as we know it—and this includes the history of the avant-garde. In all these respects, the paratactical, nonlinear structures of collage aesthetics in *The Mother of Us All* contest the accepted structures of our understanding even as it posits an alternative mode for understanding knowledge, literature, and history.[31] Furthermore, while the artistically innovative dimensions of that alternative tend to situate Stein within the ranks of the avant-garde, the epistemological underpinnings of her aesthetic produce a highly self-conscious mode of expression that repudiates the very countertraditions that emerged from the avant-garde's disavowal of literature and tradition. That repudiation is by no means a reaffirmation of literature and tradition but is rather a metacritical acknowledgment of the negative dialectical shadow of conventional literary and cultural values haunting the countertraditions of the avant-garde itself.

In that shadow, we can recognize the looming specter of the patriarch, and if, as I am suggesting, the metacritical turn of Stein's libretto is also a turn against the underlying patriarchal values of the avant-garde, that turn, I would argue furthermore, is the direct result of a profoundly significant piece of dramatic (anti)literature: an unruly libretto with a "feminist approach" that Virgil Thomson said he "could not deny"[32] and that pushed the literary, political, and historical narratives that harbor the specter of patriarchy into the illuminating three-dimensional spaces of performance. If we, in that gesture toward the performative space, are left to ponder what the commensurate mode of immediacy is for critically illuminating the meanings and knowledge that the discourses of written history elide, then the aesthetics of collage offer a certain degree of guidance. For it is within the performative immediacy of the collage event that meanings and knowledge appear that the discourses of literature and of linear historical narratives cannot convey alone. This is not to say that the performative aspects of the collage event transcend the signifying practices associated either with language or with the semiotics of the theater. On the contrary, the parallel that *The Mother of Us All* draws between the performative events of the theater and the performative acts of history (i.e., between the histrionic and the historical) calls attention to the multiple ways that the defining acts of history, like the events of theater, are never immediate—even when we are participants in those events. They are always already filtered through and thus constructed and embedded in the dominant cultural discourse.

Feminist Collage and Avant-Garde Historiographies

The performative aspects of Stein's libretto stage a disruption of the patriarchal economy of that discourse, both in the sphere of political activism and in the sphere of experimental art. Here, too, the aesthetics of collage play a pivotal role, bridging the gap between American political history and the performative history of the American avant-garde. For at its most immediate level, the nonlinear juxtaposition of historical figures like Susan B. Anthony and Daniel Webster is a provocative invitation to rethink American political history, but, grounded as that juxtaposition is in the aesthetics of collage, it is also an experimental artistic gesture linking Stein's work to the self-reflective practices that belong to the germinal expressions of the avant-garde.[33] The specific tenor of that link hinges on a dynamic between content and form. By reframing the history of American political oratory within the aesthetics of collage, *The Mother of Us All* negotiates the path from a more general critique of American political discourse into a subtle metacritical illumination and reassessment of the patriarchal assumptions governing the accepted history of the American avant-garde.

This reassessment arguably serves as the pivotal link between Susan B. Anthony and Gertrude Stein. Certainly it is a far more significant link than the coincidental biographical similarities that critics have often used to connect Stein with Anthony.[34] Indeed, the thematized plight of Anthony, who struggles throughout the libretto to find a political voice for women that is not always already compromised by political subservience to established male discursive economies, finds its implicit parallel in the artistic work of Stein. But the issue here is not so much whether Stein personally identified with Susan B. Anthony, or whether Stein uses Anthony as a vehicle to plead for recognition for her own work,[35] but rather whether the work of each woman (Anthony and Stein) constitutes effort in her respective sphere of activity to procure a full hearing for the voice of women more generally, and here we are specifically talking about a voice, the assessment of whose significance—be it political or artistic or both—does not implicitly defer authority to values or criteria established by men who enjoyed privileges from which women were either excluded or were only permitted limited, controlled access.

What Stein considers such an assessment to be has major implications for long-standing histories of the avant-garde that have consistently neglected the germinal contributions of women to avant-garde performance practices or that, at the very least, have subordinated those contributions to an already established narrative that attributes the defining moments of the avant-garde to a select group of men and measures the significance of all other work against the seemingly objective and unified precedent that cultivated attention to their work has established. In this respect, Stein's project (or more specifically, *The Mother of Us All*) initially coincides with—and affirms for the literary and performing arts—the political attitudes that she attributes to her protagonist, Susan B. Anthony. As Anthony, in the second act of the libretto, says in response to the three males (Andrew G., Thaddeus, and Daniel Webster), who pronounce themselves to be "very important persons": "Yes, so they are," but then she retorts: "I am important but not that way, not that way."[36] It is precisely such qualitative differences in importance that bridge the political activism of Anthony to the artistic work of Stein. Drawing implicit parallels between the political and artistic spheres of feminist *engagement, The Mother of Us All* thus redresses historical narratives that regularly underplay the significant contributions of women to avant-garde practice, especially when those contributions are not "important" in the same way as, or are not even necessarily reconcilable with, standards that are the product of a constructed historical narrative favoring a few male artists.

Yet the pivotal issue in the relation of Stein's general historiographical concerns to the specific history of the American avant-garde is not merely the metaphorical embrace in *The Mother of Us All* of Susan B. Anthony's feminist activism but rather the libretto's use of collage in that embrace—a use that offers a conceptual strategy for circumventing a compromising absorption into established political or cultural historical models. While the splicing Anthony's political discourse into the experimental modes of Stein's artistic work critically reframes Anthony's activism and, I would argue, thus agitates for an equal rather than subservient voice for women within accounts of radical experimental performance, it also lays the foundation for a model of historiography that, within the history of the avant-garde, aims at avoiding the very fate that Stein's protagonist admonishes against when, for example, late in the second act, Anthony's companion Anne attempts to counter Anthony's growing sense of despair. Anne complements Anthony on her willingness to fight a fight that Anne tells her she "will win." Anthony does not contest this outcome but laments its cost. Women will obtain the right to vote, she says. But "by that time it will do them no good because having the vote they will become like men."[37] Indeed, the very legacy of Anthony's work succumbs to a comparable fate at the end of Stein's libretto: a fate that is symbolized in that disembodied voice of Anthony hovering behind a statue that the surviving state has erected ostensibly in her honor; a fate, in short, that amounts to an ossified and abstract, neutralizing absorption into a larger and already established political narrative dominated and regulated by men.

The historiographical model that Stein offers as a contrast to this fate—a model based upon the radical heterogeneous juxtapositions of collage—pivots on a calculated avoidance of the suggestion that an equal voice for female experimental artists and an equal accounting of their contributions to the history of the American avant-garde are obtainable by simply finding a niche for them within the existing paradigms of a theater historiography whose pillars center on and reinforce the work of men. In this respect, the far-reaching implications of Stein's libretto exhaust the parallels that it implicitly draws between Susan B. Anthony and Stein herself. Rather than staking out a voice within the existing cultural paradigms, Stein's libretto advocates a voice whose critical modulations are audible, in their full range, only after its dissonance forces a reorientation in our habitual modes of critical reception and in our efforts to integrate the voice into dominant models of signification.[38]

It is difficult to overstate the important role that chance plays in this attempted reorientation—not so much an aesthetic tactic like that employed by John Cage, but rather chance as a focus of critical scrutiny and as a concept with unacknowledged significance to the writing of history. Indeed, through the techniques of collage, *The Mother of Us All* critically illuminates the manner in which the unacknowledged chance associations of accepted historical narratives carry the ideological footprints of patriarchal society and repeatedly situate women within a conceptual frame that renders the scope of their significance imperceptible. The irony here is that collage itself relies on the chance associations and "new possibilities of signification" that result, as Marjorie Perloff has noted, from "the transfer of words and images from their original sources to the collage construction."[39] It is such chance associations, for example, that link the projects of Anthony and Stein. But in this respect, the aesthetic at play in *The Mother of Us All* is an especially good example of the self-conscious techniques of collage, techniques that in some respects are analogous to Gris's provocative placement of a mirror fragment on the canvas of *La Lavabo* (that tool of representation which illuminates the preclusions of representation). Exploring the subtle nuances of its fundamental mechanisms for producing meaning, Stein's collage-structured libretto exposes similar mechanisms and chance associations within our dominant cultural historical narratives. The difference is that, unlike conventional historical narratives, collage does not mask the seams uniting its heterogenous elements. Before realizing the fuller potential of their own new possibilities of signification, the chance associations that emerge in *The Mother of Us All* thus provide a critical counterbalance to the chance associations that have enjoyed acceptance as historical fact. They demystify history without obscuring the radical heterogeneity of their own elements.[40]

The use of this unveiled heterogeneity as a strategy for interrogating the patriarchal foundations of historiography is most immediately apparent in the nonlinear juxtaposition of Susan B. Anthony and Daniel Webster.[41] The strategy is especially evident in the third scene of act I—arguably the most important scene in the entire libretto. Constructed in part out of various speeches that the two figures from different historical periods made over the course of their political careers,[42] the scene is a masterful collage of chance associations that initially give the impression of being integrated into a shared discursive economy but that when situated within their performative context actually pursue a course of critical decomposition. For as the performative context of this scene stresses—indeed critically strains—the seams holding Stein's libretto together, that stress, in turn, illuminates the socially constructed but largely hidden gendered hierarchies in public discourse. In this respect, the mise-en-scène demanded by Stein's stage directions (one of the few examples of clearly demarcated stage directions in all of Stein's dramatic writing) serves as a deconstructive wedge, critically severing what initially appears to be the semantic implications of her text from the acculturated habits of literacy that reinforce patriarchal prerogatives.[43] Within the performative space provoking that severance—a space that disrupts and ultimately displaces an initial appearance of discursive unity and synthesis with the radical juxtapositions of collage—*The Mother of Us All* ultimately recontextualizes Anthony's pursuit of a political voice for women within a historiography of experimental writing and performance that does not vitiate the unique aesthetic contributions of women.

The stage directions indicate that while Anthony and Webster have comparable status, they also establish competing centers of focus. To some extent these directions extend the easily overlooked precedent established in the previous scene where both Anthony and Webster are introduced and appear simultaneously on the same stage even though they move within different social orbits and never directly interact with each other. But in scene 3, they are no longer part of a chorus or of a representation of a large informal civic event where it is possible and potentially insignificant for two individuals to be simultaneously present while being sheltered from interaction by a crowd. The staging of scene 3 is stark and nonrepresentational by comparison, opening with an image of the two historical figures on a sparse stage. They are "seated in two straight-backed chairs but not too near each other."[44] Remaining seated for the entire scene, Anthony and Webster share the same stage, but they move neither physically closer to each other nor conceptually toward a synthesis of the respective views that they express. From their similar but separate positions, they thus decenter the visual field both literally and conceptually.

Initially, one might assume that the image of these two historical figures suggests the possibility of a physical point of symmetry and balance between their different positions on the stage, that is, a midpoint that could signify a negotiation between their respective political views. Yet, significantly, that space either remains empty or is only temporarily filled by the chance wanderings of the characters Jo the Loiterer and

Angel More, who pass coincidentally between the stationary figures of Anthony and Webster. The initial suggestion of a possible point of balance between Anthony and Webster thus succumbs to the alternating emptiness and chance occupation of the physical space between them. Where synthesis might logically be presumed, emptiness and chance prevail, leaving Anthony and Webster juxtaposed but not reconciled. Ultimately, the performative context of this scene gains its critical force in the illuminating counterbalance it offers to what one might characterize as the understandable tendency of the audience (or readers) to look for a thread of dialogue through the alternating sequence of statements made by Anthony and Webster. Since the performative context of this scene goes against the grain of precisely such an interpretive act; indeed, since the performative context is positioned specifically as an alternative to a repressive tradition of cultural literacy that Stein subtly equates with the semblance of dialogue in this scene, it is worth considering momentarily how the statements of Anthony and Webster are positioned rhetorically in relation to one another.

Given their sequence and diction, it is virtually impossible to interpret Anthony's and Webster's statements as a dialogue without simultaneously participating in the subordination of Anthony's statements to the authority of Webster's. As a dialogue, the text of this scene is decisively one-sided and repeatedly reaffirms Webster's authority and patriarchal prerogative. Typical in this regard is their opening exchange when, as if in reply to Anthony's statement "I hear a sound," Webster ironically asserts, "I do not hear a sound," an assertion that either implicitly refuses to acknowledge Anthony's statement or, if true, suggests Webster does not even register Anthony's presence. The statements directly following this exchange would seem to bear out the latter possibility as Webster, altogether unaffected by Anthony's subsequent comments, introduces a short allegory about a lost mariner and plots a course of conversation that is not addressed to Anthony at all but rather to a male counterpart in the senate whom he formally addresses as "sir."[45]

Webster's comments in this scene are largely fragments taken from his "most famous senatorial speech, the 1830 debate with Senator Hayne of South Carolina over the Foote resolution."[46] Yet understood as an exchange with Anthony, these fragments function rhetorically as a series of preemptive dismissals of any substantive contribution to politics that Anthony would seem to attempt, and, with Webster's repeated use of masculine pronouns, those dismissals fall along gendered lines. When read as a dialogue, the non sequitur and fragmentary dimensions of Stein's libretto gain a rhetorical quality that quickly vanquishes any semblance of neutrality within the political traditions and heritage that Anthony and Webster presumably share.[47] And inasmuch as a collage aesthetic illuminates that lack of neutrality, it also underscores the extent to which Anthony's goals are compromised from the very start by a patriarchal nepotism affecting both the semantic and structural levels of the political discourse in which she participates.[48] The voice that Anthony seeks on behalf of women proves to be a voice that ironically always speaks first in deference to male authority. Her comments, for example, repeatedly utilize words and themes that moments earlier Webster has coincidentally introduced into the text. Thus, however combative Anthony may appear to be, the echoes of Webster's statements in Anthony's encourages a judgment of them that is based upon the precedent that Webster establishes and that gives her comments the appearance of primarily being attempts to engage in a debate the terms of which Webster sets and commands.

What is significant about these appearances is that they are but one stream in the contradictory currents that are set in motion by the performative context accompanying Stein's libretto. Just as the physical space between the seated positions of Anthony and Webster never emerges as a meaningful point of symmetry between the competing centers of focus that the two figures create, neither do the overlapping themes and diction in their statements emerge as a site of balanced, impartial negotiation. Yet at the same time, the alternating emptiness and chance occupations that dominate the physical space between Anthony and Webster illuminate a strategy for understanding the libretto that potentially resists the imposition of a collective or unified sense of meaning purchased at Anthony's expense. Stein's mise-en-scène undercuts Webster's authority by overshadowing it with a staging of emptiness and chance and by offering the decentered, unreconciled image(s) of Anthony and Webster as an alternative to the illusion of a neutral discursive sphere. Indeed, the performative context of the third scene of act 1 not only reveals but also embraces the sense in which the scene's corresponding text is a masterfully constructed sequence of non sequiturs, fragments, and chance associations that do not gravitate toward synthesis but rather recoil in metacritical heterogeneity. In the light of the visual field of the stage, the dramatic text loses its semblance of unity, the individual elements of the text reasserting their autonomous significance and accentuating precisely the insignificance of the discursive terrain that they coincidentally share.[49]

To some extent, this tendency is a predictable outcome of the collage principles at play in Stein's libretto. As David Graver has observed, the heterogeneous elements of collage never settle "within the frame of the artwork." Although stripped away from their "quotidian context of meaning and use," the collage fragments persistently point "back to the world from which they came" and constantly assert their own "disruptive autonomy."[50] Yet what is significant about this disruptive autonomy in *The Mother of Us All* is that it reverberates well beyond the frame of Stein's libretto. As the borrowed citations embedded in her text point back to the world from which they came—in this case, back to the public sphere of common political discourse—they do so with a disruptive force garnered from the performative context of the collage event into which they have been placed. While the collage elements recoil from the artificial unity constructed by Stein, that same artificial unity indicts and undercuts the authority of the ostensibly neutral political discourse to which Webster and Anthony presumably both subscribe despite their political and generational differences. In short, the collage structure of Stein's dramatic text associates the presumption of equity within that public discursive sphere with a vacuity that is comparable to the empty space between Anthony and Webster and with a disingenuousness that Anthony herself illuminates when she later dismisses Thaddeus Stevens's admonishment to "remember [that] humanity comes first" as an underhanded way of saying that "men come first."[51]

Thoughts on a Feminist Historiography of Avant-Garde Performance

Illuminating the illusory neutrality in the discursive space shared not only by Anthony and Webster but also by spectators and readers whose acculturated habits of literacy reinforce patriarchal prerogatives, the performative context of Stein's libretto fosters a radical break with history that, on the one hand, is indicative of the avant-garde's uneasy relation with conventional notions of history but that, on the other hand, self-consciously and critically folds back into the experimental traditions of the avant-garde itself. Inasmuch as that break is geared toward a demystification of the illusion of a common political heritage—especially when affiliation with that heritage necessitates a masking of subservience beneath the repressive guise of dialogue—the implicit parallel that Stein draws between American political history and the history of the avant-garde arguably aims not at a fundamental rejection of the history of the avant-garde per se but of the underlying assumption of unity in the terms and concepts upon which that history is based. In this particular respect, Stein's use of collage aesthetics begins to fragment those terms and ultimately dispels the illusion of a unified, linear narrative of experimental performance that they create. *The Mother of Us All* thereby develops an aesthetic strategy that contains the rudimentary structures of the feminist historiography of avant-garde performance shaping the subsequent chapters in this book.

At the very forefront of that strategy is a manner of artistic expression that, highlighting the seams of its own constructedness, illuminates the socially constructed, gendered foundations of the very aesthetic (anti)values and concepts that comprise the institutionalized history of avant-garde performance. Concomitant to such illuminations is a conceptualization of historiography that is intimately tied to the experimental dimensions of modern theater and to that theater's explorations of the relation of performance and text. But the stakes here and in the chapters to come surpass a basic recognition of the inadequacy of the written word as a tool for representing either theatrical or historical events. *The Mother of Us All* admonishes us not only to recognize the inadequacy of the written word but to see in experimental performance, and in collage events in particular, the tools for exploring the ideological dynamics that govern that inadequacy. In this respect, *The Mother of Us All* lays a foundation for understanding the stakes not only of its own aesthetic agenda but of the widespread use of collage aesthetics in the performative work of women experimental artists in the United States in the early part of the twentieth century. But even here the radical juxtapositions that Stein utilizes in the construction of *The Mother of Us All* encourage a historiography that is based upon a juxtaposition of disparate materials and events and that is devoid of a gesture aiming to corral materials and events into a unified, coherent narrative. Consequently, this study does not aim at a comprehensive overview of American avant-garde performance, but rather at partially registering the ways that the performative practices of women experimental artists, in drawing upon the aesthetics of collage, force us to engage the basic concepts of the avant-garde and to consider their gendered histories.

CHAPTER FOUR

Between Material and Matrix

Yoko Ono's *Cut Piece* and the Unmaking of Collage

> All my works in the other fields have an "Event bent" so to speak. People ask me why I call some works Event and others not. They also ask me why I do not call my Events, Happenings.
>
> —Yoko Ono, "To the Wesleyan People"

Introduction: Getting to YES

A *Ceiling Painting* so small that a magnifying glass was necessary to decipher its content: this is what awaited John Lennon when in November 1966 he climbed the ladder placed beneath the painting that was mounted to the ceiling of the Indica Gallery in London. That journey up the ladder was Lennon's first introduction to the work of Yoko Ono, whom he also met for the first time that evening. It's hard to say whether Lennon was aware of the nihilism traditionally associated with the historical avant-garde, but when he scrutinized the painting with the magnifying glass attached by chain to its frame, he was relieved to discover "YES" minutely inscribed on the otherwise blank canvas. "It's a great relief," he later told Jann Wenner, "when you get up the ladder and it doesn't say *no* or *fuck you;* it says YES."[1] Never mind the fact that Lennon overlooked the semiotic conundrum that Ono created by selecting a word as an object of painterly representation or that he overlooked the dialogue between Eastern and Western aesthetics that was summoned by the piece's allusion to calligraphy. Never mind that he disregarded the ladder's playful, critical allusion to high and low art or that he ignored his own reflection in the Plexiglas covering the canvas. Never mind that he overlooked how the magnifying glass attached to the frame of the painting not only transformed the painting into a three-dimensional collage but also, together with the ladder beneath the canvas and the reflections on the Plexiglas across it, actually structured a collage event as well—a performance event—since it required the spectator's action, the spectator's literal and figurative reflection and, of course, the spectator's interpretation to realize the canvas's multivalent semantic potential. However limited Lennon's initial grasp of the subtleties of the piece called *Ceiling Painting (YES Painting)* might have been—and we really don't know how limited his grasp actually was—his introduction to Ono's work strikingly focused precisely on an affirmation that critics have gradually recognized as a crucial tenet of Ono's aesthetics.

Given the close association that Ono developed with John Cage in the early 1950s, it is tempting to find in her "YES" an echo of Cage's definition of art as "an affirmation of life," the life that he famously found to be "so excellent,"[2] and to cite *Ceiling Painting (YES Painting)* as yet another example of the sweeping influence that Cage exercised across the landscape of America's postwar avant-garde. But before yielding, it is worth pausing to better understand not just what this temptation entails but what it perpetuates. Above all, it perpetuates the questionable tendency of translating the enormous critical (and well-deserved) attention that Cage has received over the years into credit for breaking a path that, while perhaps running parallel to his own, was nonetheless distinct in the contours of affirmation that it facilitated. For if there is a lesson to be learned from Lennon's ascent to the ceiling of the Indica Gallery, it is that getting to "YES" is only as significant as the questions motivating the search in the first place. Indeed, Joan Rothfuss has suggested that *Ceiling Painting* is "reminiscent of those stories in which a man climbs a mountain to ask a monk the meaning of life, but for all his arduous effort receives an indecipherable reply."[3] The subtext of this parable, if we might venture into the obvious, is that the problem lies not with the monk's answer but with the traveler's question, and the wiser traveler learns to reformulate the question to match the answer that she encountered by surprise. This is another way of saying that once the relief at having discovered "YES" subsides, it behooves us to ask ourselves what we've just delighted in affirming.

Not only do such questions underscore the fact that affirmation is never unmediated; they also remind us that while the work of Ono and Cage may overlap in expressions of affirmation, the expressions affirm substantially different social realities. On its own, the "YES" of *Ceiling Painting* may be too enigmatic for viewers to flesh out the social particulars of those realities. But it does provide a beacon, illuminating an underlying optimism in other works where the sociopolitical sphere is more identifiably present. In this respect, one need only recall the optimism emanating from the "WAR IS OVER! IF YOU WANT IT" billboards that Ono and Lennon installed internationally during Christmas of 1969. Aside from offering us perhaps the most memorable example of Ono's and Lennon's involvement with the antiwar movement, those billboards are indicative of an aesthetic through which Ono has repeatedly, creatively, and optimistically imagined the sociopolitical alternatives advocated in her work.

Critics have noted the Eastern philosophical foundation of that aesthetic and its concomitant optimism, a foundation that has not only encouraged an understanding of Ono and Cage in similar conceptual terms but that also literally brought the two of them together in the 1950s when they met and became friends at a New York lecture by D. T. Suzuki and subsequently started moving within the same artistic circles.[4] Indeed, at a philosophical level, there is much room for a consideration of the complementary ways that Cage and Ono both participated in the avant-garde's critique of Western rationalism, which was partially facilitated by a postwar embrace of non-Western aesthetics. But the complementary turns to contrast when one shifts from philosophical abstraction to the materiality of performance. For it is at the level of performance that the political undercurrents of Ono's work surface and that the distinctions between Ono's and Cage's competing senses of affirmation emerge with a clarity beyond the blur of their philosophical affinities.

Crucial to this contrast, as I will be arguing in the pages that follow, is Ono's status not as a woman of Asian descent whose philosophical training[5] and aesthetic sensibilities "played a key role in the transmission of Eastern aesthetics"[6] to the postwar international avant-garde but rather her status as a woman of color—and I am specifically referring here to a contrast between the abstract and the material, that is, between the philosophical and the performative. For it is my contention that within the realms of performance, Ono's Asian female body remained doubly marked as an exotic Other within a Western patriarchal tradition that was subtly underwritten in the aesthetic assumptions governing the American avant-garde in the 1950s and 1960s. That tradition thrived amid and in spite of the legendary influential embrace of Eastern philosophical traditions by artists like Cage. In this respect, my examination of Ono's performances aims at facilitating a long overdue consideration of the extent to which Cage's influence inadvertently provided a kind of ideological diversion from the postwar avant-garde's perpetuation of the West's long-standing problematic fascination with the East, a fascination that not only had strong ties to colonialism and racism but that was also conceptually gendered, perpetuating an image of the East as effeminate, passive, and receptive to domination.

My interest here is less in Ono's Event Scores or in their performance generally speaking. It is rather in Ono's particular performances of those scores as a woman subjected to Western constructed stereotypes of Asian femininity. While American avant-garde groups associated with Cagean aesthetics—groups like the happening and Fluxus artists—were obviously not the source of those stereotypes, neither did they create a significant space of opposition to them. Indeed, Kathy O'Dell has noted that women artists who departed from the norm and whose work renegotiated "body-text relationships[s]" along feminist lines—artists like Kate Millett, Carolee Schneeman, Schigeko Kubota. and Yoko Ono—frequently found themselves excluded from artistic programs or, at the very least, ostracized by their male counterparts.[7] Within this male-centered context of what O'Dell describes as women artists finding recognition only by "playing ball, so to speak, in the boy's gym,"[8] one of Ono's great artistic achievements was to position her work in such a way that it exposed an ironic undercurrent of complicity between those pushing the boundaries of theater and performance and those securing the normative patriarchal values of the social mainstream. Working against the pull of that undercurrent—a pull that had a surprisingly unacknowledged sway within the larger context of American experimental performance in the 1960s—Ono's performances enacted a unique process of critical excavation and rehabilitation of collage aesthetics. The larger implications of that twofold process of critique and reclamation ultimately distinguishes the affirmative gestures in Ono's work from the affirmations associated with the works of John Cage.

If that process illuminated and ultimately gestured beyond the undercurrent of sexism and racism within the American avant-garde, nowhere was the process better exemplified than in Ono's performances of *Cut Piece.* Whether intended or not, those performances exposed a fundamental conflict between abstract and material realities in the aesthetics of the postwar American avant-garde. They exposed how that conflict provided safe harbor to regressive sexual and cultural politics. The catalyst for this exposure was *Cut Piece*'s critical restructuring of the aesthetics of collage, and Ono's specific performance of this piece positioned that restructuring within a tense juxtaposition of seemingly unrelated traditions. On the one hand, the techniques of collage in her piece harmonized with the influential chance operational format that John Cage, drawing upon the philosophies of the *I Ching,* extended to the realms of experimental performance and that in the 1960s critics like Richard Kostelanetz argued were "designed to help *man* develop a more immediate relationship with *his* surroundings."[9] [my italics.] On the other hand, Ono's use of collage technique also exposed how chance operations easily accommodated a fetished, voyeuristic humiliation of her own person, which in turn underscored the darker side of the dominant aesthetics in the American experimental performance communities of the 1950s and 1960s.

Yet inasmuch as the juxtaposition of these two seemingly unrelated currents exposed how the former unwittingly accommodates the latter, so too, I would argue, did the juxtaposition and the critical perspective it facilitated foreshadow a rehabilitation of collage and signal the affirming, potential alternatives imagined in Ono's performances of *Cut Piece.* Those alternatives were directed outward as a kind of activist challenge, focusing on how the piece could conceivably unfold in the hands of the audience who, in a manner of speaking, might arrive at the "Yes" later explicitly incorporated in Ono's *Ceiling Painting,* or who, as Jill Dolan has recently argued in another context, might recognize a utopia beyond patriarchy "not as some idea of future perfection that might never arrive, but as brief enactments of the possibilities of a process that starts now, in this moment" of radical, experimental performance.[10] But as alternatives, these possibilities existed *in potentia:* as stark contrasts to the sociopolitical strictures that, as Ono's performances of *Cut Piece* revealed, were equally accommodated within the ranks of the avant-garde and within the social mainstream—sociopolitical strictures that would dictate how women practiced art, how women functioned in society, and how women defined themselves.

What fuels the realization of those alternatives is a kind of dialectic that opens aesthetic spaces of progressive sexual politics in the opposition that *Cut Piece* constructed in its critical attitudes: toward the privileged status of collage as an artistic practice; toward the presumed authenticity and immediacy of what Michael Kirby so famously called "non-matrixed performance";[11] toward the idealized notion of audience/participants in experimental performances; and, more generally, toward the myth of neutrality in chance operations. In this respect, Ono's *Cut Piece* also occupies an important position in the arguments of this book. Whereas in the first chapter we saw how the work of Elsa von Freytag-Loringhoven set unacknowledged precedents in the history of American avant-garde performance, exposing and indeed challenging the gendered economies that have governed our understanding of concepts like Artaud's notion of the plague or the collage-related notions of the *objet trouvé* (found object) and the readymade; and whereas in the second chapter we saw how the collage of historical documents in Gertrude Stein's *Mother of Us All* queries the production of historical meaning in a patriarchal society and does so in a manner that lends itself to parallel reflection on the male centered historiography of the avant-garde, Ono's *Cut Piece* is remarkable for its own self-reflective sense of the historicity of collage. Perhaps its most significant and yet most subtle accomplishment centers on a critical positioning of collage not as mere method or technique but as a historical category. This constituted a crucial step toward its reclamation.

Collage in History / Collage as History

While taking account of the alternatives suggested by *Cut Piece* certainly distinguishes the affirmations to be found in the work of Ono from those to be found in the work of Cage, it also points to a larger critical, if not subversive, rapport that Ono's work developed in relation to the postwar American avant-garde more generally. That rapport reached a pinnacle of sorts with her performances of *Cut Piece* in the years (and even months) directly prior to the Indica gallery exhibit where John Lennon saw *Ceiling Painting* and Yolo Ono for the first time. Indeed, if there is a work where Ono's problematic relation to the American avant-garde is not only identifiable but where it also constitutes a pivotal aspect of the work itself, then it is *Cut Piece,* arguably her most famous contribution to experimental performance. Performed five times between 1964 and 1966, *Cut Piece* was a deceptively simple conceptual work in which Ono entered a performance hall, sat on the stage floor with her legs tucked beneath her and after having placed a pair of scissors in front herself, invited members of the audience "to come up on the stage, one by one, and cut a portion of her clothing (anywhere they like[d]) and take it."[12] Yet beneath this deceptive simplicity and beneath the seeming emotionless passivity of Ono who stared blankly into the distance while audience members slowly cut away her apparel, a germinal experimental feminist performance aesthetic was at play whose caustic reworking of the dominant troupes of the postwar American avant-garde has largely eluded scholarship. This is not to say that Ono's *Cut Piece* has been neglected, but rather to say that the reception of *Cut Piece* has done little to explicate how radically the piece subverts the conceptual models of avant-garde practice that historians have used to define experimental performance in the early and middle 1960s. Neither has the reception of *Cut Piece* articulated the work's imagined alternative for the theory and practice of experimental performance. Such is the task that I pursue in this chapter.

By almost any measure, *Cut Piece* is a more demanding and significant work than *Ceiling Painting*, and comparing the two pieces might be unjustified were it not for the insight, in general, that *Ceiling Painting* offers into the optimism underlying Ono's work and for the common aesthetic strategy, in particular, that both pieces share in their use of a structured collage event to query the spectator's traditionally passive role. Granted, by the midsixties, aesthetic challenges to audience passivity were not particularly unique on their own. Nor was the framing of those challenges within the aesthetics of collage. After all, challenging audience passivity was integral to the Duchamp-Cage aesthetic,[13] and the conceptual ties between collage and Cage's use of chance operations were both recognized and adopted by the happening artists of the late fifties and early sixties.

Those artists consciously deployed the aesthetics of collage as a strategy for disrupting the spectator's traditional role as passive consumer. Allan Kaprow, for example, who would later describe his happenings as an extension of an "action-collage technique,"[14] argued in his essay "Happenings in the New York Scene" (1961) not only that happenings enlarge the concept of theater just as collage enlarges the concept of painting but also that in happenings "audiences, or groups of visitors, are commingled in some way with the event, flowing in and among its parts. . . . [and that there] is thus no separation of audience and play" as there is in traditional theater.[15] If, in this respect, action-collage technique contributed to an expanded concept of theater, the risk of this expansion, as Kaprow himself admitted a in 1967, was that the action-collage technique's commingling of audience and event, like any aesthetic technique, could very well lose "the clarity of its paradoxical position of being art-life or life-art," regress into habit, and ultimately "lead Happeners to depend on certain favored situations and to perfect them in the manner of conventional artists."[16] The risk, in short, was the specter that has always haunted the avant-garde: a regression of vitality and innovation into sterility and style.

By the time that Kaprow articulated these concerns, consciousness of them was already evident in events like *Cut Piece* and in the radically different conceptual model that *Cut Piece* offered for collage aesthetics. For what is significant about *Cut Piece,* what distinguishes it over and above works like *Ceiling Painting* and indeed what positions it critically in relation to the Cagean-influenced happenings, is its highly self-conscious use of collage as an aesthetic form. That use highlighted the ideological shadow of bourgeois normative values that haunted many of the happening artists who employed variations of the action-collage techniques described by Kaprow. Those values, which tended to reinforce mainstream notions of gender, repeatedly surfaced in unexpected forms. For example, they emerged in the conceptual vision of happening artists like Claes Oldenburg whose expressed enthusiasm for what he presumed to be the unmediated naturalness of quotidian objects and actions led to equations of the urban environment with a feminized notion of nature:

> I dont [*sic*] consider myself in struggle w nature but in harmony w *her.* Neither arrogance nor humility but harmony and identification. Nothing is not nature (natural?) And nothing not suitable for the living organizational capacity which is "art."[17]

Just as John Cage's wide influence inadvertently provided cover for an exoticized and gendered image of the East as effeminate, passive, and receptive to domination, so too did Oldenberg's equation of city life with a feminized conception of nature not only imply that the city like nature could be dominated, but the domination, by extension, was also patriarchal in structure. Equated with a feminized notion of nature, the urban playground was tantamount to women as playground, and the anything-goes of Oldenberg's "Nothing is not nature" was little more than an old recipe for the subjugation of women to patriarchal authority.

Against the backdrop of such currents within the avant-garde, Ono's self-conscious use of collage recognized that collage's very viability depended upon a mode of artistic expression capable of critically rethinking its basic principles. The larger stakes in this critical embrace can be understood vis-à-vis how we conceptualize our understanding of collage as an aesthetic medium: whether we fix our notions of collage in terms of form, style, and technique, or whether we conceptualize them in terms of process, performance, and becoming; whether we perceive collage as a fixed structure for expression or whether—following Ono's quip to McLuhan that the "Message is the Medium"[18]—we perceive it as part of the evolving content of expression itself; and finally, whether we understand collage as an established aesthetic model with a history of applications or whether we understand it as a model of history itself with an unfolding history of its own—an unfolding that is neither necessarily linear, progressive, nor homogeneous. If, as I obviously want to suggest, we ally Ono's *Cut Piece* with the latter side of each of these contrasting propositions, then the innovative length to which *Cut Piece* pushes the aesthetics of collage can thus be seen as a turning point in the history of collage itself, that is, as one of those invaluable dialectical moments when a specific work of art or a specific performance salvages a particular aesthetic form by illuminating and breaking from its past and by turning against the form itself. In this respect, the very title of *Cut Piece* is a double entendre, denoting not only the work's basic performative gesture but also its radical severance from the performative notions of collage promoted in the work of Ono's male counterparts, particularly in the work of happenings artists like Kaprow, Dine, Oldenberg, and Grooms.

Unmaking Collage / Remaking History

We can sharpen our sense of the historiographical dynamics of that severance by pausing momentarily to consider the extent to which Ono's performances substantially broaden the scope of the "bad memory" that was structurally cultivated by the happenings. In his article "Bad Memory: Text, Commodity, Happenings" Mike Sell argues that "the fragmented 'structure' of the Happenings" disrupted memory because it divided the audience in such a way "that no spectator could achieve a synoptic vision of the piece."[19] Though more limited in the simultaneous variety of occurrences that they facilitated,[20] the fragmented structural juxtapositions employed in *Cut Piece* also created a context that divided synoptic vision. But so too did those juxtapositions point to larger divisions within the avant-garde performance communities of the 1950s and 1960s, divisions that had a decisively gendered character. In this respect, the most radical juxtapositions of Ono's performances of *Cut Piece*, ironically, were found not so much in the piece itself but in the critical position that Ono's performances of it occupied in relation to performance practices of her male contemporaries who built upon on the legacies of the Duchamp-Cage aesthetic. Indeed, one of the best illustrations of that critical position is to be found in the "bad memory" shadowing the histories of Ono's performances.

As is the case with so many of the happenings and with avant-garde events in general, the accounts of Ono's performances of *Cut Piece* have left us with often conflicting images of what actually transpired. Generally speaking, the basic structure of her performances appears to have remained consistent with Ono's general score: in each performance, Ono positioned herself sitting on the stage, placed a pair of scissors at the spectators' disposal, which they, in turn, then used to cut Ono's clothing from her. What happened beyond that, however, is not entirely clear. By Ono's own accounts, the audience was invited "to take" the pieces of clothing with them, and film documentation of her Carnegie Hall performance suggests that this is exactly what happened, at least in New York.[21] Subsequent performances may have varied. In the late 1980s, for example, Alaster Niven (who was the administrator of the Africa Centre in London in 1966 when Ono performed *Cut Piece* for the last time) recalled not only that Ono invited the audience to cut away her clothing but, in contrast to Ono's own recollection, Niven also recalled that the audience was requested "to fix the pieces [of her clothing] to a large canvas on an easel at the side of the stage."[22] Remarkable in Niven's account is his recollection of the canvas, its location, and, in particular, the request to fix the pieces of Ono's clothing to it. All of this suggests an odd symmetry: while members of the audience dismantled Ono's appearance by cutting away her clothing, others constructed a collage in the margins of her performance. Nevin's recollection thus offers us a graphic image—a performative juxtaposition—of a collage constructed at Ono's expense.

That image lends itself to multiple readings, not the least of which is its visual reinforcement of what I want to argue was the critical dichotomy that Ono's performance established between events like her own and the performance events of those whose embrace of action-collage technique fell in line with traditions of the Duchamp-Cage aesthetic. Granted, there is a degree of uncertainty as to whether Niven's account is accurate regarding the canvas on the stage with Ono, and yet, ironically enough, this historical uncertainty has everything to do with the force of that dichotomy. At the most immediate level, of course, the canvas's indeterminate historical status underscores the "bad memory" woven into the very fabric of any narrative history. Its vacillation between presence and absence, between historical fact and fabrication, is a subtle reminder of how the construction of one history always—*always*—erases, elides, or suppresses another. But so too is this moment of historical uncertainty a moment of profound haunting. As such, it gives an eerie substance to the critical dichotomy that Ono's performance established between *Cut Piece* and the male-centered traditions of the Duchamp-Cage aesthetic. Indeed, the uncertainty regarding the canvas in Ono's event echoes the uncertainty surrounding what is widely viewed as the ur-event that set the experimental precedent for the happenings: namely John Cage's untitled event at Black Mountain College in 1952.

Of the variety of ways that one might understand the provocative juxtaposition of Ono and the canvas in *Cut Piece,* the fact that the canvas initially was blank and was situated as an object within a larger performance makes it startlingly reminiscent of the white paintings that Robert Rauschenberg reportedly placed in the margins of John Cage's untitled event. More importantly, the historical indeterminancy of the canvas contributes to this reminiscence as well since there is as much uncertainty about the Rauschenberg canvases as there is about the canvas in Ono's own event. In this regard, it is worth remembering that in a 1967 interview, Merce Cunningham told Martin Duberman that "Rauschenberg showed his paintings"[23] in Cage's untitled event. Nonetheless, there are real questions about whether the paintings were present at all. For like Nevin's account of Ono's performance, Cunningham's account of Cage's untitled event is unique among the numerous accounts that Duberman amassed in his book on the history of Black Mountain College. Just as Nevin is alone in his recollection of a canvas accompanying Ono on the stage, so too is Cunningham alone in his recollection of Rauschenberg's paintings in Cage's untitled event. A fluctuation between presence and absence characterizes the historical status of both.

Within the larger context of Ono's performance of *Cut Piece,* that fluctuation means that her event is and is not like that untitled event at Black Mountain College. While both events have canvases flickering in the margins, the on-again / off-again fluctuation of the canvas in Ono's *Cut Piece* situates Cage's untitled event in the margins of her own performance, vacillating, as it were, between presence and absence. Haunted as the indeterminate canvas in Ono's piece is by the specter of the uncertainties surrounding Cage's own event at Black Mountain, the canvas in *Cut Piece,* I would suggest, becomes a semiotic sign for that which haunts it: in short, there is a way to read the canvas as a sign for Cage's untitled event and, if we can venture so far, for its legacy in the action-collage techniques of the happenings. In this reading, the composite of Ono's performance event consists of a radical juxtaposition of contradictory trajectories, with Ono on one side and the legacies of Cage's untitled event on the other. Not only does such a reading underscore the dialectical relation that Ono's performance of *Cut Piece* has to Cage's untitled event, but it also goes a long way toward clarifying the feminist critique of the Duchamp-Cage aesthetic to which Ono's performance of *Cut Piece* gave voice. The nature of that critique becomes increasingly apparent the more one recognizes the contradictory activities that Ono's performance offered to her audience: an aggressive dismantling of her attire on the one hand, and a construction of a collage on the other, neither of which the piece endorses. But inasmuch as *Cut Piece* suggests that the latter is premised upon the aggressions of the former and inasmuch as the latter subtly alluded to Cage's seminal untitled event, Ono was thus positioned in her performance in a dialectical opposition to the pivotal aesthetic traditions embraced by her male contemporaries. For lack of a better term, we might call this dialectical opposition *the unmaking of collage* since it worked contrary to the action-collage techniques that, drawing upon the traditions of the Duchamp-Cage aesthetic and of action painting, artists like Kaprow and Oldenburg employed in what became known as the happenings.

At what point, *Cut Piece* implicitly asks, does the making of a collage become untenable when its construction simultaneously entails a progressive violation of women? At what point, the piece also implicitly asks, does the action-collage technique of the happenings become similarly untenable? These questions pointed toward the unexamined repressive spaces accommodated by the aesthetics of action-collage technique, and if, to us as cultural historians, these questions seem to be the product of a false dichotomy—given that the canvas in *Cut Piece* is historically suspect[24]—it is worth pausing momentarily to consider how much more pressing the questions become when the severed articles of Ono's clothing do not find their way onto a canvas but are distributed like spoils among the perpetrators. At such a moment, the indictment rings just as clearly since the disappearance of the canvas clears the way for a much more focused realization of how naively and idealistically the happening artists conceptualized their notions of the audience/participants. With or without the canvas, *Cut Piece* conjures up a tradition, the critique of which emerges as Ono becomes a casualty of spectator participation.

Much of that critique pivots on the type of casualty that Ono becomes. Indeed, her status as an Asian women has everything to do with how *Cut Piece* set the unexamined repressive spaces of action-collage technique in critical relief. In this respect, it is worth noting how strikingly consistent the critique emanating from Ono's performance event is with the more general observations that Shannon Jackson has recently made regarding the gendered and racist ideologies that always lurked in the shadows of the happenings:

> As numerous commentators have noted, such performances often reified a number of gendered, racist, and classed conventions in order to stage absolute reduction. The attempt to lay bare the essentials of performance often led toward a display of the primal with familiar sexual and racial codings. The number of "naked girls" who appear in the documentation and descriptions of the happenings of Allan Kaprow, Al Hansen, Richard Schechner, and others is somewhat overwhelming. Meanwhile, the spectacle of mostly white participants performing all-too familiar "rituals" of circling, drumming, and sacrificing testifies to the primitivist fascinations that propelled the search for the real. Such reifications did not go unnoticed at the time.[25]

Although Jackson does not mention Ono, one would be hard pressed to find a more concise summary of the political-aesthetic position that Ono's performance of *Cut Piece* staked out vis-à-vis the action-collage techniques championed by her male contemporaries.

If the radical juxtaposition of Ono and the canvas signified two competing, mutually exclusive traditions, so too did the performances of *Cut Piece* where the canvas was not present at all. In those performances members of the audience were left with the elements of collage at their fingertips. Carrying the remnants of Ono's clothing with them or discarding the remnants as they returned to their seats, the spectators unknowingly participated in a literal deconstruction of collage—a deconstruction of the absent canvas as collage and, more importantly, a deconstruction of the collage that Ono herself was in the stylized fabrics of social convention (i.e., her clothes). The turning point of this latter deconstruction was in the irony that increased as each article of clothing was cut away. Rather than moving Ono increasingly toward the literal, the concrete, the real, and the actual (all of which were the prized ideals of the happeningers),[26] the denuding of Ono magnified her status as a fetishized and exotic object of voyeuristic fascination. Rather than moving closer to the real, the audience moved deeper and deeper into the patriarchal ideologies that their actions reinforced. The consequence of this deconstruction—this *unmaking of collage*—was that placing the tools, remnants, and artifacts of collage squarely in the hands of the audience, fundamentally questioned the widespread embrace of the audience that had emerged out of the Duchamp-Cage aesthetic and that had long been touted as a path out of the problematic sphere of aesthetic absolutes. So too did the feminist underpinnings of this *unmaking of collage* radically challenge the assumptions governing the mode of performance that Clement Greenberg and Michael Fried had "designated as 'literalist'"[27] and that Michael Kirby associated with the emergence of an entirely "New Theatre."

Action-Collage, Collocation, and Submatrix

At a time when many of Ono's contemporaries assumed that the application of the aesthetics of collage or of chance operations to the theater would subvert audience passivity while simultaneously achieving what Michael Kirby was subsequently to call a "non-matrixed performance,"[28] Ono's *Cut Piece* took a decisively critical turn against the cultural practices of the "New Theatre." By handing the audience the basic instrument of collage (the scissors) and by simultaneously positioning the exposure of her body as the consequence of the audience's actions—an exposure subject to the audience's voyeuristic and fetished fascination with an Asian female body—Ono exposed a *submatrix* functioning beneath the presumably "nonmatrixed performance" practices of experimental theater in the sixties. In no uncertain terms, that submatrix is a disruptive—indeed, deconstructive—element in Kiby's famous binary between matrixed and nonmatrixed performance because it exposes the unacknowledged matrices lurking in the shadows of Kirby's privileging of the "nonmatrixed."[29]

We can garner a sense of the critically disruptive force of this exposure by briefly conceptualizing its relation to some of the traditions of Western drama that, despite a radical rethinking of theatrical conventions, the action-collage techniques of Ono's male counterparts left intact and that, despite Cage's influential interest in Eastern philosophies, never even registered as being worthy of critical consideration. In this regard, James Moy's important study *Marginal Sights* is particularly helpful. In the introduction to his study of staging the Chinese in America, Moy argues that the history of representing people of Asian descent in Western drama evinces a "need to demean or dehumanize these othered people . . . [in order] to maintain or reestablish an advantage for the dominant culture."[30] This need, which Moy ties to the imperialistic underpinnings of a naive anthropological fetishization of Asian peoples, can be traced back to "the beginning of the Western tradition in drama."[31] In the theater, that need to demean has manifested itself in what Moy later calls "the empowering gaze," which, under the sign of altruism, has subordinated Asians to repressive stereotypical representation.[32]

For the present discussion, Moy's argument is particularly intriguing because it develops a conceptual dynamic that lends itself in important ways to an assessment of the repressive Western traditions that *Cut Piece* excavates from the working aesthetics of action-collage technique. I refer specifically to Moy's argument that "by the middle of the nineteenth century two forms of the empowering gaze become clear, the serial and the voyeuristic."[33] Both of these forms converge in Ono's implicit, radical critique of the action-collage techniques of her male contemporaries. Certainly, it is difficult to imagine that the members of the audience who were willing to publically disrobe Ono with a pair of scissors did not recognize the extent to which their actions involved them in a process of demeaning or dehumanizing her, and though one might balk at the suggestion that this process deliberately aimed at reestablishing the audience's gendered, racist advantage, the issue here is not so much conscious objective as it is the authoritarian baggage that always accompanies acts that demean or dehumanize others. Consciously or unconsciously, the audience participated in a uniquely dialectical production of "the empowering gaze," a production that, on the one hand, was achieved at Ono's expense and that, on the other hand, simultaneously illuminated the parallels between collage technique and "the popular form of the serial, or survey"[34] (what we often refer to today as bricolage) that emerged at the turn of the century as a mode of anthropologically rationalized appropriation of cultural artifacts for random display.

Like collage itself, the serial relied on a process of displacement and "collocation of objects to create the *potential* for meaning."[35] Indeed, the sources that scholars have historically cited as the wellspring for the Cagean-inspired college events known as the happenings coincide with the very traditions that Moy cites as those that provided the structural foundation for a theatricalized display that subordinated Asian Americans to a bevy of stereotypes. Not only does Moy argue that "Chineseness first appeared in America within the displacing structure of the variety stage,"[36] but his description of the anthropological serial reads almost as if he were summarizing the performative traditions that, according to Michael Kirby, gave rise to the happenings. Whereas Kirby describes the happenings as "compartmented" in format and devoid of an "information structure"[37] (i.e., a narrative), Moy notes that the serial was "panoptic in sensibility and usually nonnarrative" in structure.[38] Whereas Kirby notes that "the materials of Happenings . . . are taken from and related to the experiential world of everyday life"[39] and likens happenings to the "circus,"[40] Moy notes that the serial "employed displacement as a structural force and included museum displays, vaudeville" and "circus" elements.[41] Important in this regard is the manner in which the "nonnarrative" of the empowering gaze, which was the consequence of collage-like act of collocation and which bears such an uncanny similarity to Kirby's notion of the nonmatrixed structure of the happenings, still leaves space for the oppressive fictional fabrications known as stereotypes, fabrications that are directly connected to the voyeuristic undercurrents governing the audience's participation in *Cut Piece.*

Before moving into a more detailed consideration of the voyeuristic, one preliminary conclusion is well within our grasp. If Ono's *Cut Piece* achieved nothing else, at the very least, it underscored the extent to which action-collage technique, while rejecting one theatrical tradition, tacitly reaffirmed a far more repressive one. In this respect, the overlap that I have highlighted between Kirby's notion of the "New Theatre's" nonmatrixed performance and Moy's history of the repressive theatrical tradition of "the popular form of the serial, or survey" is merely one example among many of the ugly baggage carried along with action-collage technique that still remains to be unpacked. Whereas the former rejection was bound to the abstract realms of a crisis in aesthetic representation, the latter reaffirmation continues to bind countless individuals to the oppressive stereotypes that mediate their experience not in the theater but rather in the public sphere. In this specific respect, *Cut Piece* began to illuminate a history of collage that is no longer selective in what it highlights and in what it celebrates. Indeed, *Cut Piece* opens collage to the contradictory trajectories of its own legacies in the West. And if this gesture also had strong feminist undercurrents, they were the consequence, in part, of the position that Ono herself occupied in relation to New York's avant-garde during the 1960s.

Rethinking the Role of the Audience

With the privileged hindsight of the critic and historian, it is possible to read far into the implications of *Cut Piece*'s exposure of the gendered and racist submatrices in "the New Theatre" and to see in those implications a larger illumination of the problematic relation that action-collage technique bore to an unacknowledged diversity of theatrical traditions. But such a reading, I would suggest, is only really possible in light of the critical perspective that Ono's performance developed in relation to the central pillar of Duchampian aesthetics: his embrace of the spectator. More than on anything else, that embrace was grounded in the conclusion that Duchamp drew in his short but important 1957 essay "The Creative Act." The conclusions that Duchamp draws in this essay had governed his work since early days of New York Dada. But by 1957, his embrace of the spectator had already paved the aesthetic path that many among the American avant-garde would take in the middle decades of the twentieth century and that was central to the performative avant-garde's innovative attempts to disrupt audience passivity. In the final paragraph of that essay Duchamp maintains:

> All in all, the creative act is not preformed by the artist alone; the spectator brings the work in contact with the external world by deciphering and interpreting its inner qualifications and thus adds his contribution to the creative act.[42]

Following the lead of Cage, the happening artists had pushed this specific dimension of Duchamp's aesthetic into an increasingly conscious envelopment of the spectator's creative contributions.

That extension of Duchampian aesthetics pivoted on the development of a variety of strategies for provoking the spectator out of passivity, and while Ono's performance of *Cut Piece* initially would appear to overlap with this project of disrupting the spectator's passivity, the disruption provoked by *Cut Piece* was unlike any of those scored by her contemporaries. Through the process of a subtle dialectical inversion—achieved when Ono assumed the passive stance that she invited her audience to abandon—Ono's performance of *Cut Piece* engendered a critical rerouting of the assumption of immediacy and authenticity that underlies the Duchampian embrace of the spectator. What was primarily responsible for this critical shift was a deconstructive playing of one sense of passivity off another, which literally disrupted the disruption of audience passivity, broke the idealistic spell cast about the spectator's newly acquired active role, and demonstrated that the spectator's creative contributions—not despite but precisely because of their "contact with the external world"—are potentially as repressive as they are liberating. Indeed, Ono's performance of *Cut Piece* exposed some of the ugliest of the fabricated absolutes that mediate the public sphere and that, once exposed, gave the lie to the rhetoric of authenticity that was embedded in the aesthetics of the happenings.

In the happenings, that rhetoric pivoted on a constructed binary, which equated the transformation of spectators into active agents with a blurring of art and life and with the creation of an event that was presumed to be more immediate, concrete, and "authentic" and that thus stood in contradistinction to what Michael Kirby described as the matrixed events constituting traditional theater. Claus Oldenburg specifically stated, for example, that his happenings aimed at using " 'real' material" (which included real "people") set "*in motion*" in "a particular 'real' place" like his store.[43] For happening artists like Oldenburg, disrupting audience passivity was thus a gesture of revolt against the fabrications and fictions associated with traditional theater, a revolt that coincided with—indeed was precipitated by—an embrace of the presumably accessible immediacy and authenticity of a performance event or spectacle. But if happening artists like Oldenburg framed this embrace of immediacy in contrast to the matrixed, fictional constructs of conventional theater, Ono, in the very early sixties, had already recognized that the most powerful, enduring, and pernicious fabrications were carried into the theater rather than produced by it!

Her performance of *Cut Piece* gave a dramatic illustration of this very conviction, but it was a conviction that she expressed through numerous venues. Witness her 1962 essay "The World as Fabricator," an essay marked by a profound (even if somewhat ambivalent) postmodern aesthetic sensibility. At the very least, that essay is important because its arguments foreshadow the conceptual structures that arguably inform *Cut Piece* and that radically question the binary opposition between matrixed and nonmatrixed performance that Kirby subsequently posited as the conceptual signature defining the happenings. In that essay, Ono argues:

> I cannot stand the fact that everything is the accumulation of "distortion" owning to one's slanted view. I want the truth. I want to feel the truth by any possible means. I want someone or something to let me feel it. I can[not] trust the . . . manipulation of my consciousness. I know no other way but to present the structure of a drama which assumes fiction as fiction, that is, as fabricated truth.[44]

To conceptualize the world as a "fabricator," as Ono does in her essay, is to perceive it as a site of endless construction where the very concepts of truth, authenticity, and the "real" are inextricably tied to the manipulations of consciousness. Moreover, a recognition of those concepts for the constructs that they are is a necessary prerequisite for recognizing their use as tools of political and ideological manipulation. Ono' s distaste for distortion notwithstanding, her articulated desire for truth resolves itself not in a dichotomy between distortion and authenticity but rather between the naive assumption of authenticity on the one hand and the recognition of the manipulations of consciousness as a foundation of human experience on the other. The acknowledged limitation of knowing "no other way but to present the structure of a drama which assumes fiction as fiction, that it is, as fabricated truth" is thus an acknowledgment that plays manipulation against itself by announcing fiction to be fiction rather than pretending that is truth.

Following the logic of Ono's notion of fabrication, a logic that resurfaces in her performance of *Cut Piece,* the "real" of Oldenburg's happenings was thus arguably as much a constructed matrix as any matrix to be found in conventional theater—except that it was perhaps a little more dangerous because it so successfully masqueraded as its opposite. Building on this logic, Ono's performance of *Cut Piece* did much to cast new and critical light on the Duchampian-inspired embrace of the spectator that had done so much to finally liberate art from the sphere of conceptual aesthetic absolutes. In its simplest terms, *Cut Piece* revealed the manner in which that embrace covertly (re)constructed one set of absolutes even as it deconstructed another. The catalyst for this exposure, as I have said, was a simple exchange of roles.

Rather than merely commingling the audience with the event, *Cut Piece* orchestrated an inversion of the audience/performer divide that produced at least three significant and related effects: it gave free reign to the spectators' voyeuristic inclinations; it linked those inclinations to the construction and maintenance of ethnic and gendered stereotypes; and it linked both tendencies to the aesthetic practices of Ono's contemporaries because it simultaneously positioned Ono physically at odds with the practice of collage. Indeed, while Ono assumed the passive role traditionally assigned to the spectators, placing the scissors in front of her transformed the spectators into active agents whose conduct defined the practice of collage in gestures shaded by implicit violation of or overt hostility toward Ono as a woman and/or as a person of color. To cite one explicit example of that hostility, it is worth recalling that during the first performance of *Cut Piece* at the Contemporary American Avant-Garde Music Concert in Kyoto in 1964, "a man came on to the stage and raised the scissors over Ono's head, threatening her for a long time as if ready to stab her."[45] The Japanese context of this threat reminds us that the issues raised by the audience's responses concerned not only stereotypical notions of race but also stereotypical notions of gender as well—particularly those notions that attribute passivity to women and that, at one level, the man who raised the scissors above Ono attempted to reinforce with the threat of physical violence.[46]

Ono's response to that threat is telling because it illustrates the critical position that she adopted in relation to the practice of action-collage technique. Accounts of this tense moment remark that Ono watched her would-be attacker with a kind of "dismay"—a dismay, I would argue, that dramatically punctuates the critical distance that *Cut Piece* established between the practice of collage and Ono's own work.[47] Shaped as that distance is by the threat of violation and violence, Ono's position not as the agent but as the target and potential victim of collage challenged both the assumptions governing the experimental collage events staged by Ono's contemporaries and the value systems brought into the performance of *Cut Piece* by the audience.

That dual challenge resulted from a subtle blurring of the traditionally distinct roles of artist and audience—a distinction that, for all Kaprow's commingling of audience with event, was still central to his work. Ultimately, the blurring set the stage for a fundamental critique of the immediacy that experimental artists in the United States associated with abandoning both painterly representation on the one hand and text-based dramatic theater on the other. Nothing was more crucial to that blurring than the object that mediated the audience's relationship to Ono. By handing the audience the most basic tool of collage—that pair of scissors with which the prerequisites for collage constructions occur—

Ono not only echoed Duchamp's acknowledgment of the audience's role in producing any work of art. She extended that acknowledgment and, in an illuminating reversal of the experimental trends away from dramatic fictions, *Cut Piece* conceptualized the audience in such a way that individual spectators not only commingled with the event; they unknowingly became actors.

One by one spectators became performers, cast in the role of the artist enacting the fundamental performative gestures of collage aesthetics, and they did so in an environment where their ethically problematic decision to prey upon Ono implicitly doubled as a profound indictment of the latent racist and sexist assumptions that were still extant in the avant-garde's belief that some essential immediacy could be achieved in the action-collage techniques of the happenings. Indeed, the spectators' decision to actively prey upon Ono struck at the very foundations of collage technique, tied symbolically as those decisions were to the act of cutting. As Kristine Stiles has noted, the Latin *decidere,* which means "to cut," is also the source for the English verb *to decide,* and if as she suggests *Cut Piece* is thus at one level a "decision piece" in which the audience had to choose how far they individually would take the piece and how far they collectively would allow it to go, then the dramatic structure of the *Cut Piece* simultaneously spliced those decisions into a semiotic system that symbolically equated the audience's ethically questionable violation of Ono's person with the practice of collage itself.[48]

This equation was not limited to the ethical decision that the audience had to make about whether or not to participate in a voyeuristic frenzy that necessitated a demeaning of Ono. Accompanying the cutting were far more significant, albeit subtle, acts of construction that mediated the passive position Ono assumed on the stage. That passivity became its own constructed role, one that was constructed more by the spectators than by Ono herself and one that was grounded in their fetishized fascination with Ono's Asian body. Furthermore, it was a stereotypical role that was directly connected with the voyeurism unleashed by the spectators' enactment of the fundamental gestures of collage. Cutting was indistinguishable from stripping, stripping was the stimulus for voyeurism, and voyeurism, however reductive its processes may be, contextualized Ono within the frame of a specific social stereotype, one that subordinated her to the defining authority of a Western male gaze. The authoritarian underpinnings of voyeurism are well known. But in the cross-cultural sphere, the mechanisms of the voyeuristic gaze, which tend to reaffirm "the authority of the looker . . . at the expense of the object," often function, as James Moy has argued, by reducing the object to a "stereotype."[49]

Scholarly discussion of what that stereotype in *Cut Piece* entailed is virtually nonexistent, at least in any detailed terms. What we find instead are general references by scholars like Kristine Stiles to Ono's occasional interlacing of "strong proto-feminist elements" with "commentary on race and class"[50] or an implicitly critical citation, by scholars like Kevin Concannon, of how Ono's artwork was received in the popular press. "Even before she became the so-called 'dragon-lady' who destroyed the Beatles," Concannon notes, "Ono endured a particular type of 'gaze' reserved for women of color," and Concannon specifically cites a *Daily Telegraph and Morning Post* review of Ono's London performance of *Cut Piece* from September 29, 1966, in which Sean Day-Lewis recounted the event during which "Miss Ono sat looking inscrutably Japanese (she is actually Japanese) while members of the audience took it in turns to cut off her clothes with a pair of scissors."[51] It is unfortunate that Concannon, who is careful to document his claim, chose not to explore in greater detail the gaze that he rightly argues Ono had to endure. Perhaps at one level, the problems with describing Ono's passive posture as "inscrutably Japanese" may well be obvious enough that commentary would appear unnecessary, but amid the obvious it is easy to overlook the more subtle mechanisms that sustain the very stereotypical images that we would openly repudiate.

In theater studies a larger sense of those mechanisms took shape at the end of the 1980s with the premier of David Henry Hwang's *M. Butterfly*. We began to receive a critical scholarly discussion of what Hwang himself identified in the "Afterword" to his drama as "pulling a Butterfly" or "playing the submissive Oriental number."[52] What Hwang is referring to, of course, are gendered, racial stereotypes, and in light of the debates provoked by Hwang's drama, it would be difficult today not to recognize, at least at some general level, the critical confrontation that Ono's performance of *Cut Piece* orchestrated with the cultural stereotype of the Asian woman as being characteristically passive and submissive. But the real significance of that confrontation is the result of what is the most important but most neglected aspect of Ono's performance in this regard: the fact that it was not Ono who was "pulling a Butterfly" but rather the spectators who constructed her as Butterfly and who in doing so betrayed their agency in the construction of ethnic and gendered images that maintain a Western patriarchal order. Nowhere is this crucial point more readily apparent than in the fact that Ono's score for *Cut Piece* makes no reference to the ethnic origin of the performer whatsoever.

It is hard to overestimate the importance of that lack of reference to the performer's ethnicity. But if recent studies of the effects of stereotypes in popular culture can serve as a provisional gauge, this lack of reference is arguably a pivotal element in the critical distance that *Cut Piece* established between the practice of collage and Ono's own performative work as a person of color—especially since those studies help us to conceptualize the audience's agency in *Cut Piece* in terms that illuminate the parallels between the forging of stereotypes and the techniques of collage. Certainly, Moy's discussion of the serial helps to move us in this direction, but here I am thinking more of Josephine Lee's identification of the underlying conceptual violence in the construction of stereotypes themselves. Although Lee does not discuss Ono in her book *Performing Asian America* (nor, for that matter, does Moy),[53] her understanding of the implicit violence that accompanies the mechanisms of stereotyping finds a ready echo in the tense critical atmosphere that characterized Ono's performances of *Cut Piece* and that thus positioned Ono simultaneously at odds with the construction of stereotypes and the construction of collage. Lee argues:

> Stereotypes in popular culture and art enact a violent dismemberment that focuses attention on particular body parts and features (in the case of Asians, eyes, noses, and hair, as well as skin) by highlighting or visually severing them from the rest of the body. This dismemberment preserves the fantasy of the oppressor's self as unified, coherent, orderly, and rational.[54]

In *Cut Piece,* each individual act of shearing Ono's clothing rehearsed this play between highlighting and visual severance. Couched in the techniques of collage, the gradual cutting away of Ono's attire thus highlighted a body, the features of which were already severed, decontextualized, and collocated within a fetishized stereotypical construction. Combined, the cutting and construction thus effected a profound indictment against the unexamined, racist legacies that found shelter in the practice of action-collage technique.

At this point, it is, I think, important to underscore my use of the phrase "finding shelter," not so much for the sake of avoiding the suggestion that individual happening artists were consciously racist—there is no direct indication that they consciously were—but rather to emphasize the entanglement of action-collage technique in conceptual and institutional structures where arguably more virulent instances of racism occur because they are covert and undetected and can thrive even among those of us who know better. More than anything else in this regard, the underlying myth of immediacy in the aesthetics of the happenings (and that myth's concomitant assumption of authenticity) harbored those legacies, and perhaps the single most important accomplishment of Ono's performance of *Cut Piece* was a critical exposure of that myth and of the false dichotomy upon which it depended. For if, as Michael Kirby suggested, the happenings pivoted on the presumption, first, of a possible departure from the matrixed fabrications of traditional theater and, second, of a contrasting movement into a sphere of nonmatrixed performance, then Ono's performance of *Cut Piece* exposed the concept of nonmatrixed performance as an idealized fabrication obscuring the repressive social matrixes that continued to thrive beneath the surface of what Kirby called the "new theatre."

Whether Ono consciously set out to debunk the governing myths of that new theater is a matter of speculation, but it is worth noting that in the same year that she performed *Cut Piece* for the last time, she directly confronted, in retrospect, the assumption that cutting away her clothing would uncover a presumably natural, unmediated, or authentic self. As Ono was to explain in her short "Biography/Statement" from late 1966:

> People went on cutting the parts they do not like of me finally there was only the stone remained of me that was in me but they were still not satisfied and wanted to know what it's like in the stone [*sic*].[55]

Geologists will tell us that the answer to this query varies from stone to stone, but generally speaking the substance within a stone coincides with the substance on the surface, and in fact this type of material consistency is necessary for the sculptor's trade. For the essence of sculpture is not what is within a stone but rather what the artist makes out of it. Similarly, the disrobing of Ono's body was not so much a movement toward some presumed essence or immediacy of her being as it was a constructing of her body within a repressive sociopolitical matrix.

If Ono's critical consciousness of the ethnic undercurrents to that matrix were not immediately evident in her performances, then at the very least the performances would appear to have cultivated an acute awareness that she began to articulate in "Biography/Statement"—and it is not just her comments comparing herself to a stone that are evidence of this awareness. Directly following her metaphorical comments on the audiences' dissatisfaction with their encounter with Ono's nonessentialist conception of the self, Ono triumphantly added the postscript: "P.S. If the butterflies in your stomach die, send yellow death announcements to your friends."[56] This playful allusion to the Asian stereotype (butterfly) and its visually severed marker (i.e., yellow skin) not only consumes the narrative of Puccini's opera but specifically positions Ono as an active agent willfully moving beyond the passive suicidal long-suffering that the stereotype would attribute to her. For she does not fade like a butterfly, but rather presides over the death of a stereotype.

Arguably, this gesture leads us into a sphere of affirmation where a full vetting of the sexist and racist baggage of action-collage technique clears a path for a radically reconceptualized notion of collage itself. The beating of that path is nowhere better evident than in Ono's critical foray into uncharted aesthetic realms where the basic categories that have long shaped our understanding of the happenings and Fluxus events of the 1960s are not only inadequate but also cultivate a misleading and ultimately repressive conceptual imprecision, an imprecision that Ono's performances of *Cut Piece* expose. If for no other reason than this exposure, Ono's performances of *Cut Piece* thus merit our attention because they critically illuminate the unexamined reactionary shadows cast by the structural relation of the categories of *audience participation* and *nonmatrixed performance.*

Heretofore, the former category has widely served as a characterization of a basic technique for achieving the latter. Yet *Cut Piece* would encourage us, at least by way of implication, to consider the extent to which the category of nonmatrixed performance—as an aesthetic goal or as an end in itself—has actually served as a kind of ruse that exaggerates the significance of the performative avant-garde's departure from the fictional constructs of traditional dramatic theater. This is not to say that the departure is insignificant, but overemphasizing its significance has diverted attention from a much needed critical scrutiny of the sociopolitical matrixes that the audience inscribes across any performance regardless of whether that performance is based upon fictional dramatic constructs or upon the illusion of immediacy and regardless of whether the audience remains spectator or becomes participant.

Scoring Optimism in the Construction of *Cut Piece*

While it is certainly possible to imagine a progressive audience whose participation moves a work of art in a politically radical direction, Ono's performances of *Cut Piece* remind us that, even in the volatile sixties, the conceptual, sociopolitical matrixes that spectators bring to a performance tend to reaffirm the normative, patriarchal values of white America. In this respect, Ono's performances offered a substantial challenge to the underlying assumptions that governed the experimental performance community's extension of Duchampian aesthetics into the "New Theatre." Echoing the precedent set by Duchamp, that extension had taken a decisive step away from the rigid hierarchies of aesthetic absolutes and gestured, at least implicitly, toward a further democratization of the arts—a gesture exemplified in the avant-garde's embrace of the audience. But that embrace was largely of an audience always already defined.

Ono's performances exposed the extent to which this seeming gesture toward a democratization of the arts was entangled in a subtle form of patronization that reaffirmed white male privilege "even as it allegedly contest[ed] the practices that construct" that privilege.[57] Ono's performances, in short, were positioned at odds with a precalibrated democratization that, despite fanfare to the contrary, subtly reaffirmed the existing structures of cultural authority. This point was profoundly illustrated in the form of participation that the audience adopted in *Cut Piece.* But for those who took the time to look, it was also evident in the composition of the audiences who generally frequented the happenings, Those audiences were largely comprised of people who moved within New York's chic gallery culture: hip but mainstream, middle- to upper-middle-class whites.

Given the attitudes that surfaced in Ono's performances of *Cut Piece,* one might seriously question why Ono bothered to address her performances to this audience at all, especially since the advantage of hindsight allows us to recognize her critique as part of a larger current of dissatisfaction that in the mid-1960s people of color began to express regarding theater that catered to white audiences by default. In 1968, for example, John O'Neal, who was one of the founding members of the Free Southern Theatre, specifically admonished black artists not to succumb to the "divided consciousness" that, he argued, is necessary in order to address white audiences and that, he maintained furthermore, is a product of engaging "cultural, political and economic institutions that incorporate the premises of racism."[58] O'Neal concluded that "as long as the victims of racism accept the judgements of their oppressors and rely on the approbation of that society, they are locked in."[59] O'Neal's comments coincided with a growing sense of militancy and cultural nationalism within the black community.

Although there is no corresponding sense of militancy or nationalism in Ono's work, she was careful to distinguish her sense of performance from what she critically described as the "get togetherness" of the happenings.[60] In contrast to the happenings, her events, she argued, were characterized by two related concerns. Reflecting the nascent forms of identity politics that began to emerge in the 1960s, Ono argued that unlike the "get togetherness" of the happenings, her events were foremost "a dealing with onself," which she described as being motivated by "something that starts it moving—the closest word for it may be a 'wish' or 'hope.'"[61] It is the sense of optimism in that "something" called a "wish" or a "hope" that kept Ono engaged with audiences whose inclinations proved to be more reactionary than they perhaps realized before Ono invited them onto the stage. In this respect, the "dealing with oneself" that Ono referred to cut in both directions because the implicit wish or hope in her performances of *Cut Piece* clearly referred not just to a coming to terms with herself vis-à-vis the audience's constructed stereotypical images of Asian women; it also implied the need for the audience to deal with its own tacit if not active perpetuation of sexist and racist legacies.

Unspecified in its initial articulation, that something called a wish or hope arguably resurfaced in a contrast between what was and what might be the particular forms taken in a performance of *Cut Piece,* a contrast that Ono carefully articulated when she finally published a score of the event some four years after she had performed *Cut Piece* for the last time. Ono included a description of *Cut Piece* in the 1970 edition of *Grapefruit,* which was an updated popular press version of the book of instructions that she had originally published privately in 1964, the same year that she began performing *Cut Piece.* In this new edition of her book, the instructions for *Cut Piece* are notable because unlike the other instructions, which are limited to abstract imperatives, the instructions for *Cut Piece* include a third-person account of Ono's own performances that culminates with a suggestion about how the piece might be performed differently in the future. Whereas instructions like those for *Lighting Piece* direct us to "Light a match and watch till it goes out,"[62] the instructions for *Cut Piece* are fragmentary, containing only a portion of the detailed instruction that Ono wrote for the unrealized concert/exhibition *Strip Tease Show* that was planned for 1966. They are literally already cut. Containing only a partial instruction, the score for *Cut Piece* is supplemented with a description of Ono's performances from which we can derive not only the full instruction but arguably the sociopolitical alternative imaged by the piece itself:

> CUT PIECE
> Cut.
> This piece was performed in Kyoto, Tokyo, New York and London. It is usually performed by Yoko Ono coming on the stage and in a sitting position, placing a pair of scissors in front of her and asking the audience to come up on the stage, one by one, and cut a portion of her clothing (anywhere they like) and take it. The performer, however, does not have to be a woman.[63]

It is easy to overlook the significance of Ono's remark that *Cut Piece* need not be performed by a woman, especially since rhetorically the remark is positioned almost as an afterthought. But the importance of this remark lies in the fact that it reflects upon the past and projects into the future. While the implied alternative here is presumably that a man might perform the piece,[64] the absence of a specific reference to a male performer is noteworthy. It suggests, for example, that the performer need not be a woman as a woman is defined within a patriarchal society. At the same time, the absent sign is a telling reminder that the envisioned performer is someone who only potentially exists in the sphere of social cultural possibilities, someone, in short, who is receptive enough to the deconstructive practices of collage that his assumption of a passivity within the performance would provoke a radically new construction of masculinity within an enactment of a rehabilitated action-collage technique.

CHAPTER FIVE

Between Dialectics, Decorum, and Collage

Sabotaging Schneemann at the Dialectics of Liberation Congress, London 1967

> Is this Blitz Heaven or another skit from the mango factory?
> how strange it compared with the black and white aquarian
> stalinists ranting and raving from the platform at the Dialectics
> of Liberation.
>
> —Heathcote Williams

Dinner Party Politics: An Introduction

On a midsummer evening in 1967, Carolee Schneemann found herself on London's East Eisham Street, far away from the dinner party across town on West Eisham to which, only begrudgingly, she had been invited. Having already been told rather cooly "to arrive *after* the dinner," Schneemann had some cause to believe the directions that led her to East instead of West Eisham were not accidental. An invited but unwelcome guest, Schneemann recalls that, once she finally arrived at the party, no one spoke to her and she was left isolated in the "deadly, impenetrable atmosphere . . . [of] men in huddles passing wine to each other."[1] It is tempting to liken the passive-aggressive atmosphere of this scene to that of private conversations between members of a gentleman's club being interrupted by the premature arrival of the evening's questionable entertainment. For, invited though Schneemann may have been, her assumed place among the other guests is not too difficult to glean from the fact that she was greeted with an air of hostility and suspicion—an air that implicitly cast Schneemann's work as a performance artist within the realm of the morally and politically suspect and which, questioning the legitimacy of her artistic claims, relegated her work to a category of entertainment that could be privately relished while publically rejected. In simplest terms, Schneemann's arrival at West Eisham breached decorum with those who did not desire to take her seriously, and her arrival did so because it demanded entrance to the party rather than accepting the role of merely providing entertainment to the party-goers. In this regard, likening the party to a gentleman's club is not too far off the mark. For both are closed-door affairs regulated by the economies of sexism and privilege, and both, with their comparable notions of entertainment, mesh well with that onerous mechanism of authoritarian culture that Herbert Marcuse called "repressive desublimation."[2]

At first blush, looking to Marcuse for an understanding of the unwelcome reception that Schneemann encountered at this midsummer party might appear to be an odd choice. But the choice is not gratuitous. While the broader reaches of Marcuse's theory of repressive desublimation attempt to characterize the underlying psycho-political structures that perpetuate industrial bourgeois society, two things bring his theory to the heart of that midsummer party. First, the hostility and suspicion that greeted Schneemann there largely pivoted on the assumption that her work was a prime example of what Marcuse characterized as the central failing of art within the larger context of desublimated society: namely, a kind of complicity in which artistic expression frequently neglects its critical responsibilities, opting instead for the "function of entertaining without endangering" the status quo.[3] It was hardly a stretch for the members of the party to make such an assumption since Marcuse had suggested as much in his own writing, specifically singling out the American avant-garde tradition to which Schneemann belonged as an example of art that had settled on a path of clever entertainments rather than forging a path of critical opposition to one-dimensional society and thought.[4] Second, if I seem to give Marcuse's ideas high currency among the partygoers, that is because Marcuse himself was among the wine-sippers snubbing Schneemann, and he was conversing with like-minded men. Indeed, whatever the similarities that those huddled men at the party bore to a gentleman's club, they fancied themselves to be anything but the last remnants of a stodgy rear-guard.

The dinner was, in fact, a welcoming party for a collection of radical thinkers. The men who attended were prominent figures in the New Left, a "curious pastiche of eminent scholars and political activists"[5] like Lucien Goldmann, Herbert Marcuse, John Gerassi, Jules Henry, Gregory Bateson, Erving Goffman, Paul Goodman, Stokely Carmichael, and even Allen Ginsberg—all of whom had been brought to London by an independent and loosely structured organization that called itself the Institute of Phenomenological Studies. This institute was headed by a small group of radical antipsychiatry psychiatrists, the core of which included R. D. Laing, Joseph Berke, Leon Redler, and David Cooper. Despite its established-sounding name, the institute was little more than a name, a mailing address and a vaguely articulated agenda on a one-page flyer that Berke, Cooper, and Redler appear to have mailed to every progressive intellectual they had every heard of—and archival evidence suggests that they had heard of many. Less than a year old, the Institute of Phenomenological Studies, whatever its programmatic airs, had in actuality no identifiable function other than that of organizing and administering the Dialectics of Liberation Congress[6] to which the collection of individuals mentioned above had been invited and which convened during the last two weeks of July in 1967 at the Roundhouse, an old Victorian train station in London's Chalk Farm that the playwright Arnold Wesker had transformed into "an experimental theatre and center for the arts."[7] Although her name never appeared on the Congress program, Schneemann was also invited. In fact, she was the only woman among the core Congress participants, having been invited to create a performance event for the last evening of the Congress, an event that Schneemann entitled *Round House* and that, though advertised as "a Happening" she described as an example of what she called "kinetic theater."

It was amid her hostile reception at the welcoming dinner to the Congress that Schneemann apparently began to realize that the absence of her name on the printed program was more than mere oversight. It was part of a pattern of erasure, neglect, attempted censorship, and deliberate sabotage, all of which not only served as the backdrop to Schneemann's actual performance but which also, I would argue, became the part of the very fabric of the performance's significance as an event both within and beyond the Congress itself. I single out *Round House* in particular because the more one examines the sociopolitical context of this largely disregarded piece, the more one recognizes its striking singular paradigmatic achievement among Schneemann's numerous generative accomplishments as a painter, filmmaker, and performance artist. Seldom has Schneemann's work so directly challenged the patriarchal avatars of the Western intellectual tradition, and what especially singles out *Round House* in this regard is that this challenge took shape against the backdrop of organized events that were shrouded in the aura of the progressive politics associated with that tradition. At the simplest level, then, the argument here is that Schneemann's work exposed a repressive undercurrent in the assumptions about liberation that dominated the Congress. But what makes that exposure significant is that it took shape within an irreconcilable conflict between the method of dialectics generally espoused at the Congress and the conceptual strategies of kinetic theater practiced in Schneemann's work. Out of the immediate particulars of this conflict, I would argue, Schneemann's kinetic theater, grounded as it was in the aesthetics of collage and in the sensual social immediacy of performance, not only offered but *enacted* a radical political alternative to the critical methodology repeatedly reaffirmed in the work of the other Congress participants. Indeed, Schneemann herself characterized that reaffirmation as a kind of intellectual nepotism in which the other participants, while often embroiled in heated arguments, nonetheless "validated each others [*sic*] work" and their ostensible "transgressions of established culture" by maintaining a singular unity in their uncritical acceptance of the governing assumptions of their own common discourse.[8]

If the alternative enacted in Schneemann's work transcended the immediate context of the Congress, it did so because the methodology it challenged was not a product of the Congress itself. Grounded in the tenets of logocentrism, that methodology, which, in fact, was a derivation of the scientific method, united the other Congress participants not just in a shared belief in reason but in reason specifically empowered by the assumed stable referential authority of the Word. Critical theorists have long decried the problems haunting such assumptions. Indeed, one of the basic lessons of poststructural theory is that beneath the veneer of referential authority a host of problematic binary oppositions frequently regulate not only the structural dynamics of signification and meaning but also the economies of dominance and power. On this point, the Congress did not prove to be an exception. Its assertions of authority, couched though they may have been in the rhetoric of dialectics, antiauthoritarianism, and progressive politics, were purchased nonetheless with a range of restrictive binaries, not the least of which were the unquestioned oppositions between the categories of science and art, and, correspondingly, of male and female. That the Congress pushed the discourse of science at the expense of art ought not be too surprising, given that the Congress was dominated by social scientists. That the Congress also privileged male prerogatives at the expense of women, on the other hand, was far too commonplace a phenomenon to write it off as a product of the Congress being dominated by men. That dominance was symptomatic, not generative, of the patriarchal hierarchies it reinforced—hierarchies that regulated gender, that put Schneemann on all too familiar terrain, and that, as a consequence, activated some of the most important strategies she had developed as an artist. Indeed, I would go so far as to argue that Schneemann's response to that dominance ultimately stretched the borders of her performance back from its officially scheduled slot in the Congress proceedings into the daily activities of her workshops and into her tense interactions and encounters with the Congress organizers and other participants during the two weeks leading up to her performance at the end of the Congress.

Of Decorum, Found Restrictive Behaviors, and the Word

By the time that Schneemann arrived at the Dialectics of Liberation Congress in 1967, she already had almost a decade's worth of work behind her that went against the grain of the expectations imposed upon women by intellectual, aesthetic, and social paradigms that privileged the work of the men who forged them and measured the work of women against standards they seldom had any role in setting. Some sense of this very point is evident in Schneemann's reflections on the effects of claiming aesthetic proprietorship over her own body in works like *Eye Body* (1963). Those reflections are particularly salient because the patriarchal attitudes she attributes to the American avant-garde of the late fifties and early sixties could easily double for the attitudes she encountered a few years later at the Dialectics of Liberation Congress—hence, as will be evident momentarily, my opening comparison of the Congress participants with a gentleman's club. Recalling her experiences as a woman artist working in the long macho shadow of the American abstract expressionists, Schneemann writes:

> In 1963 to use my body as an extension of my painting-constructions was to challenge and threaten the psychic territorial power lines by which women were admitted to the Art Stud Club, so long as they behaved *enough* like the men, [and] did work clearly in the traditions and pathways hacked out by the men.[9]

Humorous though Schneemann's sarcasm about the "Art Stud Club" may be, the important point here is that breaking with these traditions and refusing to conform to the gendered expectations of "Stud Club" aesthetics seldom led a response that one might characterize as a serious reflection on the conflicting artistic sensibilities located in the contrast between a male-dominated artistic tradition and a calculated break with that tradition by a female artist. As Schneemann was quick to recognize, breaking with the aesthetic discourse established by her male counterparts led not to dialogue but to exclusion, isolation, and ostracization—all of which were regulated by the subtle but forceful presence of the conventional and prescriptive notions of gender that give shape to commonplace quotidian experience in the social mainstream and that, ironically enough, had free reign beneath the progressive political rhetoric of the Dialectics of Liberation Congress.

From the vantage point of the twenty-first century, there is perhaps nothing particularly new about the discovery of conventional notions of gender regulating social interaction along the cutting edge of radical art and politics. But what Schneemann actually did with the conventional notions of gender that she discovered there is another matter. In her handling of these attitudes, Schneemann transformed the parameters of collage aesthetics by a rather undifferentiated treatment of visual objects and enacted social attitudes as basic material in the construction of collage events, a treatment that, with regard to the aesthetics of collage, marked a unique conceptual shift from the graphic to the performing arts. Whereas in the graphic arts collage artists had used a radical juxtaposition of found objects and everyday detritus to provoke a fundamental questioning of art and its boundaries, Schneemann, in the collage events of her kinetic theater, extended the category of found objects beyond physical material to include human actions that she would "dislocate" and "disassociate" from their normal context and that she would in turn juxtapose with a wide variety of "waste material" and "varied media" in order to challenge basic social conventions and thereby facilitate new and "unpredictable relationships."[10] Since the moments of dislocation and disassociation involved human actions, there was an inherent social, and, indeed, political dimension to the relationships her work ultimately encouraged and facilitated. But what made these moments unique were the types of actions that Schneemann built upon.

In this process, Schneemann worked with what for lack of a better term we might call *found restrictive behaviors;* in particular, she worked with performative acts that policed gendered social mores, "repressive conventions," and "cultural taboos."[11] Disciplining gender rather than exemplifying the traditional roles they enforced, these performative acts were not examples of conformity to expected behavior but rather instances of behavior attempting to enforce expectation by regulating aberration. They were, in short, moments of *social panic* that were marked by attempts to maintain a threaten patriarchal social order and that, most importantly, Schneeman was only able to use after having first provoked them into play. As is so frequently the case with the provocations of the avant-garde, the provocations that served as a crucial prerequisite to Schneemann's performance at the Dialectics of Liberation Congress struck at the unwritten codes of propriety that quietly govern interaction in the public sphere.

Few critics have been more attuned to the nature of those provocations in Schneemann's work than the art historian Kristine Stiles who, in an immensely insightful characterization of Schneemann as an artist, has contextualized her work within the social dynamics of decorum or within what Stiles otherwise describes as "the regulatory conventions associated with social, gender, and class concepts of propriety, good taste, and good breeding that are judged according to how one comports oneself in congruity with [among other things] one's social standing."[12] Arguing that "the driving force in [all of] Schneemann's work" involves "breaches [of] decorum," Stiles suggests that unlike transgression, which may lead to "legal punishment and repudiation," breaches of decorum are "met with stony, embarrassed silence and followed by rejection" that is as "subtle and deadly" as it is invisible and severe and that emanates not so much from distant sites of power and authority as from "the social group to which one belongs or aspires."[13] We would be hard pressed to find a more concise characterization of the responses that Schneemann's work and, indeed, her very presence as an invited female participant provoked from the other key participants of the Dialectics of Liberation Congress, responses that were underscored, for example, by the sudden evaporation of the money, time, and designated space that Schneemann had originally been promised the for preparation of her performance.[14] Most disturbing of all, those responses suggest that, at least within the Dialectics of Liberation Congress, the social mechanisms regulating decorum and gendered proprieties ran much deeper than the discourse of liberation, and they constituted nothing short of a substratum of continuity uniting the radical and the reactionary.

If for no other reason, Schneemann's ability to provoke that substratum into play was important because in doing so she disrupted the operative stability of the binaries both of the radical and the reactionary, and, similarly, of the radical and the status quo. These binaries constituted absolutely pivotal antinomies in the notion of dialectics posited at the Congress, and Schneemann's presence at the Congress had a profoundly disruptive effect on them both. If a unity or synthesis of antinomies constitutes the working logic of dialectics, Schneemann's breaches of decorum spotlighted a deeply problematic and embarrassing unity that not only challenged the authority of Congress participants' selective construction of dialectics and liberation but that also ultimately destabilized their notions of the radical itself. Bringing this unity of the radical and the reactionary to the fore, Schneemann's breaches of decorum may have initially been met with stony silence, but the rejections that followed were hostile, and, if nothing else, those hostile rejections reflected an amazingly perceptive understanding both of the implications of Schneemann's work and of the stakes in not reigning it in. Similarly, those same breaches of decorum disrupted the notion of the status quo upon whose negation the Congress's ideas of liberation hinged. Some small sense of this disruptive effect was evident even at the dinner party where only a select and privileged few were invited, where Schneemann was in fact met with a "stony, embarrassed silence," and where, following Marcuse's notions of desublimated society, her work was implicitly dismissed as the type of art that entertains "without endangering" the status quo.[15]

Ironically enough, that very dismissal embodied its own affirmation of a powerful but unacknowledged status quo—one that Schneemann's breaches of decorum set into motion and with which her work was at odds. Indeed, the stony, silent dismissal of her and her work reaffirmed a patriarchal status quo that rigidly defined not only who could speak, but also when and under what circumstances. This disturbing reaffirmation was not unique to the dinner party, and its various manifestations did not go unnoticed even by those who were favorably disposed to the goals that Laing, Berke, Redler, and Cooper had set in convening the Congress in the first place. In fact, for many the answer to the question of who could speak and under what circumstances became the signal failure of the Congress as a collective project.

The Congress itself was billed as one of the decade's major events, and the organizers played up its importance in carefully orchestrated (albeit somewhat pretentious) news conferences[16] and in stories fed to sympathetic members of the press. Six months before the Congress convened, for example, Roger Barnard of *Peace News* wrote that the international collection of intellectuals and activists coming together for the Congress would initiate a necessary "long-term project of *subversive re-education.*"[17] The focus of this reeducation was broadcast in posters distributed across London, which announced that the Congress would "demystify human violence in all its forms, the social systems from which it emanates and . . . explore new forms of action."[18] The call to convene at Chalk Farm was thus a call for a general collective articulation of radical political alternatives to repression, to alienation, and to inhumanity at all levels of society—an articulation that the Congress organizers believed would only be possible with a requisite illumination of the hidden forms of authority and aggression that sustain Western industrial society. "The dialectics of liberation begin," they argued in the printed program to the Congress, "with the clarification of our present condition."[19]

Unfortunately, disentangling the present condition from its clarification proved to be one of the Congress's greatest challenges. If that present condition was, in fact, one characterized by enforced hierarchies of privilege and authority, then the Congress frequently did more to replicate than illuminate those hierarchies—and this was not only evident in dinner-party politics. Even the most sympathetic press accounts of the Congress proceedings returned time and again to the organizers's inability to break down basic structures of authority at the simplest levels. The same Roger Barnard who had played up the pending Congress in February, found himself in early August criticizing the "air of false rigidity and pretentiousness," which dominated the Congress itself and which, he bitterly noted, "is absolutely inimical to anything purporting to be an authentic educational project." He specifically criticized the Congress for the way its organizers "were apparently trying to 'structure' everything in advance, blocking genuine dialogue by means of a very effective tyranny of the microphone."[20] Similarly, Raymond Donovan in a piece commissioned for the *New Statesman* wrote: "At the best of times communication between the audiance [*sic*] and the platform was bad. No travelling microphone was available in order that the main speakers could be challenged on their own terms."[21] Clearly, the issue for these journalists was more than merely that of who controlled access to the microphone. But leave it to the press to sniff out a small anecdote that tells a larger story, and here the larger story of unapproachable authority appears to have been repeated in a wide variety of forms throughout the

Congress, not the least of which involved a concerted effort to thwart the critical dialogue that Carolee Schneemann proposed as an essential facet of the performance that she planned for the end of the Congress.

If those efforts at thwarting dialogue exposed a conventional notion of hierarchy and privilege functioning beneath the radical discourse of the Congress, Schneemann discovered the workings of that substratum almost immediately after her arrival. In fact, the first rumblings surfaced on the opening day of the Congress. Prior to that wine-sipping, passive-aggressive dinner party on the next evening, Joseph Berke began the opening day of the Congress by introducing the keynote speakers and guests, among whom he counted Schneemann since he was in fact the one who had invited her to perform at the Congress. This introduction involved some brief explanation of their work, and when, after having been introduced, Schneemann proceeded to explain that her planned performance would include a collage event that drew upon "dominant issues and elements of the congress," the other participants not only balked; they also mounted what in retrospect bears a striking similarity to an assertion of textual authority over performance, protesting what they presumed would be the performance's infringement on the integrity of their own discursive prerogatives. As Schneemann herself recounts, Paul Goodman, in particular, "sprang up from the audience" and objected to the event on the grounds: first, that it would be intrusive; and second, oddly enough, that the other invited guests "weren't consulted about inviting" this woman Schneemann in the first place. Goodman summed up his objection with the rhetorical question: "Why in the world would we want her to do this sort of thing?"[22] Why, indeed?

That this question came from Goodman who, in addition to being a practicing psychotherapist, was also a man of letters (a poet, playwright, and novelist) is telling, especially when one recognizes that Goodman's objection had less to do with whether Schneemann performed than it did with the substance and the implications of her performance. In subtle but significant terms, the contrast drawn by Goodman's question was more perceptive than it might first appear, for it astutely marked the competing notions of performance that came into play when Schneemann announced her plans for the piece that she had been commissioned to produce. Simply put, the mere announcement of her plans provoked a struggle between a notion of performance as a tolerated interlude from the otherwise serious work of the Congress and a notion of performance as a source of serious critical dialogue in which everything was on the table, including the Congress itself. On this point, our hindsight may be less than twenty-twenty. After thirty-some years of critical theory, during which time essays like Lacan's "The Presence of the Analyst"[23] have risen to such a prominence that considerations of our own subject position are now an accepted staple of critical discourse, we may find ourselves in a position that makes it difficult if not impossible for us to fully grasp how profoundly alarming Schneemann's proposal apparently was, even to progressive intellectuals like Goodman.

Whatever our current convictions about representation and its processes, asking why the Congress participants would want Schneemann to proceed with her plans was, in no uncertain terms, another way of calling attention to the fact that Schneemann's use of the participants's words in her performance would jeopardize their control as the authors of those words over the meanings that the words would thus produce. Granted, it is debatable whether they had much control over this to begin with. But the stakes here were far more significant than a petty squabble over authorial intent. Beneath Goodman's question, and the male prerogatives it reinforced, was a gesture attempting to maintain a traditional culture of humanism (and privilege) that in no small part relied on discursive order and stable representational authority. It is worth noting in this regard that Goodman's own keynote address was simply entitled "Objective Values" and referred to a humanistic notion that he not only embraced but that under the protective guise of objectivity was beyond reproach and, not surprisingly, was regulated by mechanisms of decorum. Arguing, for example, that the hippies were "harrassed, beat-up, and jailed by the police" because they are perceived to be "dirty, indecent, [and] shiftless," Goodman suggested that rather than challenging the system from without, young people would do better to become "professionals" and challenge the system from within.[24] The unfortunate lesson of this equation, however, was that it implicitly endorsed a culture whose seeming malleability from within was accessible only for the select and the few, and certainly not for upstart young women like Schneemann.

Schneemann's plan struck at the foundation of that culture. David Cooper, one of the other Congress organizers, admitted as much to Schneemann when, many years later, they met again in London and in the form of a belated apology he told her: "We didn't welcome a woman taking an equal space among ourselves, we distrusted a theatrical form, and we certainly didn't want a very young woman putting on a performance which incorporated our own words with a countering physicality."[25] Embedded in this apology, I would argue, are the last vestiges of the *linguistic panic* that rippled through the circle of Congress participants at the prospect that a "countering physicality" would challenge the referential authority of their words. Of what value are words if they do not connect with a corresponding physical reality? And how better to raise this very question than to give it dramatic form in an embodied space that clashed visibly with a recycled litany of phrases from the keynotes addresses. Indeed, the very real concern in this regard that participants like Paul Goodmann had was that Schneemann's proposed collage event would lend credence to sentiments like those that would ultimately later manifest themselves during the Congress when, for example, a young working-class member of the audience became disgruntled with the absence of concrete political action at the Congress, denounced the proceedings as just so much "chat, chat, chat, chat,"[26] and dramatically left the building accompanied by wild applause, loud cheers of support, and sincere but not particularly effective efforts by Herbert Marcuse to incorporate the young man's sentiments into the frame of his own comments.

Retrospectively magnanimous though Cooper's apology may have been, the apology was a telling concession at multiple levels, and here one cannot help but notice the profound irony of Cooper's acknowledgment that an antitheatrical bias—particularly a bias against experimental theater—had wide currency in a Congress that promised not only to demystify violence but to "explore new forms of action."[27] Cooper's apology, temporally separated though it may have been from the earlier events at the Chalk Farm, nonetheless betrayed the extent to which the governing assumptions of the Congress cast such explorations within decidedly cautious and conservative parameters. In its dealings with Schneemann, the Congress implicitly embraced theoretical speculation and frowned upon experimental action. It relied upon *logos* to discipline the unruly body and the body politic, and it presumed that the Word could plot the course that action would follow. In short, the Congress embraced an epistemology where performative acts are always subordinate to textual authority and where textual authority always already presumes unproblematic referential stability. Yet in doing what she proposed and transforming the "dominant issues and elements of the congress" into material subjected to an artist's critical scrutiny, Schneemann overturned the Congress's implied hierarchies of knowledge. Bucking the distrust of theatrical form to which Cooper referred, Schneemann subordinated the social scientific discourse of the Congress to the aesthetic discourses of her own performance. The radical, unreconciled juxtapositions of collage—nowhere better exemplified than in clash between the spoken word and a countering physicality—subsumed a method of dialectics that presupposed not only the objectivity of social scientific discourse but also its unproblematic representation of the objective world.

The actual collage event in which this epistemological reversal unfolded was grounded in a theatrical practice that Schneemann associated with the theories of Artaud and that owed no allegiance to literary theater. It was thus a small step for Schneemann, after two weeks of wrangling with Congress participants who attempted at numerous junctures to sabotage her work, to liberate herself from the discursive authority of the Congress and literally to walk across the "chat." At the high point of her performance of *Round House,* she, along with Michael Kustow and a few other performers, openly rummaged through papers strewn across the performance space in a mixture of detritus, pulling out textual fragments and reading them aloud to the audience who apparently had little difficulty in recognizing the fragments as pieces of the lectures and discussions that they had heard over the preceding two weeks.[28] Indeed, many of the statements were culled from some of the most contentious moments of the Congress when civil discourse had given way to shouting matches between different Congress participants and competing factions within the Congress. As other performers concentrated on an exercise that Schneemann called body sculpting, Schneemann and Kustow inundated the audience with the litany of questions and comments that they found among the waste on the floor. The content of these textual fragments ran the gamut from the abstract and theoretical to the argumentative and accusatorial. On the one hand, Schneemann and Kustow would read relatively serious questions that had been posed during the Congress, questions like: "Is it possible to develop a separate system in which we can live our lives completely outside of the existing system?" And yet as they dug through the papers on the floor, such serious questions inevitably would be answered by a series of rhetorical markers that not only signaled a breakdown of meaningful debate but that for many of those in the audience had become the most familiar refrain of the entire Congress, markers like: "Will you just let me finish? . . . I'm not finished . . . You're not listening . . . Can you hear me? . . . You're not listening."[29]

As if to offer a visual comment on nature of these latter statements, members of the chorus began slinging mud from the corners as the participants in the core group began a game of pursuit, some members running after others who attempted to avoid being caught. All the while, the large images of Schneemann's erotic film *Fuses* were projected across the participants's activities, and as the mudslinging and game of pursuit subsided, members of the core group crawled into the center of the performance space where they lay down and, submerged in the papers, looked up and watched the concluding intimate and erotic images of *Fuses.* What happened after *Fuses* ended is not entirely clear. The score for the event suggests that the central lighting was replaced by a series of slides, although the content of those slides is unspecified and forgotten. From the balcony, members of the chorus (or perhaps other assistants) began to throw foam onto the performance space, adding additional texture to the littered space where the fragments of the Congress lectures lay discarded and buried. Whatever transpired in this short interval, it quickly moved into a subsequent scene of near pandemonium.

As *Round House* ended, the audience took to the performance space, where they began to dance on and among the material strewn across the floor. The playful irreverence of this ritualized dancing across the dirtied texts of the Congress lectures is obvious enough that it may in fact obscure the genuine acts of defiance in the scenes that preceded the closing celebratory dance. Those acts of defiance were directly related to the numerous obstructions that Schneemann had encountered during the two weeks leading up to her performance. Repeatedly, she had had to contend with students of the other key participants to the Congress, who, apparently emboldened by their mentors's disdain for Schneemann, took it upon themselves to disrupt the workshops that Schneemann conducted in preparation for her performance. All in the name of keeping a group from coalescing as an independent body within the larger group of the Congress itself, these students stormed through her workshops, stole props, and banged on cans in order to keep the members of the workshop from concentrating on their work.[30]

Successfully carrying through with her planned performance despite these and other hostile acts was no small act of defiance. Schneemann thus proved that it was possible "to develop a separate system" in which to work outside of the system—and here the system subjected to scrutiny was the Congress as an organized body—a point that was further underscored by the fact that as the Congress polarized along a bitter racial divide, Schneemann's workshop emerged as the only site of cooperative diversity within the Congress. Reciting the question of whether "it [is] possible to develop a separate system in which we can live our lives completely outside of the existing system" was thus a rather blatant reminder of where the possibilities suggested by this question had in fact been realized within the Congress itself. It was also a reminder of how the Congress had worked against those possibilities.

More defiant still was Schneemann's decision to show her film *Fuses* as part of the visual texture of her performance. Indeed, no single decision would prove to be more controversial, and no decision would be more telling in the response that it elicited, for no decision was as effective in setting the inner political machinery of the Congress into play, and once that machinery was in motion the larger priorities and stakes of the Congress as a project were exposed and vulnerable. All this too hinged on a simple matter of decorum and decency. Its larger significance emerged in the disingenuousness with which the Congress organizers addressed it.

Legal Counsel, Precedent, and Priorities: *Fuses* and the Context of the Congress

When asked why she thought that R. D. Laing was so hostile toward her during the Congress, Schneemann responded that Laing was threatened by her presence, particularly as a woman who was not "one of his subjects" or who unlike "many of his students" was not "subject to him."[31] While this hostility was certainly carried over in the constant disruptions of Schneemann's workshops and in a general indifference regarding the sudden loss of time, money and space for the workshop itself, nowhere was that hostility more crystalized than in tense and disenchanting moments like the one during which Laing, Berke, and the Congress's legal counsel summoned Schneemann outside the conference building a few days before her performance event in order to inform her that if she went ahead with her plans to show her erotic film *Fuses* as part of the multimedia component of *Round House,* the Congress organizers would not extend to her the umbrella of legal protection that they had guaranteed to other Congress participants like Stokely Carmichael. As Schneemann recounts, "The lawyer said I *could* show the film, they did not want to prevent it . . . but they could not come to my defense, that I must be prepared to go to jail!"[32] It is hard to miss the disingenuousness of this manipulative support of Schneemann's plans on the part of the Congress organizers, that is, of their not wanting technically or publically to bear responsibility for obstructing her plans while at the same time privately abandoning Schneemann by refusing to extend to her the basic assurances that were supposed to facilitate individual expression and the free exchange of ideas within the Congress itself. If the organizers billed the Congress as a site of respite from the tyranny of mainstream social and political rationalizations of authority and violence, and if the Congress's purpose was to demystify the "socially approved lies"[33] that cast an ideological veil over the exercise of authority and violence both at home and abroad, then this private meeting between Schneemann and the organizers separated the illusion of respite from the intrusive realities of social authority, both with regard to its patriarchal underpinnings and its reinforcement of conventional social mores.

Although in her recollections about this conversation Schneemann presents a compelling case that such moments of manipulative support were indicative of the treatment that she constantly encountered as a woman participating in a Congress whose "conventions of intellectual address presume[d] a man's point of view,"[34] the immediate backdrop to this less-than-subtle bit of legal corralling exercised against her suggests that this "point of view" was but one aspect of a larger epistemology that provided cover for a system of rigid social hierarchies and dubious political priorities. In that epistemology, art was not only positioned as a feminized subordinate to the discourses of political philosophy and science but, in the most traditional militaristic conception of a vanguard, art was also conceived as that which, in times of crisis, could be safely abandoned or sacrificed ostensibly for the good of the whole but in actuality for the benefit of the privileged few. In fact, one of the great ironies of Schneemann's little tête-à-tête with the Congress organizers—so symbolically situated as it was just outside the sanctuary of the actual conference building—is that it exposed how vulnerable the Congress's call for a common front was to a fear of common liability. It exposed how easily the cry of comrade could be silenced with the threat of indictment as accomplice.

In the summer of 1967, these fears were not altogether irrational. A screening of the erotic film *Fuses* at the Congress, even if only to add an additional medium to Schneemann's multilayered "happening," flirted with charges of obscenity. Yet some sense of how disingenuous the legal counsel had been with Schneemann can be garnered from the fact that the threat of prosecution actually loomed less over Schneemann (an American) than it did over the Congress organizers themselves, who were either British citizens or residents of Britain. In one respect, then, when the Congress organizers dangled the prospect of jail in front of Schneemann, they were in effect bullying her with legal bluff, manipulating her with the threat of prosecution in order to protect themselves. Certainly, there is some room for speculation about whether, as practicing psychiatrists, the organizers of the Congress may have had more to fear from a conviction on charges of obscenity than Schneemann did as an artist. But beyond this immediate possible concern with their own careers, the organizers's move against Schneemann appears to have been motivated, in part at least, not by an abstract threat of prosecution but rather by a threat that, like growing storm clouds on the horizon, had become an increasingly ominous potential as the Congress progressed. Like all gathering storms, this one emerged from a combination of elements, and it was as much a consequence of what was transpiring within the Congress as it was of the fallout from the Destruction in Arts Symposium (DIAS) that some ten months prior to the Dialectics of Liberation Congress had convened (in September 1966) in London's Africa Centre and that, as Kristine Stiles has noted, was largely the prototype for the Dialectics of Liberation Congress itself.[35]

The fallout from DIAS proved to be a small disaster for the Dialectics of Liberation Congress in both practical and conceptual terms, and at the end of this section, I want to return to the conceptual dimension of the relation of DIAS to the Congress and consider the implications of the fact that a symposium of the experimental arts served as the prototype for a congress of the social sciences that was largely skeptical of the role that art by artists like Schneemann (and ultimately like those who contributed to DIAS) could have in forging meaningful alternatives to the repressiveness of Western society. But first, it is important to understand the more immediate, tangible, and practical ways that the shadow of DIAS hovered over the Dialectics of Liberation Congress. For that shadow arguably had a significant impact on the Congress's dealing with Schneemann and her plans to show *Fuses* during her performance.

The Destruction in Arts Symposium had attracted a wide array of exceptionally provocative and controversial artists and intellectuals, including members of the Dutch PROVOS, a number of Fluxus artists, and a prominent contingent from the Vienna Actionists. The French happenings artist Jean-Jacques Lebel participated in DIAS. George Maciunas was present. Yoko Ono performed *Cut Piece* there. Fluxus artist Al Hansen began collaborating with the Vienna Actionists at DIAS, and even the psychiatrist Joseph Berke (one of the organizers of the Dialectics of Liberation Congress) gave a paper at DIAS.[36] Many of the performances there were controversial, but none was so scandalous as that which was presented by the Viennese Actionist Hermann Nitsch, who on September 16 at London's St. Bride Institute attempted to stage a performance of the *5th Abreaction Play* of his Orgies Mysteries Theatre. This was a multimedia event that, among other things, facilitated a idiosyncratic screening of Nitsch's film *Penis Rinsings.* The performance included a segment in which the 8 mm film of a twenty-year-old man's penis (which had been covered with cow brains, blood, water, and egg yoke) was projected onto the bloody carcass of a lamb that had been crucified on a section of the wall covered with a white sheet.[37] This multimedia confluence of graphic, sexualized, and sacrilegious imagery proved to be a highly effective provocation. Ten policemen stormed the performance space, confiscated what they thought was the film, and, in a little performance all their own, subjected Nitsch to a search "in the toilet."[38]

As one might expect, the police action brought widespread attention to DIAS, increased critical acclaim for Nitsch, and ironically even paved the way for a reception of Nitsch's work in the United States. But indictments did follow, and, as is their want, the indictments had a chilling effect that rippled not only through London but even through American artistic communities. While Nitsch himself—it is important to note[39]—was never charged, Gustav Metzger and John Sharkey, who had organized DIAS but had not performed in Nitsch's Abreaction Play, were charged with "unlawfully causing to be shown and presented an indecent exhibition contrary to Common Law."[40] Word of these indictments had even reached Schneemann as she was in the planning stages of what would become the piece entitled *Round House.* Roughly a month before the Dialectics of Liberation Congress, she sent a letter to Joseph Berke (dated June 9, 1967) in which she outlined some of her ideas for the performance and in which she wrote:

> I'm taking a film job this week and will make a print of [the] Fuses film and also [the] Viet-Flakes film which I'll use in [the] London performance somehow. There are some bad rumors here about people named Metzger . . . [and] Fraser, charges against them by armored moral rearmament? Is it so? My film could be dangerous/ . . . . ? What do you think?[41]

By the time the Congress actually convened in the last two weeks of July, the rumors that Schneemann had heard about Metzger and Fraser had proven to be grounded in increasingly harsh political and legal realities.

In fact, at the exact same time that the Dialectics of Liberation Congress convened, the London papers were reporting the trials and convictions of the two people mentioned in Schneemann's letter.

In the year prior to the Congress, the fashionable gallery owner Robert Fraser (aka "Groovy Bob") had been arrested "for showing erotic drawings by Jim Dine."[42] Once again, it was not the artist Dine but the gallery owner Fraser who was arrested. Then in February 1967, Fraser had been photographed in a police van famously handcuffed to Mick Jagger after the two of them had been busted for drug possession in a raid on Keith Richards's home, and in the last week of June, as the final preparations for the Congress were being made, Fraser, Jagger, and Richards were subsequently tried and convicted on drug-related charges. Fraser was sentenced to a year in prison in a court proceeding that was widely criticized for being hasty, overzealous, and draconian.[43] While conjecture is hardly a precise science, one cannot help but suspect that the harshness of the sentence against Fraser was at least indirectly tied to a lingering distaste for those nasty drawings by Dine that he had hung in his gallery.

If Fraser had the good fortune of being convicted along with Jagger and Richards, whose notoriety as rock starts caused enough of a public outcry that the convictions were overturned later that August, Gustav Metzger and John Sharkey were not so lucky, and the prosecution of the case against them cast a long a shadow over the Dialectics of Liberation Congress since their case, which was draconian in its own right, not only went to trial during the Congress itself but ended after only three days. Metzger and Sharkey were convicted before the Congress concluded and, more important still, before Carolee Schneemann had presented her multimedia performance piece.[44] The legal wrangling around her plans to use *Fuses* in that performance unfolded against the backdrop of this conviction—a conviction, it is worth noting, that played to the classic distinction between cinema and theater. Indeed, much of the case against Metzger and Sharkey pivoted on the attempted confiscation of Hermann Nitsch's film *Penis Rinsings* and on "a series of photographs taken during Nitsch's event."[45] Apparently, the artifactuality of celluloid and film negatives provided evidence that was far more tangible than the notoriously elusive ephemerality of performance.

The conviction of Metzger and Sharkey was a sobering moment. One of the few published critical accounts of the trial notes: "The real threat of a maximum six-year prison term hung over their heads regardless of the fact that they had the artists indemnify them, prior to participation in DIAS, against responsibility for the destruction of material and/or the possibility of danger to life and property."[46] Ultimately, Metzger was only fined one hundred pounds and Sharkey, as his chief assistant, was "given a conditional discharge,"[47] But the warning emanating from the conviction itself was writ large and unmistakable, especially since Metzger, though not on the program, was a visible presence at the Dialectics of Liberation Congress, where, interestingly enough, footage of him siding with Carolee Schneemann in a group discussion on art and violence was taken by Peter Davis and later included in Davis's short documentary on the Congress.[48] Despite Metzger's own comments in Davis's film that he "very much agree[d] with Carolee in emphasizing the protectiveness of art toward the individual," the successful prosecution of Metzger must have been alarming for Laing, Berke, and the other Congress organizers, who had little faith that art could protect anyone and who, at one level, had legitimate cause to be concerned that a screening of *Fuses,* as Schneemann had suggested in her letter, could actually be dangerous. The potential parallels were certainly alarming enough. The general consensus is that the charge of obscenity against Metzger was a calculated strategy to sanction him for organizing DIAS in the first place.[49] Similarly, Laing, Berke and the other organizers of the Congress had genuine cause to fear that a public screening of Schneemann's film might give the judicial authorities a pretext to punish them for bringing Stokely Carmichael to London, where in a very short time he displayed an amazing ability to provoke a major political controversy that attracted the attention not only of the press but of the House of Commons and the ruling British Government.[50]

Armed with a charismatic and incendiary mastery of the political philosophies of Frantz Fanon and Che Guevara,[51] Carmichael's addresses to the Congress advocated a violent, revolutionary overthrow of white society that was so uncompromising in rhetoric and so militant in tone that he stunned the Congress participants, whom he openly taunted as naive and pretentious white liberals. If nothing else, Carmichael's short stint in London demonstrated his brilliance as a provocateur. His presence was not only polarizing within the Congress; it virtually eclipsed the Congress itself—especially since Carmichael was able to use his participation in the Congress skillfully, both as a platform for political agitation among the Congress participants and as a springboard for cultivating other talks and interviews with members of the press. The press turned out to be as polemically divided in their opinions about Carmichael's embrace of revolutionary violence as the Congress participants themselves, and in response to newspaper interviews with him, editorials appeared in the press demanding that the Government take action to remove this "dangerous man" from Britain.[52] There were daily reports in the newspapers on Carmichael's activities, and though in these reports the Congress became a mere footnote "incidently mentioned as a meeting where Carmichael made a speech,"[53] the Congress was nonetheless the immediate and direct cause of Carmichael's presence in England. Questions raised about Carmichael implicitly rebounded back to the Congress and its organizers, and those questions were being raised in the highest circles of Government. As Gajo Petrovi reported shortly after the Congress ended: "A question about Carmichael's activities was asked in the House of Commons . . . and after an inquiry had been set up the Home Secretary ruled not to allow Carmichael to re-enter Great Britain."[54] By the time that the home secretary issued this ruling, Carmichael was already safely in Cuba at another conference—in 1967, he was a speaker in high demand—but it is pretty obvious that those who conducted the inquiry into Carmichael's activities were very much aware of the Congress of prominent left-wing intellectuals that had financed Carmichael's trip to England and provided him lodging while he was there.

If the political storm generated by Carmichael proved to be more than Laing, Berke, Cooper, and Redler had bargained for when they invited him to participate in the Congress, so too did the conception of art that informed Schneemann's performance practices, particularly with regard to the risks she was willing to incur in order to facilitate new, and hence understandably controversial, relationships. Since that conception clashed with the assumptions held by many of the organizers and participants alike, it is worth pausing momentarily to consider what the pressure that the Congress organizers exerted against Schneemann tells us about their understanding of art and the role it has to play in the public sphere. In this respect, recognizing the move against Schneemann as a defensive maneuver against the political fallout from Carmichael's activities is an important first step in also recognizing the conventional humanistic notion of art that prevailed among the Congress organizers and among many Congress participants as well. In simplest terms, that conception rehearsed a traditional understanding of the relationship of art and politics, one that posited them as two separate spheres of activity; and, moreover, that in a rather Hegelian gesture relegated art to a position subordinate to the discourses of philosophy and the social sciences.[55] To assert, then, that the Congress organizers saw Schneemann's use of *Fuses* as a point of vulnerability in their defense against potential governmental retribution for sponsoring Carmichael is ultimately to argue that they conceptualized art as an expendable luxury in the calculated pursuit of what they posited in contrast as serious politic struggle.

Interestingly enough, the Congress organizers primarily located this struggle not so much in direct political action as in a privileged sphere of political discourse, which, as a variant of scientific discourse more generally, they presumed to be grounded in reason, to possess a largely unproblematic immediacy in representation and thus to have an access to genuine human experience that was unavailable either in the seeming irrationality or creative ambiguities of aesthetic expression. Witness, for example, the participation of Allen Ginsberg and Julian Beck in the Congress. Both were implicitly commissioned to speak, not as one might expect, through the respective discourses of the literary or performing arts but rather from within the general discursive parameters of the social sciences. They thus provided lectures that, while often addressing questions of art and politics, had no direct artistic pretensions. Although Ginsberg did read some poetry during the Congress and also chanted mantras[56] (for which he was roundly attacked by an Indian member of the audience who accused him of grotesque Western cultural appropriation), he was invited to the Congress less as a poet than as a prominent representative of the American counterculture, and his primary participation in the Congress was as a panel member during numerous sessions. There he presented a rather incoherent paper entitled "Consciousness and Practical Action," and he contributed to roundtable discussions, probably the most memorable of which was one that included David Cooper, R. D. Laing, and Stokely Carmichael and that devolved into petty personal attacks between panel members and the audience. Beck, who had been invited at the last minute to the Congress, figured much less prominently. Appearing without any other members of the Living Theatre, he merely presented a paper entitled "Money, Sex, Theatre,"[57] in which he described the communal structure of the Living Theatre.

Although Ginsberg vacillated, at times magically, between the roles of serious speaker and sardonic, chaotic presence during those last two weeks of July 1967, the willingness that he and Beck displayed in their papers to adapt to the discourse expected by the Congress tended to reinforced a second-class status for art—a status that, not surprisingly, was also given to women at the Congress as well, none of whom had any direct say in the actual organization of the Congress and none of whom, except "wives and girlfriends"[58] of course, were invited to stay at the separate accommodations that were arranged so that the core Congress participants could have what Berke described as "a sustained dialogue away from public intervention."[59] Neither were any women listed on the Congress program nor even among the principle Congress participants—and this despite the fact that the two women most directly affected by this slight, Carolee Schneemann and the poet Susan Sherman, had made major contributions to the Congress. Throughout the entire two weeks leading up to her performance, Schneemann participated in discussion groups (like the one that included Metzger) and conducted workshops in preparation for her performance at Congress's closing. Sherman had even picked up some of the administrative work of the Congress (due in part to her close editorial collaboration with Berke on other projects), for which she never received acknowledgment.[60] The short of all this is that within the gendered, disciplinary hierarchy of the Congress, art was relegated to a stereotypical feminine sphere where, at best, it could play a complementary but nonetheless always subordinate role to the presumably more serious and masculine discourses of science and reason. When it came to the work of Schneemann, art, in a very literal sense, was considered to be the maidservant to philosophy and politics.

Perhaps such a paradigm would partially align the underlying assumptions governing the Congress with the more orthodox Marxist notion that culture is only really possible after a radical reorganization of the body politic. But neither Laing, Berke, Cooper, nor Redler was a Marxist in any orthodox sense. Indeed, in the flyer accompanying their many letters of invitation to the Dialectics of Liberation Congress, they described their orientation as that which would "best be called phenomenological."[61] Whatever tenuous philosophical allegiances this group of antipsychiatrists attempted with their idiosyncratic embrace of this term, or, for that matter, of the term *dialectics,* they placed their political stock in *logos,* that is, in the primacy of the Word and reason. But even this allegiance was idiosyncratic and curried with a mixture of pretense and populism.

Above all, their philosophical and political allegiance to *logos* was manifested in a belief that, once removed from an academic setting, the discourses of philosophy, psychiatry, and sociology could circumvent what the organizers called "preconceptual schemata" and "rigid systems of knowledge" and then provide "a maximal clarification of our field of experience."[62] Strategically positioning themselves at odds with established institutions of learning and with what they characterized as "all manner of socially convenient academic convention,"[63] the Congress organizers implied that the failure of philosophy to deal effectively with human violence was the failure of the stewards of the Word rather than of the Word itself. However appealing this anti-institutional rhetorical may have had been in the summer of 1967, tapping astutely as it did into the increasing antagonism between the student movement and university administrations, it placed the Congress squarely within the traditions of philosophical idealism and fundamentally reaffirmed the high modernist assumption that language and signification, while perhaps moribund, could nonetheless be redeemed—in this particular instance, redeemed if snatched from the wasteland of established academia.

Initially, the calculated, timely, and fashionable appeal of this anti-institutional gesture,[64] with its implicit hailing of the Congress and its organizers as the countercultural stewards of a rejuvenated political philosophical tradition of dialectics and liberation, may well have been heady enough to obscure the populist demagoguery and subtle authoritarian proclivities thriving beneath the Congress's embrace of *logos*. Conceptually at least, this anti-institutional rhetoric allowed the Congress organizers to posit an alternative—albeit hypothetical—public space where social scientific discourse presumably could function as an unproblematic tool of representation capable of demystifying human experience without producing mystifications of its own. More recently, however, this fashionable gesture has led to a trenchant criticism of the Congress as a crass example of "radical chic."[65] Indeed, in definitive studies of the Destruction in Arts Symposium, Kristine Stiles has argued that the Dialectics of Liberation Congress not only amounted to a vitiated popularization of issues first addressed by the artists involved with DIAS but also neutralized the subversiveness of DIAS by using language to filter, discipline, and ultimately contain the radically unpredictable meanings, the slipping significations, and the irreverent play of artistic expression.[66] In short, the Congress disciplined the unruly subversive provocations of artistic expression with the authority of text and word—and this, ironically, in the same year that Derrida published the seminal critique of that authority.[67]

Stiles's criticism comes as part of a broad contrast that she draws in passing between DIAS and the Dialectics of Liberation Congress. As a general characterization of the Congress, her criticism is quite persuasive and indeed noteworthy if only because her very short discussion of the Congress is one of the very few existing theoretical critiques of it. But within the Congress itself there were differing and frequently contentious views on almost every subject addressed, and in this regard, questions about the role of art were no exception—especially when one remembers that a number of participants in the Destruction in Arts Symposium, like Metzger himself, were wandering around the Congress, and he was not alone. The Dutch PROVOS, for example, who were active both in DIAS and the Dialectics of Liberation Congress, fell into the spotlight first when John Gerasis dismissed them as a group that posed no threat to the status quo[68] and then again when Herbert Marcuse, in what was widely viewed as the most important address of the Congress, singled them out along with the Diggers as a source of legitimate creative rebellion.[69] In that same address, Marcuse argued that "creative imagination and play" were crucial aspects of social transformation, and he reminded everyone that "one of the oldest dreams of all radical theory and practice" was the creation of "an 'aesthetic' reality" and the construction of "society as a work of art."[70] Although Marcuse prefaced his comments with a telling apology for resorting to aesthetics,[71] he could hardly be accused, with comments that spoke of an "aesthetic reality" or "society as a work of art," of writing art off as a luxury. Yet despite his nod to the PROVOS and Diggers and to creative imagination, Marcuse's comments ultimately fell back to a conception of art held up not as a means to an end but as the end of politics: in other words, as its goal and as its dream. And if the end of politics is art, that is, the creation of an "aesthetic reality," a subtle but distinguishable border always separates the two.

Whatever conceptual space Marcuse's comments may have supplied for art, the Congress provided precious little room for the creative imagination or play that he embraced, and this more than anything else distinguished DIAS from the Dialectics of Liberation Congress. Whereas Metzger had structured the former around exhibitions and wildly unpredictable performance events that were supplemented by lectures and unexpected provocations, the Congress organizers, for all their antiacademic pretensions, adopted an academic conference format that ultimately proved to be more conducive to containment and discipline than to dialectics and dialogue. At the very least they significantly limited the parameters of the new forms of action that they promised to explore. If in its relation to DIAS, the Congress's cloak of radicalism was thus exposed as a cover for a proclivity for restriction, particularly with regard to artistic expression, nowhere was that proclivity more evident than in the Congress organizers's dealings with Schneemann and her proposed use of *Fuses* in her performance.

Even Joseph Berke, who was far more sympathetic to Schneemann's work than R. D. Laing and who attempted to forge a compromise that would provide some legal cover for everyone concerned, finally resorted to a format that tended to reaffirm the gentleman's club mentality that dominated the Congress as a whole. Suggesting that the "way around" the legal problem presented by Schneemann's film was to allow "entrance . . . by 'membership' "only,[72] Berke implicitly framed Schneemann's film as a backroom affair catering to those of prurient interests. In doing so, he conceded to the charge of indecency—even though the charge had not actually been made nor ever was—and he thus cast a shadow of pornography over a film that, in its disruptive use of the explicit body, was calibrated for a recuperation of female erotics from the dominance of the male gaze.[73] Not only was there a strong case to be made that the film was counterpornographic, but Schneemann had conceptualized its use within her performance as "a sorely needed reference to dismantling the structures of rationalized power"[74]—the very structures that ironically her rather indecorous plans to use the film had set into motion and that were exemplified in the actions of Laing and Berke.

Initially, the threat of potential legal vulnerability forced Schneemann to consider making adjustments in her performance score. The two existing scores from her performance (one from Schneemann's personal files and a later version, dated July 26, that is printed in *More Than Meat Joy*) list *Fuses* as part of the multimedia component, but the later version has the word "Slides" penciled in directly above the reference to the film, suggesting that consideration was given to eliminating *Fuses* from the performance altogether. In fact, the actual program that was handed out at the performance event contains a short disclaimer explaining that "Existing English 'obscenity' laws have made it impossible to use 'Fuses,' an erotic film which is central to the imagery of this work (while the film of Vietnam war atrocities, 'Viet-Flakes,' is not considered obscene)."[75] Despite this printed disclaimer, Schneemann actually showed both films, and it speaks to her courage, her playfulness, and even her lack of decorum that despite having announced in writing that she would not show *Fuses,* she decided—apparently in defiance of her own textual authority—to do so anyway. For in the final analysis, Schneemann decided that the idea of "ending up in a London prison . . . was a silly and unlikely issue."[76]

Whether this dismissal of potential prison time was the product of astute perceptiveness or reckless disregard for her own wellbeing, Schneemann's willingness to defy the Congress organizers and risk what they characterized as looming incarceration not only called the bluff on their legal gamesmanship; it also turned Laing's antiauthoritarian rhetoric on its head. For in his own keynote address, "The Obvious," Laing had first chastised "those who, no matter what they think they know or don't know . . . , will *just do what they are told,*" and he then praised those "who know they don't know" but "who will not necessarily do what they are told." Whether or not one agrees with Laing's exaggerated characterization of this latter group as "the last surviving *human beings* on the planet,"[77] Schneemann's plans outed Laing as one who belonged to another category still: to those who are inclined to tell others what to do. In this regard, Schneemann's defiant screening of *Fuses* ultimately may not have positioned her as one of "the last surviving *human beings* on the planet," but it certainly positioned her as one to be reckoned with at the Dialectics of Liberation Congress.

Conclusion: An Epic Farewell

Toward the very end of the one-page program that Schneeman handed out for her performance of *Round House,* she cited the writings of Simone de Beauvoir, Antonin Artaud, and Wilhelm Reich as sources of inspiration for her work, and while there are a variety of reasons for citing each of these writers, one might have expected to find Brecht's name there as well, and not merely because his name might have dispelled some of the distrust of theatrical forms that pervaded the Congress by reminding Schneemann's audience of the important role that the performing arts have had in political activism. But if Brecht's name did not appear on Schneemann's program, his work certainly haunted her performance, providing a powerful frame of reference both at the beginning and ending of *Round House.* Even for those who were only minimally familiar with Brecht's work, this haunting was difficult to mistake, particularly at the beginning of the piece when, once the audience was seated in a semicircle, the lights dimmed, bells began ringing, and members of Schneemann's chorus pulled a livery wagon onto the stage. Not only did this beginning recall the opening scene of *Mother Courage and Her Children* when, in one of the truly great opening moments of modern drama,

Courage and her sons pull her wagon onto the stage, but *Round House* like *Mother Courage* both began and ended with the image of that wagon and of its integral connection to the circular logic of war. Moreover, the haunting presence of Brecht's play suggested a stinging critique of the raucous, bitter acrimony that had marred the Congress proceedings, for despite her seeming efforts to the contrary, Mother Courage loses all her children while she haggles with others.[78] As if to provide a shorthand of the import of Brecht's play, the wagon in *Round House* arrives already full of bodies that, like the casualties of war being carried from the battlefield to their grave, are carted onto the stage and unloaded where moments later they come to life amid a multimedia construction of Beatles music, newsreels, slides, and the two films, *Fuses* and *Viet Flakes.* When the piece concluded some ninety minutes later, these same bodies—now wrapped in a cocoon of detritis [a poor (wo)man's makeshift shroud]—were piled together and then, as if headed for another grave site, they were loaded onto the wagon again and carted away.[79]

Three things make this imagery particularly important to the significance of *Round House,* not only in its relation to the Congress but also in its relation to the historiography of the American avant-garde. First and foremost, while traces of *Mother Courage* frame Scheemann's piece, *Round House* owes no allegiance to the literary text that haunts it. There is no subordination of performance to literature in *Round House,* and rather than aiming at a faithful representation, Schneemann's piece merely samples Brecht's text, taking broad interpretative liberties with it by combining the implicit allusions to *Mother Courage* with elements drawn from diverse sources (like the keynote addresses of the Congress, for example). In this regard, Schneemann's performance piece not only offered a countering physicality to the logocentric social scientific discourse of the Congress; it positioned performance in a comparable critical relation to the canon of modern literary drama as well.

To some extent, this critical relation coincided with currents that were already astir within the American experimental performance community, and in fact offering a radical reinterpretation that challenged the authority of the literary dramatic text was a staple of experimental theater in the 1960s. Yet the presence of such challenges to textual authority in the work of Schneemann, particularly within the context of the Dialectics of Liberation Congress, put the critique of patriarchal authority at the center of such endeavors, and this is where Schneemann's work marks a profound departure from and, indeed, finds itself surprisingly at odds with the tradition of dissembling and reinterpreting canonical texts that came to prominence in American experimental theater in the mid-twentieth century. While it is certainly possible to see this gesture as a variation on the widespread avant-garde practice that Erika Fischer-Lichte has called "*Sparagmos*" or "the tearing apart and incorporation of textual bodies in which we symbolize our cultural traditions,"[80] the link between patriarchal and textual authorities that *Round House* teased into play is arguably strong enough to push assessment of Schneemann's work beyond the category of "variation" and into that of "dissent." We can certainly label that dissent as a refusal to conform to "Stud Club Aesthetics," but to take it seriously arguably necessitates a fundamental questioning of the aesthetic categories that heretofore critics have used to write a history of avant-garde performance where opposition to the unholy alliance of *logos,* patriarchy, and literary culture never even makes an entrance, let alone finds its way to center stage in the history itself.

Perhaps some sense of the need for a rewriting of that history is what makes the subtle allusions to *Mother Courage* in *Round House* so compelling. Perhaps that same need is what makes the absence of Mother Courage herself in those allusions so noticeable. As is widely known, in the early productions of Brecht's play, when the character of Mother Courage moved from page to stage, the effect was unruly enough that Brecht went back and rewrote her into a more consistent conformity with the didactic purposes of his play. The challenge here is quite the opposite: it is to move from the unruly presence of Schneemann at the Dialectics of Liberation Congress into the unwriting of the narrative that the organizers attempted to construct and then to move into a rewriting of the histories with which she does not conform. The point is not to write a separate and isolated history of women experimental performance but rather to write a history in which the dialogue with others that the work of artists like Schneemann initiated is not always already cast in terms that preclude the equity that dialogue presupposes. In this respect, we can close with the image of that wagon at the beginning of Scheemann's piece.

Once the wagon was situated in the performance space, the core members waited for the chorus to shovel them out of the wagon and onto the floor where the dead weight of their bodies began to impress the mounds of paper, which included fragments from the keynote addresses to the Congress, giving it new shape and form. Similarly, Schneemann's work would press upon us to give new shape and form to the historiography of the avant-garde.

CHAPTER SIX

Forget Fame

Valerie Solanas, the Simplest Surrealist Act, and the (Re)Assertion of Avant-Garde Priorities

After the ambulance had rushed a near mortally wounded Andy Warhol from the Factory to a hospital on June 3, 1968, a small brown paper bag still remained on a table close to where he had been talking on the phone when Valerie Solanas shot him. An incongruous and foreign object, the bag contained three items: a pistol, Valerie Solanas's address book, and a woman's sanitary napkin. Solanas had placed the bag on the table as she was departing from the scene of chaos that her violent act created. In a small but not insignificant way, its discordant contents echoed a sense of incongruity that had been hovering about Solanas for some time. Though it was a hot summer day, Solanas had donned a turtleneck sweater and a trench coat reminiscent of Hollywood spy movies, and rather uncharacteristically she was also wearing makeup. Having already been thrown out of the Factory earlier that afternoon by Paul Morrissey (the coproducer of Warhol's films), Solanas waited for Warhol outside, and when he arrived, she accompanied him back into the Factory, where she shot him and Mario Amaya. She probably would have shot Warhol's manager, Fred Hughes, as well, had her gun not jammed. Hughes pleaded with Solanas to go, which she then did, leaving not only a near mortally wounded Warhol behind but also the paper bag which she had placed on the table.

Significantly, this act of terror was couched in the accouterments of a performance comparable to—but in effect far more militant than—the guerrilla theater tactics that in the sixties followed the student and social unrest into the streets and quickly became a mainstay of contemporary radical experimental theater. The makeup, the trench coat, and the mysterious bag—containing the address book that identified her, the second gun that carried phallic connotations, and the sanitary pad that transgressed decorum by calling attention to basic feminine experiences that were publically taboo—all served, as Laura Winkiel rightly asserts, as "props to stage the assassination" even though, I would add, the sheer, actual violence of Solanas's act served as a harsh reminder that the assassination was not merely staged.[1] But if these props underscored the performative nature of Solanas's act of violence, she was by no means positioning herself as an actress—at least not in any conventional sense of the term. Rather than referring the press to a script she was following when they inquired why she had shot Warhol, she referred them to the manifesto that codified her beliefs and her political agenda. After voluntarily surrendering herself to a traffic policeman a few hours after shooting Warhol, Solanas told reporters at the police station: "I have a lot of very involved reasons [for shooting Warhol]. Read my manifesto and it will tell you what I am."[2] More importantly, when the *New York Daily News* reported in the morning headlines that Solanas was an actress ("Actress Shoots Andy Warhol"), Solanas quickly demanded a correction, which she obtained. Warhol himself recalls that the evening edition of the same paper contained a front page picture of Solanas with "a copy of the day's earlier edition in her hand. The caption quoted her correcting, 'I'm a writer, not an actress.'"[3]

Though never really discussed, Solanas's corrective is actually quite telling. Asserting her identity as an author was a roundabout way of asserting her autonomy and independence from Warhol. In effect, her corrective was a kind of shorthand for saying that she was not one of Warhol's actresses and that she had a vested interest in resisting the maelstrom pull of his influence. When she voluntarily surrendered to a traffic officer shortly after shooting Warhol, she explained to him that she shot Warhol because he "had too much control of my life."[4] But if Solanas was not an actress, neither was she only an author. Somewhere between asserting her own author-*ity* and somewhere between the props and the pistol shots, Solanas constructed a mode of performance that absolutely defied the conventions of mainstream theater and that tore at the very conceptual fabric of the avant-garde. Indeed, such a explanation is one of the few ways to reconcile the deliberate theatricality of Solanas's violent act (i.e., the makeup, the trench coat, the props in the paper bag, etc.) with her rejection of the media's depiction of her as an actress and with her subsequent representation of herself as a writer and "a social propagandist."[5] For in rejecting the designation of actress while nonetheless consciously staging her attempted assassination of Warhol as a performance, Solanas not only asserted her independence from Warhol; she also aligned herself with the historical avant-garde's rejection of the traditional structures of bourgeois theater even as her militant hostility toward patriarchal society pushed the avant-garde in radically new directions. In this respect, the seemingly insignificant paper bag left on the table at Warhol's Factory has a major part to play not only in establishing Solanas's act as a calculated aesthetic performance but also as a performance that like the sanitary napkin among its contents transgressed decorum by calling attention to basic feminine experiences that were publically taboo and tacitly elided within avant-garde circles.[6]

It is hard to overstate how far afield such a conceptualization of Solanas's assault on Warhol is from the accepted interpretations of her actions, interpretations that by and large are based upon Warhol's own reduction of Solanas's act to a mere attempt to use him as a trampoline to fame. "Being famous isn't all that important," Warhol subsequently claimed in *The Philosophy of Andy Warhol.* "If I weren't famous, I wouldn't have been shot for being Andy Warhol."[7] At the time of the shooting, this clarification—subordinating Solanas as it did to Warhol and his agenda—was quickly picked up by the mainstream media, which was only too happy to depict Solanas as a product of Warhol himself, that is, as an expected outcome of what they considered to be the morally suspect world that Warhol encouraged.[8] While the fleeting sensationalism of that event and the moral drum roll against Warhol have come and gone, Warhol's account of Solanas's actions has endured even in projects implicitly aimed at finally giving Solanas her due.

One such project is Mary Harron's film *I Shot Andy Warhol,* which I will briefly address momentarily, but first I want to give a sketch of the movements through which my argument will be progressing as I propose an assessment of Solanas that understands her shooting of Warhol as the pivotal gesture in a radically subversive project, the implications of which demand a recalibration of the trajectory of the American avant-garde. To this end, the first section of my chapter counters Warhol's influential accusation that Solanas was fame-trolling. It conceptualizes Solanas's act of violence as a calculated, performative exhaustion of the antiart agenda of pop art culture. The second movement of my chapter situates this initial reconceptualization of Solanas's act within what I will be arguing is the implicit theoretical, feminist critique of the avant-garde that Solanas articulates in her polemical *SCUM Manifesto.* Returning to questions of vanguard performance in the third section of the chapter, I will explore how Solanas's manifesto has an important additional but unacknowledged function as a prop within a version of guerrilla theater that I argue Solanas had long practiced on the streets of Greenwich Village and that culminated in her shooting of Warhol. The concluding section of my chapter is a short meditation on the scaring of Warhol's body both as a metaphor for the rupture that Solanas's act caused in the history of the avant-garde and as a politicized cultural artifact.

Forgetting Fame: Solanas and the Narratives of the Avant-Garde

The appearance in 1996 of Mary Harron's film *I Shot Andy Warhol*[9] was one of those ambiguous moments that all too frequently accompany long histories of neglect. Evincing the almost incomprehensible power of the cinema, the film arguably did more to give Valerie Solanas's name a lasting place in the cultural imaginary than did her actual attempt to kill Warhol. In this respect, a subtle irony shadows the tagline printed on the poster advertising the film. That line claims, "You only get one shot at fame," despite the fact that the film has given Solanas a second and rhetorically more powerful shot at what the poster portrays as a one-time opportunity. As many will recognize, the line also plays upon Warhol's well-known promise that in the future everyone will enjoy fifteen minutes of fame.[10] Even though the film trumps this promise by actually giving Solanas 103 infinitely repeatable minutes in celluloid, the riff on Warhol is more than merely a witty slogan for marketing an independent film. The play on Warhol's promise, like the title of the film itself, frames Solanas in a position subordinate to Warhol and Warholian aesthetics. This act of subordination, which is wholly consistent with the media's portrayal of Solanas some thirty years ago, arguably culminates in the visual imagery of the poster itself, which is a modified reproduction of Warhol's 1964 silkscreen of Elvis Presley absurdly cast by Hollywood in the role of a gunfighter, pistol drawn and ready for action. In the advertisement for Herron's film, Elvis's head is missing and supplanted by an image of Lilli Taylor, the actor who plays Solanas in the film.

The ambiguities of Harron's film crystallize in this constructed image. Even though, at one level, beheading Elvis makes good on Solanas's call for a "Society for Cutting Up Men" (SCUM), the subsequent, constructed representation of Solanas as a pistol-toting cowboy necessitates cutting up or beheading Solanas (Taylor) as well and arguably makes as much fun of as it makes good on the radical program that Solanas proposes in her *SCUM Manifesto.*[11] More importantly, the constructed image of the poster, relying as it does on Warhol's silkscreen of Elvis, presents Solanas as a figure completely and literally subsumed not just within a Warholian frame but within the aesthetic contours of Warhol's own fascination with stardom. In this respect, the film makes a case for a reassessment of Solanas, which it simultaneously undermines because it privileges Warhol's own interpretation of Solanas's attempted murder as a perverse gesture at cashing in on his promise of fame. For all the attention that the film cultivates on Solanas's behalf, it thus uncritically perpetuates a narrative of fame-fishing that significantly underestimates what I will be arguing is Solanas's importance in the cultural history of American experimental performance.

Whatever the publicized motivations of Solana's act, somewhere seething beneath the glitzy media spectacle of taking a pot shot at perhaps the most popular icon of pop art culture a much more significant historical narrative transpired, one that has never really been told, perhaps because its telling positions a deadly act of violence within an unsettling liminoid sphere of cultural legitimacy that is potentially as seductive as it is dangerous. That narrative, as I will be arguing momentarily, only really emerges when the moments of terror that Solanas brought to Warhol's Factory are situated within the context of the radically changing landscape of American avant-garde practice in the late 1960s. The foundation of that narrative thus lies not in a depiction of Solanas's act of violence as a perverse shot at fame or publicity, but rather in the recognition of that act as a carefully orchestrated and radically disturbing aesthetic performance—so disturbing in fact that Robert Rauschenberg, upon hearing of the back-to-back shootings of Andy Warhol and Robert Kennedy, reportedly "fell to the floor, sobbing," asking in dismay whether guns were the new medium of artistic and political expression.[12] For Solanas, guns had clearly become both, and, in this respect, her conscious and deliberate theatricalization of a radical and violent enactment of her own anarcho-libertarian political agenda—complimented as it was by her use of the manifesto as a literary form—situated her within a long-standing anarchist tradition of avant-garde practice.[13] In fact, the uniting of radical art and radical politics was, by the 1960s, such a familiar trope of the avant-grade that the greatest irony in accusing Solanas of wounding Warhol in order to take a shot at fame is the way that such accusations have consistently denied Solanas the attention she deserves as the orchestrator and agent of perhaps the most deeply provocative and profoundly subversive moment of American avant-garde performance in the 1960s.

At one level, acknowledging that denial is the first step forward toward correcting the neglect. But the larger issue in that corrective pivots on a recognition that Solanas's act of violence is as antagonistic toward the prevailing standards and histories of the avant-garde as it is hostile toward the patriarchal bourgeois mores of American society as a whole. Indeed, the two are linked in their reinforcement of a notion of patriarchal privilege that Solanas sought at every turn to disrupt—as is subtly indicated by the seemingly indecorous contents of her strategically placed brown paper bag. Consequently, any recognition of Solanas's significance within the history of the American avant-garde simultaneously introduces an acerbic, hostile, and irreconcilable element into that history, an element that is consciously defiant and deliberately incorrigible and that seeks neither an acknowledgment according to established aesthetic standards nor a place within the accepted narratives of American avant-garde history. On the contrary, Solanas's act implicitly aims at subverting the underlying assumptions and standards upon which that history depends. Parallel to the attitude that SCUM maintains in its relation with the body politic, Solanas's assault on Warhol sought, as a transgressive performative act, "to destroy the system, not to attain certain rights within it."[14] Solanas's significance as a figure within the avant-garde is thus inseparable from her overtly hostile outlaw status within its culture. It is from this position, which Solanas herself describes as necessarily "criminal,"[15] that she fashions a conception of performance that, in its combination of revolutionary anticapitalist and antipatriarchal sentiment, not only mapped out a radically new course for the traditional political priorities of the avant-garde but also initiated a militant critique of the underlying assumptions of the American avant-garde itself.

Warhol's role in that critique is not merely that of an unfortunate victim. Solanas punctuated her vision with bullets that were calibrated with political and artistic ambiguity. In a world where anything could be art—a world Warhol helped to create[16]—Solanas's gun menacingly fired the unanswerable questions: is this art, is this revolutionary politics, "is this the new medium"? The significance of that moment hinges on the recognition that, though intimately related to her manifesto, Solanas's act of violence was the real testing ground for the cutting edge of American avant-garde performance. Some sense of the underlying dynamics of that cutting edge can be garnered from the model that Stephen Foster proposes for conceptualizing what he terms "event-based arts." Foster maintains that the function of event-based arts is to challenge dominant artistic traditions by "largely abandoning historically sanctioned aesthetics" and by consciously embracing as art activities that by prevailing standards would be judged to be "nonart."[17] There is perhaps no better description of the provocation wrought by Solanas's assault on Warhol even though the sanctioned aesthetics that Solanas abandoned in shooting Warhol were arguably a product of the very antiart traditions that Foster addresses in his article. Nevertheless, Solanas's act owed much of its significance to the fact that, in trying to kill Warhol, she exposed the unspoken criteria functioning beneath the then prevalent notion that art no longer had definitive criteria. At a time when the distinction between art and nonart was largely considered to be no longer viable, she thereby proved that the distinction between art and nonart was very much alive in the celebrated antiart agenda of pop art culture. As an event, indeed as a performance, the shooting of Warhol thus placed Solanas directly within the radical antiart traditions of the avant-garde even as her act profoundly tested those traditions.

It is in the testing of those traditions that Solanas's position in relation to Warhol's own vanguard aesthetic takes shape. Although Warhol was cleverly manipulating critical categories already associated with the historical avant-garde's critique of high culture, Solanas was actively engaged at a much more fundamental level in a radical evolution of that same critique, and though she shared the historical avant-garde's emphatic contempt for the very idea of being absorbed into capitalism, such sentiments only scratch the surface of the irreconcilable aesthetic agendas finally separating her activities from those of Warhol. A glimpse at the antagonism separating those two agendas is evident in the far-reaching scope of Solanas's attempt to revitalize and reenvision what critics like Peter Bürger have described as the historical avant-garde's critique of the institution of art. In Solanas's revisions, however, the focus shifts to the patriarchal underpinnings of the concept of the artist—not so much as producer but as someone who presumably possesses "superior feelings, perceptions, insights and judgements" and who is presumably a man.[18]

What is striking about Solanas's critique of the "artist" is the absence in it of terms normally associated with artistic production, terms like "talent," "technique" or "skill." This is not to say that Solanas was subtly reinstating a bourgeois notion of the artist. Her amusing characterization of artists as "conceited, kooky, funky females grooving on each other and on everything else in the universe" is a far cry from the bourgeois artist who was the object of the historical avant-garde's scorn, and her aestheticized act of violence was as much an attack on the institutional category of the artist as producer as it was an assault on Warhol and all he stood for culturally and politically.[19] Indeed, by choosing to focus her critique on the presumed superior sensibilites of "great artists" rather than directly parodying the artist as producer, Solanas pushed the aesthetics of the historical avant-garde beyond assumptions that the pop cultural avant-garde had accepted without question and that even today largely serve as the foundation for Warhol's reputation as an artist.

Both in her manifesto and in the breach of "sensibility" manifested in her act of violence, Solanas recalibrated the avant-garde's critique of the artist as producer, generating a blistering militant feminist critique of the artist as genius in its stead. In fact, the critique was long overdue. For all the avant-garde's radical questioning of the artist as producer, it continued to embrace a notion of genius that had its origins in eighteenth-century aesthetics. That notion has direct historical connections with the unequal social construction of gender and class (and of race as well), and one of Solanas's fundamental artistic accomplishments was to question not only the role of the artist as producer but to do so in such a manner that she was simultaneously able to expose the bourgeois, patriarchal notions of genius lurking in the shadows of the avant-garde itself.

The Margins of the Manifesto: SCUM and the Critique of the Avant-Garde

On a theoretical level, this immanent critique of the antiart traditions of the avant-garde and of their ties to a long history of patriarchal privilege was already present in the manifesto to which Solanas referred reporters when they inquired about her motivations for shooting Warhol. But much of that critique has been lost in the balancing act that feminist historians have attempted in their accounts of Solanas's significance to feminist theory more generally. Rather than viewing Solanas's manifesto and her act of violence as separate and equal components of a larger, radically antipatriarchal avant-garde sensibility, feminist historians have tended to interpret Solanas's statement to reporters that they should read her manifesto[20] as a indication that Solanas was acting under the guidance of its dictates and that her act of violence was an understandable albeit misguided reading of the vitriolic implications of her own text. Following this interpretation, Solanas becomes a symptom of real social problems that real women face but not a part of the real solutions finally and seriously endorsed. In simplest terms, however, the limits of this interpretation are to be found in its unexamined subordination of Solanas's actions to the text of her manifesto. Although Solanas's *SCUM Manifesto* certainly contains passages that advocate a "selective and discriminate" use of violent destruction and that speak of "SCUM . . . coolly, furtively stalk[ing] its prey and quietly . . . [moving] in for the kill,"[21] there is no clear indication in Solanas's ambiguous statement to reporters that the contents of the manifesto would explain the specifics of her actions, at least not in the sense of providing a script for them.

While I absolutely agree with the moral imperative against attempted murder that underlies much of how feminist historians have recuperated Solanas, I think that much of her cultural historical significance is lost in the numerous attempts that critics have made to recuperate Solanas by implicitly accusing her of a bad performance of a text that they otherwise would be at pains to embrace. Leah Hackleman notes, for example, that in the history of radical feminist thought Solanas has been "valorized for her revolutionary courage" but "dismissed for her lunacy."[22] Similarly, Melissa Deem suggests that Solanas, like Lorena Bobbitt thirty years later, had justifiable anger that unfortunately regressed from "dissent" and "disharmony" into "violence, and madness."[23] Deem's recuperation is to subtly push Solanas into the margins. It is not a matter of coincidence that Deem's article bears the title "From Bobbitt to SCUM" rather than "From Bobbitt to Solanas." As the title of her article suggests, Deem erases Solanas and Solanas's assault on Warhol, rhetorically sweeping both beneath a discussion that characterizes the *SCUM Manifesto* as a feminist variation of Deleuze and Guattari's conception of a "minor literature."[24] A similar shift from Solanas to the manifesto also dominates Marcie Frank's "Popping Off Warhol." She specifically advocates a separation of Solanas's shooting of Warhol from discussion of the *SCUM Manifesto.* "An amazing piece of writing," Frank notes, "*The SCUM Manifesto* deserves attention less as an explanation for why Solanas shot Warhol than as an angry, urgent cry for the reevaluation of gender identity."[25]

Although all of these readings have their own merits, they tend not only to pull the curtain on Solanas's most transgressive and anarchistic proclivities, but also to reinscribe her into the kind of classic privileging of text over performance that the performative avant-garde repeatedly challenged. In this respect, readings like those posited by Hackleman, Deem, and Frank have one major oversight in common: they do not consider the implications of Solanas's choice of genre. They do not consider how that choice allies her with a performative vanguard. As a medium of expression, the manifesto has a long history as an apparatus of the avant-garde, and, as Martin Puchner has noted, "Both performative intervention and theatrical posing are . . . at work in all manifestos."[26] As an apparatus, the manifesto—and here I am specifically referring to the *SCUM Manifesto*—is an extension, but not the source, of performative acts, even a violent act like the shooting of Warhol. It is but one element in the complex performative dynamic that encompassed Valerie Solanas as a cultural figure. For this reason, the performative traditions of the avant-garde offer what is perhaps the best paradigm for understanding the subtle relationship between Solanas's manifesto and the theatricalization of her shooting of Warhol. These traditions grew out of a concerted interest in exploring performance as an art form in its own right, and they ultimately spearheaded a liberation of performance from its traditionally subservient role to the literary dramatic text. In that the avant-garde historically has defined performance in a very broad sense, its traditions accommodate and make sense of Solanas's theatricalization of her shooting of Warhol, and they offer a valuable alternative to a reception of Solanas's activities that privileges her manifesto at the expense of her militant act of violence

Exploring the compelling force of that alternative begins, I would argue, with a fundamental realignment of the respective cultural values that critics have given to Solanas's manifesto and to her act of violence. It begins with a leveling of the significance attributed to each. For the avant-garde dimensions in Solanas's activities are located in the dynamic between the text she produced (i.e., the manifesto) and the performance she enacted (i.e., the shooting of Warhol), a dynamic that arguably corresponds to the theatrical avant-garde's reconceptualization of text and performance as a radical juxtaposition of two equally weighted, autonomous art forms. In this respect, Solanas's admonishment to read her manifesto because it will tell you what she is has less to do with providing an explanation of why she shot Warhol than it does with identifying her cultural status. What her comments in fact suggest is that the manifesto will establish her identity (i.e., "it will tell you what I am") and thus serves as a credential.

The referral to the manifesto, especially when one considers its hyperbolic rhetoric, positions Solanas among the likes of avant-gardists Filippo Marinetti, Tristan Tzara, and André Breton. The irony of this positioning has not been lost on critics like Martin Puchner, who has recently noted the peculiarity of Solanas's embrace of the manifesto as a form:

> The widespread misogyny of futurism has led many . . . to argue that the manifesto itself was a masculine genre. This claim is certainly true of futurism, which makes it all the more surprising that later feminists, such as Valerie Solanas, felt free to adopt this genre for their own purpose.[27]

But it is not so much that Solanas "felt free to adopt this genre" for her own purpose; it is rather that she owed so little allegiance to the genre that she felt free to turn it on its head. Indeed, the force of her rhetoric, which in its militant—at times absurdly gargantuan—embrace of a "misandrous tradition," goes toe-to-toe against a long history of misogyny that the historical avant-garde uncritically absorbed from the very bourgeois, Western culture whose values it ostensibly opposed.[28] The *SCUM Manifesto* thus usurps the mantle of the avant-garde by skillfully inverting and thereby exposing its historically unacknowledged, gendered tropes.

Engendering a Titular Critique, or Castrating the Cutting Edge

This strategy is nowhere more immediately evident than in what is probably the most famous but oddly the least discussed aspect of Solanas's work: the acronym included in the title of her *SCUM Manifesto.* At its more literal level, *SCUM* alludes to the derisively low social status that, according to Solanas, women have in patriarchal society, and in this regard her title represents one of the first instances of an individual or a group publically embracing and appropriating an offensive characterization for a political agenda running directly counter to its derogatory implications. SCUM thereby subverts an accepted linguistic order as a titular point of departure for a group of women actively and radically engaged in subverting the social order that represses them.[29] Conjoined as the acronym is with the proclamation of "resolute oppositionality" and of participation in a "struggle against oppressive forces" that, according to Janet Lyon, is implicit anytime someone chooses to identify his or her work as a manifesto, the composite title of the *SCUM Manifesto* signals a critical trajectory of overlapping voices from the margins.[30]

While initially it may be helpful to conceptualize this trajectory as emanating from a position comparable to the notion of "double marginality" that Susan Suleiman has used to characterize French experimental writings by women, there is, in Solanas's work, a fundamental and uncompromisingly irreconcilable antagonism between the cultural margins occupied by the avant-garde and the cultural margins occupied by women.[31] Speaking from the latter indicts the former. This antagonism—once again, so subtly but insistently suggested by the indecorous contents of Solanas's strategically placed paper bag—is in many respects paradigmatic of a cultivated radical dissonance that reverberates not only through the title of Solanas's manifesto and through its content, but also through the critical position that Solanas ultimately assumes in relation to Warholian aesthetics. Indeed, that antagonistic dissonance becomes the crux of a radically subversive and startlingly fresh avant-garde aesthetic. From the perspective of avant-garde historiography, the aesthetic echoes the dynamic, decentered tensions of collage. For it recoils in critical dissonance as a disharmonious and disruptively nonassimilable element within the dominant system of avant-garde aesthetics of its time.

This same antagonistic dissonance seethes beneath the surface of the manifesto's title, always threatening destructive retribution for the indignities suffered by women who are treated as the social dregs both within the ranks of the avant-garde and within society at large. *SCUM* is, after all is said and done, an acronym for "Society for Cutting Up Men." Thus at the same time that the title subverts and appropriates a derogatory characterization of women, SCUM's acronymic function implicitly threatens a graphically violent response to the violence that historically has been perpetuated against women. In this respect, the *SCUM Manifesto* is typical of what Janet Lyon has noted is the historical connection with violence that the manifesto as a genre has: "Linked with the form's passion for truth-telling is its staging of fervid, even violent rage. David Graham Burnett has offered the thesis that the 'manifesto' derives etymologically from a Latin composite of *manus* and *fectus,* or "hostile hand" . . . and this translation acknowledges the nascent fury embodied in the form."[32] The only real difference here centers on the gendered inversion of the projected object or recipient of that fury.

While rhetorically the notion of "cutting up men" may strike directly at male anxieties about dismemberment, there is a more subtle allusion in Solanas's acronymic title. It recalls perhaps the most innovative aesthetic strategy of subversion historically employed by the avant-garde, namely the subversive cutting up, recontextualization, and radical juxtapositions that are the basic techniques of collage itself. Inasmuch as this allusion identifies the cutting up of men with a tradition of experimental art, the manifesto, in its implicit embrace of collage aesthetics, rhetorically positions itself as a hostile usurper and unassimilable agent, commandeering an avant-garde aesthetic strategy that it employs to disrupt the avant-garde itself.[33] The manifesto, once again, thus positions itself not as a petition for recognition within the existing traditions of the avant-garde but rather as a countervailing point of critical tension in a radical juxtaposition of irreconcilable, mutually exclusive aesthetic agendas.

Pop's Money Problems: Of Anticapitalism and the Critique of Patriarchy

Moving from the title into a closer consideration of the manifesto's content, one quickly discovers how crucial within Solanas's work the collage strategy of radical juxtaposition is to her retooling of the basic tropes of avant-garde expression. The most important example of this strategy is Solanas's juxtaposition and equation of capitalism and patriarchy—an equation that a decade later Hélène Cixous would repeat in her own manifesto "The Laugh of the Medusa." It is worth noting that Cixous considered the equation to be so fundamentally subversive that in her manifesto she describes its effects as "volcanic," "subversive" and capable of "shatter[ing] the framework of institutions, . . . [of] blow[ing] up the law . . . [and of] break[ing] up the 'truth' with laughter."[34] Although Cixous was probably unaware of Solanas's manifesto at the time, her essay echoes Solanas's own equation of capitalism with patriarchal society when, for example, she argues that the repression of women has its own dialectical role in the enlightenment of woman, enabling them "to see more closely the inanity of 'propriety,' the reductive stinginess of the masculine-conjugal subjective economy, which she doubly resists."[35] Peppered with statements paralleling the anticapitalist sentiments that have long been a mainstay of the revolutionary avant-garde, Solanas's own manifesto combines these same statements with assertions that fundamentally link a genuine revolutionary anticapitalism with nothing short of the complete destruction of patriarchal privilege. To eliminate either one necessitates the elimination of the other. The "total elimination of the money-work system" will liberate women, Solanas argues, because it will finally strip men of "the only power they have over psychologically-independent females."[36]

Two precedents set the context for the critical significance of Solanas's equation of capitalism and patriarchy. Both come from within the established ranks of the avant-garde. The first can be traced back a half a century to Berlin Dada and to the work of Raoul Hausmann, and the second comes directly from Warhol himself. Just as Solanas's subtle embrace of collage aesthetics usurps an avant-garde strategy that it employs to disrupt the avant-garde itself, so too does the link that she establishes between capitalism and patriarchy echo sentiments that Hausmann promoted in avant-garde circles in Berlin and that Solanas some fifty years later turned against the avant-garde aesthetics of pop art culture. Not only did Hausmann's writings for the journal *Die Erde* express a fervent anticapitalism that was grounded in anarchist and communist logic, but his essay "Weltrevolution" from 1919, like Solanas's later manifesto, specifically linked that anticapitalist sentiment to "the creation of a feminine society." Indeed, the essay argued that "the restructuring of bourgeois society into communism" absolutely necessitated "opposition to the masculine model of a patriarchal family."[37] While this strategy of equating capitalism and patriarchy has very obvious concerns with the structures and organization of society at large, in the hands of Solanas it assumed a pointed if somewhat coded critique of the direction that the American avant-garde had taken under the influence of Warhol.

Warhol had his beginnings in commercial art, and as has often been noted, he never really left those beginnings behind. Sally Banes, for example, after observing that in the early sixties "commercial art was considered by some [to be] the first truly democratic, widely accessible American art," emphasizes that "Andy Warhol, above all, asserted the commercial connection as something to exploit, not as something to apologize for."[38] The irony of this assertion, as Banes implicitly suggests later on, is that for all its supposedly democratic potential, the "commercial connection" embraced by Warhol often led pop artists like Warhol himself "to adopt uncritically—even at times salute—the dominant culture's representations of women both as a consumer and as a sexual object to be consumed."[39] That this uncritical embrace of sexist commercialism had patriarchal underpinnings, especially within the avant-garde activities of figures like Warhol, was acknowledged, however inadvertently, by Warhol himself when he cited "the paternal signifiers lurking in both 'pop' and 'dada'" and when he then stated that "dada must have something to do with Pop—it's so funny, the names are really synonyms."[40]

The Simplest Surrealist Act

Even though in common parlance the names "pop" and "dada" both affectionately refer to the father, Berlin Dada had set a political precedent that was very much at odds with Warhol's embrace of commercialism and, more importantly, that Solanas later appropriated in a full-scale critique of the avant-garde. Certainly, Dada had its own patriarchal baggage, and perhaps this is why in Solanas's manifesto there is no clear embrace of her Dada predecessors, but even this moment of ambivalence is but one example in a whole series of critical inversions that cleverly position Solanas firmly within the antitraditions of the avant-garde. As Lora Rempel has noted, the avant-garde has always had an ambivalent relation to its predecessors: "The act of symbolically killing one's aesthetic parents has been, historically and historiographically, an important initiation rite for entrance into the ranks of the artistic avant-garde—an expected impudence."[41] While Solanas's manifesto may implicitly have taken a critical snipe at Dada, her gunshot at pop explicitly took "the symbolic killing of one's aesthetic parents" to a shockingly new and unexpected level of impudence.

This double-edged strategy of forging a critique of the avant-garde by subversively appropriating its tropes is perhaps the most consistent pattern in Solanas's activities. While her militant anticapitalism positions her antithetically to the commercialism of pop avant-garde figures like Warhol and thereby aligns her with a revolutionary agenda frequently associated with the historical avant-garde, her antipatriarchal convictions strike at the foundations of the historical avant-garde itself, forwarding its evolution by means of an immanent critique. That immanent critique is embedded both in her manifesto and in her act of violence. On the one hand, the anticapitalistic sentiments of the manifesto are accompanied by an embrace of crucial dimensions from Marinetti's 1909 "Founding Manifesto of Futurism" like "the love of danger, the habit of energy and fearlessness," and "the destructive gesture of freedom-lovers"; on the other hand, Solanas's unabashed contempt for men radically inverts the futurists' openly expressed "*scorn for woman.*"[42] Furthermore, in shooting Andy Warhol Solanas subversively pushed the hyperbolic militant rhetoric of the avant-garde manifesto to its logical conclusion. The shot was an unparalleled act in the history of the avant-garde, one that cut not just through the rhetorical posturing of the futurists but also through André Breton's surrealist bravado. Indeed, the shot finally called the bluff on Breton's assertion that "the simplest Surrealist act consists of dashing down into the street, pistol in hand, and firing blindly, as fast as you can pull the trigger, into the crowd."[43]

In 1968, that crowd happened to be the fashionable one at Warhol's Factory, and in ripping through the crowd with an array of bullets, Solanas not only lived up to the rhetorical call of her manifesto to cut up men, but she unleashed a violent aesthetic process that turned Warhol's body into a kind of permanent collage.[44] In this respect, Solanas's manifesto has to be seen as providing a context for a profoundly subversive interpretation of the historical avant-garde's long-standing fascination with collage, a fascination that dominated Hanna Höch's work in Weimar and that on a more general level served as a crucial venue for the feminist undercurrents of the historical avant-garde. Not only do Höch's photomontages coincide with the avant-garde's general strategy of using montage to radically question the role of the artist as producer, but one might also go so far as to argue that Solanas's "work" on Warhol literalized what is arguably Höch's most famous piece: *Cut with a Kitchen Knife through the Last Weimar Beer Belly Culture Epoch.* Although functioning on a more militant level of graphic expression, Solanas's assault on Warhol at the very least shared Höch's strong identification with "the political empowerment of women, who she [Höch] envisioned, would soon 'cut' through the male 'beer-belly' culture of early Weimar Germany."[45]

However grotesque, the physically disfiguring effect that her attack had on Warhol was thus without question the quintessential act of appropriating and then turning the tropes of the avant-garde against itself—both with regard to the radical juxtapositions of collage aesthetics and with regard to the hyperbolic rhetoric of the avant-garde manifesto. In the process of that violently subversive act of critical inversion, Solanas's own manifesto occupies an ambiguous status. First of all, it lays the theoretical foundation for the critique of the avant-garde that was implicit in Solanas's assault on Warhol. But at the same time, it served—like the brown paper bag later would—as a prop in a series of performances leading up to and ultimately defining the shooting itself as an avant-garde performance. Indeed, as a performance, Solanas's violent encounter with Warhol was arguably as much an enacted critique of Warholian aesthetics and their reaffirmation of patriarchal culture as it was a crystallization of the confrontational performative tactics that Solanas had already employed in selling her manifesto.

Print as Props: The Presence and Absence of Text in Solanas's Performative Practices

To a great extent, the theoretical complexities of Solanas's act of violence have less to do with the actual content of the *SCUM Manifesto* than they do with the role that the manifesto played as a physical, material object in Solanas's activities prior to the shooting, activities that clearly constitute their own brand of experimental street theater. Indeed, the avant-garde dimensions of Solanas's act of violence are, in this regard, not only closely associated with the *SCUM Manifesto* as a physical text but also with the drama *Up Your Ass,* which Solanas penned in the years directly prior to her shooting of Warhol. Oddly enough, the significance of these two texts has to do with the ominous presence of the former and the troubling disappearance of the latter. But in both respects, each of the two pieces facilitated an important critical variation on the radical reconceptualization of performance that accompanied the historical avant-garde's rejection of the classic privileging of text over performance in mainstream bourgeois theater.

With regard to the manifesto, that reconceptualization pivots largely on the expansive redefinition of performance that accompanied the avant-garde's antagonistic disavowal of literary masterpieces and of the high-brow culture that valued them. While the makeshift quality of Solanas's self-published *SCUM Manifesto* (1967), mimeographed copies of which she sold on the street at two dollars a copy for men and one dollar a copy for women, certainly coincides with the avant-garde's traditional hostility toward the established institutions of official literary culture, the political agitation built into Solanas's street-level distribution of the manifesto functioned as a guerrilla theatrical performance that took direct aim at the patriarchal underpinnings of a literary culture that she described as having been "created by men" and endorsed by male critics.[46] But the more important issue here is the manner in which the assumptions governing Solanas's provocative street theater tactics for distributing her manifesto extended the avant-garde's broad redefinition of performance to include the structural foundations of bourgeois culture as well. With regard to questions of gender, those tactics were based upon the assumption that literary culture was by no means unique as a creation by men. Solanas argues throughout her manifesto that the dominant notions of gender were largely such a creation as well, and the guerrilla theater tactics she employed in distributing her manifesto were arguably calculated to shock passers-by into an awareness of their own performance of gender. Just as the makeshift quality of Solanas's manifesto chafed against the male-dominated institutions of official literary culture, her direct street-level confrontations (openly penalizing men an extra dollar because of their sex) agitated not only against male economic privilege but more generally against the unacknowledged quotidian performance of socially constructed gender roles that perpetuated a patriarchal culture that was tacitly endorsed by the avant-garde as well.

Generally speaking, Solanas was a marginal figure in the mid-1960s milieu of Greenwich Village. Yet her provocative guerrilla theater tactics, accentuated as they were by the wildly polemical rhetoric of the *SCUM Manifesto,* were incendiary enough to give Solanas some local notoriety. This notoriety landed her an interview with the *Village Voice*—even though the interview did not become newsworthy until after she shot Warhol.[47] More importantly, her provocative behavior also caught the attention of Ultra Violet, who was one of Warhol's actresses and who, by reading excerpts to Warhol from Solanas's manifesto, unknowingly set in motion a chain of events that nearly cost him his life. In this respect, the manifesto served the additional function of introducing Solanas to Warhol's circle, where she was emboldened to directly approach him about producing *Up Your Ass,* a satirical play she had written in 1966–67. Though Warhol accepted the manuscript, he apparently was never really interested in producing the play, and the manuscript was lost, not to be found for another for another thirty years.[48] Critics have questioned the literary merits of this play, which, much in the vein of Alfred Jarry's *Ubu Roi,* is rather adolescent and contrived. Based on a plot about a woman who "is a man-hating hustler and panhandler" and who, somewhat more successful than Solanas, actually ends up killing a man, the play is perhaps better understood as a provocation than as a work of dramatic literature.[49] Indeed, assessing its "literary merits" would seem to fly in the face of Solanas's own arguments that the criteria for assessing literature always already have as their first objective the reaffirmation of standards derived from work produced by male artists and male critics.[50] An actual assessment of the merits of *Up Your Ass,* if one is to follow Solanas's argument to its logical conclusion, would thus first of all necessitate a complete feminist deconstruction of "the entire system" of literary history.[51]

Until that fundamental restructuring of literary history occurs, the real significance of Solanas's drama has to be located with the radical unscripted performance occasioned by the drama's disappearance. For if any one event technically prompted the shooting of Andy Warhol, then it was the misplacing of Solanas's manuscript among the boxes of lighting equipment and film paraphernalia in Warhol's Factory. Solanas tried desperately to recover the play until it became obvious that it had been carelessly misplaced and could not be found. Making matters worse, Warhol apparently assumed that offering Solanas the opportunity to perform in one of his films would compensate for the script he had misplaced. The offer subtly replaced the lost text with another, supplanting Solanas as author and casting her in a subordinate role to Warhol's own text and agenda. To some extent, this subordination was a consequence of Solanas's persistent demands that Warhol return the manuscript that he had lost, but the gesture was replete, at least symbolically, with the very attitudes and privileges that Solanas had positioned herself against in her work. As Victor Bockris recalls, when Warhol "told her that he had lost . . . [the manuscript], Solanas started calling regularly, asking for money. Finally, he [Warhol] said she could come over and earn twenty-five dollars by being in one of his movies."[52] Financially, Solanas was in no position to decline, and thus she made cameo appearances in Warhol's *I, a Man* (1967) and *Bikeboy* (1967). Whether deliberate or not, the films symbolically subordinated Solanas beneath an assertion of masculinity. Solanas revolted against this subordination both with and after the shooting.

Ironically, these combined acts of careless disregard and gendered insensitivity harbored an amazing, culturally symbolic cache—and not merely because the loss of a play about a woman shooting a man led to the aestheticized event of Solanas actually shooting Warhol. In its relation to the shooting of Warhol, the misplacing of Solanas's drama counts as one of those truly peculiar moments of history that serendipitously offers an allegorical parallel to the cultural struggle for which it provides a context. For just as foundational gestures of avant-garde performance can be found in a liberating casual disregard of dramatic texts (as was done, for example, with the Performance Group's adaptation of *The Bacchae* in *Dionysus in '69* [1968]), so too did the careless handling of *Up Your Ass* promote a violent improvisational vanguard performance related to but so fundamentally distinct from the dramatic text to which it was tied that it demands an assessment on its own terms, an assessment that literally pivots on a distinction between acting and performance. Such was, in a nutshell, the history of the rise of avant-garde performance as an art form in its own right, and such was also the pretext that fashioned the aesthetic context of Solanas's assault on the ruling figure of pop art culture.

This distinction between acting and performance is more than a serendipitous consequence of the loss of Solanas's drama. The confrontational guerrilla theater tactics that she employed not only in the distribution of her manifesto but also in the attack on Warhol erased the artificial boundaries that bourgeois theater erected to separate actors and audience. Certainly Solanas was not the first to erase these boundaries, but it is worth noting, in passing, that this gesture crucially distinguishes the shooting of Warhol from what Kathy O'Dell characterizes as "arguably the best-known example of performance art—Chris Burden's 1971 performance *Shoot*."[53] Performed three years after the shooting of Warhol, Burden's *Shoot* shocked its audience, which watched in dismay when Burden allowed a marksman to shoot him in the arm from a distance of ten feet. Ironically, this performance piece, which critics have praised for exposing the voyeuristic fascinations of the audience, reinstated as its point of departure the very notion of the audience (as distinct for the performer) that it set out to challenge and that Solanas's direct engagement radically rejected altogether. Whereas Burden's later piece implicitly and retrospectively asked the audience why it did not intervene, Solanas assumed the responsibility for intervention herself and thus simultaneously acted to bring about a radical change of theatrical practice and a revolutionary shift in social politics and to create a common forum for both.

Warhol's Body, Legacy, and the Seams of Avant-Garde History

When Solanas emerged from the elevator at Warhol's Factory, pulled a pistol, and started firing at Warhol, she did more than cut up his body with bullets. Her violence reasserted radical politics as a central priority of avant-garde practice, and while it is true that experimental performance groups like the Living Theatre also sought to unite art and politics in their performances, Solanas's act was unique in its deeply disturbing ability to push the paradigms of experimental avant-garde performance beyond their limits while simultaneously critically indicting the very position into which avant-garde culture would and did inevitably recoil in abhorrence to her action. Given the violence of Solanas's own act, it may at first be difficult to perceive that the tenor of this indictment involved a brazen gesture of appropriation that, by means of a laconic inversion, pulled the veil on the violent and barbarous proclivities buried in the very bourgeois attitudes that were offended by her action—attitudes that historically have assumed a posture of cultural and moral rectitude even as they tacitly condone countless direct and indirect acts of violence against women, minorities, and the economically disadvantaged. In this respect, the shooting of Warhol pivoted on what implicitly amounts to a deadly serious interpretation of Walter Benjamin's assertion that "there is no document of culture which is not at the same time a document of barbarism."[54] As a document of culture, Solanas's act differs from other cultural documents primarily in its candor about its own barbarity and in its use of that barbarity to expose the barbarity seething beneath the surface of the avant-garde culture that was appalled by her action. Solanas's was an ugly act exposing an ugly history, and what the shooting of Warhol left in its wake was an aporia in avant-garde history, that is, a moment when the historical narrative was, like Warhol's body itself, no longer seamless and when, in a conceptual fashion reminiscent of collage aesthetics, the incongruous juxtaposition of irreconcilable trajectories in the avant-garde were exposed.

The scarring of Warhol's belly, both by Solanas's bullets and by the surgical hands that pieced him back together, quickly became the focus of intense cultural and artistic fascination, serving in many respects as a counterbalance to the artistic fetishization of the female body in contemporary works by artists like Yves Klein and Piero Manzoni.[55] Solanas's "work" thus became the source of a second wave of other works, beginning with Richard Avedon's two famous photographic portraits of Warhol in late 1968. The first was of Warhol facing the camera, leather jacket pulled back and T-shirt pulled up as if to expose his scars to doubting Thomas. The second photograph was of the torso itself, defamilarized by the cutting and stitching that were necessary to save Warhol's life.[56] These photos were followed by Alice Neel's 1970 portrait of Warhol in which she, more than any other artist, seemed to understand the radical, antipatriarchal sentiments that Solanas had carved into pop culture. Neel painted a feminized Warhol sitting half naked on an unfinished sofa, his scars prominently displayed at the center of the portrait.

As examples of the absorption of Warhol's refigured body into the iconography of American culture, the work of Avedon and Neel (especially Neel's depiction of Warhol as an old, scarred woman with sagging breasts), are symptomatic of the more general, radically violent, and collage-like recontextualization that Solanas enacted on Warhol as a cultural figure. Solanas's act ultimately removed Warhol from his earlier celebratory and politically disengaged embrace of popular culture and relocated him into a politically polarized context.[57] Inasmuch as the transformation of Warhol into a political figure was the work of Solanas herself, that relocation represents perhaps the single most important counterbalance to the cultural narratives that, in their accounts of Solanas's assault on Warhol, would pull her into the Warholian center and view her through the lens of Warhol's pop cultural aesthetic.

At a conceptual level, the relocation of Warhol into a politically charged context amounted to a reorientation of avant-garde priorities that has largely gone unaddressed either in historical accounts of Solanas, of Warhol, or of the avant-garde more generally. More than mere oversight, Solanas's exclusion from the accepted histories that plot the evolution of the avant-garde arguably underscores how unruly, radically subversive, and disruptive a figure Solanas is, especially to the history of the American avant-garde. Recognizing Solanas's assault on Warhol as the most radical of performative gestures is simultaneously to recognize that the shooting of Warhol necessitates a new historiography of the avant-garde. What I have attempted here is the beginning of a historiography aimed not so much at including Solanas as it is at accounting for her subversive incompatibility with the history of the avant-garde as it has been written.

Although it is tempting to characterize the polarizing aesthetics accompanying Solanas's attack on Warhol as an example of the volatility of neo-avant-garde rivalries, that is, as one neo-avant-garde aesthetic aggressively competing with another, or even to describe Solanas's activities as a good example in the realms of performance of what Hal Foster describes in the graphic arts as first- and second-wave neo-avant-garde aesthetics,[58] to do so basically reduces the terms *historical avant-garde* and *neo-avant-garde* to mere linear temporal signifiers—something akin to "pre-" and "post-" war experimental art. As problematic as the terms *historical avant-garde* and *neo-avant-garde* may ultimately prove to be on a more general scale, with regard to Solanas and Warhol they are indicative of distinct if not mutually exclusive conceptualizations of aesthetics, politics, and history. To casually place Solanas within the temporal designations of the neo-avant-garde is to endorse a conception of history and aesthetics that Solanas's act of violence radically subverts. Indeed, much of the significance of her act lies precisely in the forceful way her violence, as an aesthetically extreme form of avant-garde performance, simultaneously revolts against exclusion from avant-garde history even as the transgressiveness of that violence consciously asserts a kind of fundamental disruptive incompatibility with the history from which it has been excluded.

That incompatibility was multiplied on numerous fronts and was perhaps most immediately exemplified in Solanas's unsuccessful attempt to reorient her arraignment before the Manhattan Criminal Court into a discussion not of whether she was legally culpable for shooting Warhol but rather whether her actions were morally justified. Asked whether she had a lawyer, Solanas demanded the right to defend herself, and when she told Judge David Getzoff, "This is going to stay in my own competent hands. I was right in what I did! I have nothing to regret!" Getzoff "struck her comments from the court record" and committed her to Bellevue for psychiatric observation. Solanas ultimately spent a year in Ward Island Hospital before finally receiving a three-year sentence for "reckless assault with intent to harm." There is some debate about whether Solanas was in and out of mental hospitals over the next twenty years, but she never abandoned the sense that her actions were justified. Indeed, in a 1977 interview with the *Village Voice,* Solanas, speaking about her unsuccessful attempt to kill Warhol, emphatically maintained that she adhered to "an absolute moral standard," that the shooting was "a moral act," and that she considered "it immoral that . . . she missed." Shortly after the interview, she disappeared until the late eighties, when Ultra Violet located her in San Francisco. Roughly six months later Solanas died of emphysema and pneumonia in the spring of 1988. She was fifty-two at the time of her death.[59]

Conclusion

Collage and Community

My earlier reading of *The SCUM Manifesto* emphasized the implicit allusions to collage in the acronym for Solanas's "Society for Cutting Up Men." Not only do those allusions locate the practice of collage in a dissembling of men, but they also touch upon the substance of the acronym itself since the title *SCUM* is a construct, pieced together from fragments of words that have been cut apart in acts of what might literally be called linguistic violence. Whether this violence against words foreshadows the actual violent acts suggested in the title is uncertain because it is never entirely clear whether readers should take the title as an admonishment for violent revolution or as a piece of vitriolic hyperbole. Indeed, Solanas's manifesto is marked by such an intense level of exaggeration that it is arguably more plausible to read Solanas's admonishment to cut up men not as an endorsement of butchery but as a shorthand metaphor for sowing seeds of division, that is, for dividing and conquering the oppressive community of men and the society that this oppressiveness sustains. At one level, then, the acronym *SCUM* enacts this strategy by cutting up the word *society* and subordinating its fragment (the *S*) to the title of Solanas's manifesto—a title in which Solanas's acronymic construct ultimately refers to a very different type of society altogether.

Looking beyond a patriarchal society, the "Society for Cutting Up Men" references a politically and aesthetically imagined community. Indeed, Solanas's *Manifesto* falls well within "the protest writing in the sixties" that, as Martin Puchner has noted, often emanated from "small groups consisting of only a handful of members or," as was the case with Solanas, "even of a single member."[1] Puchner notes furthermore that "Solanas was isolated but not alone," and he situates her within the milieu of the wide range of political activists in Greenwich Village in the late 1960s.[2] Yet the observation that Solanas "was isolated but not alone" might be better used to characterize her position within the larger context of feminist art and activism in the 1960s and 1970s, especially since this latter characterization tends to highlight the disparity between her status as a lone vanguard provocateur and the concerted efforts of other feminist artists who consciously structured the politics of their art within a community of similarly minded feminist activists. At the most immediate level, of course, such structuring was a shrewd recognition of basic political realities: namely, that collective resistance offers the only hope for real changes in the public sphere. But at the same time, the blurring of political realities and radical aesthetic agendas within the structure of feminist artistic communities and collectives suggests that they had experimental if not avant-garde proclivities.

This convergence of the political and aesthetic is so central to how scholars have conceptualized feminist theater that its significance touches not only upon the position that Solanas occupies within the history of avant-garde performance but also upon much of the work to which this book has been devoted. If this book actually has the pretense of laying the foundation for a feminist historiography of avant-garde performance, it is therefore difficult to close without at least some reflection on the notions of collaboration and collectivity that have played a pivotal role in the feminist rethinking of theater. Indeed, many feminist theater historians would argue that it would be remiss not to do so. In her book *Feminist Theaters in the U.S.A.*, for example, Charlotte Canning argues with specific regard to collaboration and collectivity: "It is probably impossible to talk about feminist theater, or indeed any alternative theater of the 1960s and after, without discussing the collective."[3] Noteworthy in Canning's assertion is a positioning of the collective as a nexus between feminist and alternative theaters. Though somewhat of a passing reference, Canning's assertion is thus an implicit argument about a connection between feminist theater and the avant-garde, an argument that, as was true of the aesthetics of the most prominent alterative group theaters in the United States in the 1960s, positions collectivity and collaboration in opposition to the coded bourgeois individualism that not only has sustained traditional, Western notions of the artist but has sustained patriarchal society as well.

According to the particulars of Canning's argument, the shared interest in collaborative creation that links feminist and avant-garde theaters came from within some of the most prominent American experimental group theaters in the 1960s, where individual members often espoused both vanguard and feminist convictions. Among those theaters, probably the most famous cited by Canning are the Open Theatre and the San Francisco Mime Troupe, both of which went through significant transitions (within or beyond the initial collective) that led members away from a dominant and charismatic male leader toward more democratic structures of collective creation and ultimately toward newly forged feminist theaters. But the embrace of collaborative creation was not uniquely an expression of a feminist sensibility. Indeed, the "intense commitment to collaboration" that characterized so many of the group theaters in the 1960s and 1970s was nowhere better exemplified than "in the work of the Open Theatre."[4] As Canning notes, with regard to the history of feminist theaters in the United States, Joseph Chaikin's leadership of the Open Theatre in its collaborative creative endeavors provided a contradictory inspiration. On the one hand, it provided models and experience for "many of the women who later founded feminist theaters on the East Coast" while at the same time forcing these same women "to acknowledge that the labor of the women [in the group] was devalued because the political commitment of the ensemble did not extend to a critique of the discriminatory actions of the ensemble itself."[5]

At one level, this contradictory inspiration underscores the obvious: that neither collaborative creation nor collectivity have any inherent relation to feminist theater as such. But if neither collaborative creation nor collectivity has any inherent relation to feminist theater, neither do they have any inherent relation to the avant-garde—particularly in a sense that would lead one to argue that the avant-garde is the "origin" or "source" of strategies that subsequently became a crucial aspect of feminist theater. Indeed, when it comes to notions like collaborative creation, originary myths are never very helpful. The more important questions, I would suggest, are forward-looking, that is, questions like what were the goals in feminist adaptations of collaborative creation, what were the goals in vanguard adaptations, and what do these goals have in common? Canning's study, for example, documents how women artists were able to adapt both collaboration and collectivity into pivotal artistic gestures of feminist empowerment: "Feminist theaters saw their tasks very clearly," she argues; "in order to work toward an end of the oppression of women they had to create organizations that would empower women both in the process of creation and in the process of performance."[6] Given the ties that some of those feminist theaters had to American avant-garde groups like the Open Theatre and the San Francisco Mime Troupe, it is worth pausing to consider the function of collective creation within the larger aesthetics of the avant-garde. To do so, I want to suggest, will ultimately lead back to the link not only between the aesthetics of collage and feminist performance but also between collaboration, collage, and conceptions of a feminist avant-garde.

Stepping back from Canning's study, even if only momentarily, provides an important opportunity for understanding not only some of the different trajectories in the American avant-garde but also for identifying the significance that those different trajectories have for a feminist historiography of avant-garde performance more generally. Indeed, there are important parallels to be drawn here between the link that Canning establishes between feminist and avant-garde theaters in their shared interest in collaborative creation and the link that I have sought to establish throughout this book between feminist and avant-garde experimental artists in their interest in collage events (particularly in the work of artists like Solanas, Schneemann, Ono, Stein, and von Freitag-Loringhoven). Those parallels can be identified when one considers that collective creation and collage technique have both participated in the vanguard critique of art as an institution and of the artist as an icon of Western bourgeois individualism as well.

A consistent trend among group theaters in the 1960s and 1970s was the use of collaborative creation as a strategy for challenging the primacy of this iconic image of the Western artist. For all the scholarly debate about the antitextuality of the theatrical avant-garde, about its cry of "no more masterpieces," and its rejection of the "bourgeois obsession with the printed word,"[7] the vanguard's privileging of performance over text was as much a critique of the institution of the author/artist as it was of literature itself. It was this critique of the author/artist and its radical questioning of established structures of cultural, social, and ultimately political authority that overlapped with the critique of patriarchy that theater practitioners like Joan Holden (SFMT) and Roberta Sklar (Open Theatre) followed in their movement toward a feminist theater. Yet, while collaborative creation was an important strategy for the critique of the institutionalized, privileged status of the Western artist, this critique was forged on multiple fronts. Indeed, collage technique and its use of found objects provided a variation of this same critique.

The most famous example in this latter respect is, of course, Duchamp's

Fountain, the inverted urinal that he submitted for exhibition to the Armory Show after having signed it with the name "R. Mutt." At the time of its submission, *Fountain* provoked a scandal because, like the later notion of collaborative creation, it radically challenged established notions regarding individual creation. Speaking specifically of Duchamp's *Fountain,* Peter Bürger argues this same point in *Theory of the Avant-Garde:*

> In its most extreme manifestations, the avant-garde's reply to this [privileging of the individual artist] is not the collective as the subject of production but the radical negation of the category of individual creation. When Duchamp signs mass-produced objects (a urinal, a bottle drier) and sends them to art exhibits, he negates the category of individual production. . . . The signature, whose very purpose it is to mark what is individual in the work, that it owes its existence to this particular artist, is inscribed on an arbitrarily chosen mass product, because all claims to individual creativity are to be mocked.[8]

Bürger's disregard of "the collective" in his analysis ought not go unnoted since it tends to reinforce a problematic lack of interest in theater and performance throughout his book. But there are more important issues at stake in his specific analysis of Duchamp that illuminate parallels between the feminist adaptation of collective creation in theater and what I have been arguing is the feminist adaption of collage aesthetics within the spaces of avant-garde performance.

If, on the one hand, found objects or readymades negate individual creation, as Bürger argues, and thereby highlight how the avant-garde's critique of the individual artist took a variety of forms beyond the strategies of collective creation, Bürger's articulation of this argument is also noteworthy for its implicit celebration not of Duchamp's "individual creativity" but of the "genius" of his avant-garde gestures. It is such celebrations of genius, as Rebecca Schneider has noted, that "feminist art historians . . . have deconstructed" as that which perpetuates "a modernist masculinist myth,"[9] that is, a conceptual model that reinforces patriarchal assumptions. That critique, I would suggest, locates Duchamp's interest in readymades in a position similar to that of Chaikin's interest in collective creation: both, if I might echo Charlotte Canning's comments on Chaikin, have served as a source of "contradictory inspiration" to feminist practitioners. Canning has argued, with regard to the case of Chaikin, that "contradictory inspiration" led practitioners like Roberta

Sklar to adapt collective creation to a feminist agenda. (Feminist theorist like Elin Diamond and Janelle Reinelt have followed a similar path in their adaptation of Brechtian theory.) Similarly, the artists that I have discussed in this book embraced collage aesthetics in ways that not only challenged the mystified category of the artist as producer and the artist as genius but did so primarily because they worked within the frame of pointed critiques of patriarchal society.

Nowhere was this critique better exemplified than in Schneemann's *Round House.* While drawing upon what I earlier described as *found behaviors,* the piece *Round House* challenged the structures of authorship and patriarchal authority that framed the Dialectics of Liberation Congress itself—a frame within which Schneemann's status as a participant, as a viable intellectual, and as a "genuine artist" had all been questioned. One can and should express legitimate outrage at the injustice and sexism that was at the source of this questioning. Yet the consequence of this sexism was to put Schneemann in a position where her use of collage technique challenged the notions of intellectual and artistic production and of authority and liberation that Congress organizers took for granted. Indeed, Schneemann's work was instrumental in exposing the extent to which these notions were consistent with the mainstream sociopolitical values that the Congress ostensibly opposed. This included a subversion of her own status as artist and of the traditional claims to originality and greatness that cultural critics have rightly associated with bourgeois and patriarchal traditions. Literally wading among the scattered textual fragments of the Congress's papers and keynote addresses, Schneemann and those whom she had recruited into her performance offered a profound critique not only of the Congress itself but of the very notion of intellectual and artistic authorship as well.

Part of that critique began in the workshop that, at that awkward inaugural dinner party in 1967 on London's West Eisham Street, Schneemann announced she would be conducting during the Congress—a workshop that ultimately functioned as a kind of alternative community within the dysfunctional community of the Congress itself. What was unique about the sense of community within the workshop Schneemann conducted is that it was largely a spontaneous construct and that its initial conceptualization was as a contribution rather than as the alternative it became to what the Congress offered. The sense of community among the women and men who participated first in the workshop and then in the actual performance of *Round House* coalesced within the tense climate of hostility that the leading figures of the Congress directed against Schneemann's work and that, rather than driving her out of the Congress's events, rallied the workshop participants into a provisional collective of their own. Within this context, Schneemann discovered community in a form and space she did not expect or plan. In a very literal sense, community was a "chance operation." Amid the various interacting elements of the college event that she orchestrated, Schneemann thus arguably stumbled into what I would like to characterize as *found community.*

Rhetorically, this characterization draws conceptual parallels with the notions of found objects and found behaviors that throughout this book I have associated with collage aesthetics. But the single most important point in this parallel is to provide a segue into a much broader assertion about the basic structures of collaborations, collectives, and communities. Ultimately, my intent in drawing a parallel between found objects, found behaviors, and found community is to underscore the sense in which every community—structured, found, or imagined—is its own collage. When Canning asserts the impossibility of talking "about feminist theater, or indeed any alternative theater of the 1960s and after, without discussing the collective," she implicitly refers to a political, aesthetic dynamic that bears unmistakable affinities to that of collage. Both are assemblages that derive meaning in the dynamic interaction of their constituent elements, and when conceptualized as part of a feminist aesthetic, both envision a radical reorientation in the body politic, the model for which they partially enact within the parameters of their own constructions.

The object here, however, is not the construction of an argument that gradually subordinates the notion of the collective beneath the rubric of collage. Far more is to be gained in the recognition that the collective in its relation to alternative or experimental feminist theaters and collage in its relation to solo feminist experimental performances are both important variations of a larger notion of avant-garde performance. I stated at the outset of this book that my primary goal in examining the women artists who have been central to this study was to push the scholarly discourse on the avant-garde in a direction where the feminist currents of their work reorients the notion of an avant-garde as such. One test of the success of that goal will be whether gender as a critical category becomes a mainstay in subsequent studies of avant-garde performance. Perhaps a better test will be whether feminist historians of theater and performance become more inclined to identify the vanguard in the feminist theaters and in the feminist artists they consider.

Notes

CHAPTER ONE

1. Jill Dolan, "Fathom Language: Feminist Performance Theory, Pedagogy and Practice," in *A Sourcebook of Feminist Theatre and Performance,* ed. Carol Martin (New York: Routledge, 1996), 3.

2. Ibid., 7.

3. Ibid.

4. Jill Dolan, *The Feminist Spectator as Critic* (Ann Arbor: University of Michigan Press, 1988), 5.

5. Alan Woods, "Emphasizing the Avant-Garde: An Exploration in Theatre Historiography," in *Interpreting the Theatrical Past,* ed. Thomas Postlewait and Bruce A. McConachie (Iowa City: University of Iowa Press, 1989), 166.

6. Indeed, the margins themselves are fluid, and as Dolan noted in the piece that she wrote for Martin's *A Sourcebook for Feminist Theatre and Performance,* even in those instances where critics initially do write from the margins, vigilance against a neutralizing absorption into the mainstream looms as a constant threat. As Dolan notes: "Rather than a site of resistance, feminism is now central to the field and to the profession, and vulnerable to the same exclusionary problems of all sites, identities, communities, and methods. But if feminism is closer to the center of theatre and performance studies, being there requires that we *continually* reflect on how the center and the margins can and should shift, on what feminists are doing, what they're forgetting, and who they serve" (Dolan, "Fathom Language," 3).

7. See in particular, Canning's chapter "Feminism, Theater, and Radical Politics," in *Feminist Theaters in the U.S.A.* (New York: Routledge, 1996), 39–62.

8. Cindy Rosenthal's study of Ellen Stewart was published in *TDR* 50.2 (2006): 12–51.

9. Günter Berghaus, *Theatre, Performance, and the Historical Avant-Garde* (New York: Palgrave, 2005).

10. In this respect, Berghaus's study bears the imprint of a long line of studies like Roger Shattuck's *The Banquet Years* (New York: Random House, 1955), Michael Kirby's *Futurist Performance* (Baltimore: PAJ, 1981), Christopher Innes's *Avant-Garde Theatre, 1893–1993* (New York: Routledge, 1993), Annabelle Melzer's *Dada and Surrealist Performance* (Baltimore: PAJ, 1994), and David Graver's *The Aesthetics of Disturbance: Anti-art in Avant-Garde Drama* (Ann Arbor: University of Michigan Press, 1995).

11. See, for example, the essays included in the anthology *Not the Other Avant-Garde: On the Transnational Foundations of Avant-Garde Performance* (Ann Arbor: University of Michigan Press, 2006). I coedited this anthology with John Rouse.

12. Günter Berghaus, *Avant-Garde Performance: Live Events and Electronic Technologies* (New York: Palgrave, 2005).

13. They are similar enough in content, for example, that they both bear the title "The Genesis of Modernism and the Avant-Garde" and in their histories of expressionism, futurism, and Dada, the condensed version of which in the second book is clearly derived from the more thorough version of the same history in the first book.

14. Paul Mann, *The Theory-Death of the Avant-Garde* (Bloomington: University of Indiana Press, 1991).

15. Naomi Sawelson-Gorse, ed., *Women in Dada* (Boston: MIT Press, 1998).

16. Tracy C. Davis, "Questions for a Feminist Methodology in Theatre History," in Postlewait and McConachie, *Interpreting the Theatrical Past,* 63.

17. Arnold Aronson, *American Avant-Garde Theatre: A History* (New York: Routledge, 2000), 20.

18. Innes published a revised version of this book under the title of *Avant-Garde Theatre, 1893–1993.*

19. Republished as RoseLee Goldberg, *Performance Art: From Futurism to the Present,* revised and expanded edition (New York: Thames and Hudson, 2001).

20. Aronson readily admits in his acknowledgments the profound debt his "understanding of the avant-garde" owes to "the teaching and friendship of the late Michael Kirby" (*American Avant-Garde Theatre,* xiii).

21. Ibid., 5.

22. Ibid., 5–6.

23. Ibid., xii.

24. See Richard Schechner, *The Future of Ritual: Writings on Culture and Performance* (New York: Routledge, 1993), 8.

25. These connections have long been an established part of the histories of the American avant-garde. See for example Kate Davy's "Richard Foreman's Ontological-Hysteric Theatre: The Influence of Gertrude Stein," *Twentieth Century Literature* 24.1 (1978): 108–26.

26. Sue-Ellen Case, *Feminism and Theatre* (New York: Methuen, 1988), 32, 33.

27. Ibid., 32.

28. Ibid., 35.

29. Ibid.

30. The one notable exception here is Sarah Bay-Cheng's *Mama Dada: Gertrude Stein's Avant-Garde Theater* (New York: Routledge, 2004), which I only mention in passing because her study focuses entirely on Stein rather than on the American avant-garde more generally. Still, her careful reading of Stein leads to a multifaceted conception of the avant-garde that I not only agree with but that I would also suggest is a product of Bay-Cheng's own insightful grounding in feminist historiographies and queer theory. Rather than placing Stein as one of the two pillars of American avant-garde theater (as does Aronson), Bay-Cheng suggests a much more diffuse reception of Stein's work: "What becomes immediately clear from even a preliminary consideration of Stein's drama and the avant-garde," Bay-Cheng argues, "is that while Stein's is undoubtably a major influence on the Amer-

ican avant-garde, the path of her influence is hazy and fragmented. For this reason, among others, the temptation to treat the history of the avant-garde as linear and evolutionary is misleading at best. Rather, the history of the avant-garde is perhaps best evaluated as an intricate web of overlapping and conflated influences, Stein being only one of them" (118).

31. Sue-Ellen Case, "Re-Viewing Hrotsvit," *Theatre Journal* 35.4 (1983): 534.

32. As Case notes, "Hrotsvit," which was an adopted voice, literally means "strong voice" (*Feminism and Theatre,* 32).

33. Elaine Aston, *An Introduction to Feminism and Theatre* (London: Routledge, 1995), 8.

34. Mike Sell, *Avant-Garde Performance and the Limits of Criticism* (Ann Arbor: University of Michigan Press, 2005), 4.

35. Ibid., 20.

36. They tend, for example, to erase the significance of vanguard groups like Bauhaus. In the American context, they also brush over the strong ties that avant-garde communities have had with institutions like Black Mountain College and the New School for Social Research. Granted, Sell mentions these latter (and other) institutions that have played such a significant role in the emergence of American avant-garde theater and performance communities. But he downplays their significance in order to construct a rhetorically forceful binary between the institutions of liberal democracy and the radical and revolutionary inclinations of the avant-garde, which, he argues, is by definition "an antiliberal, antiparliamentary trend" that was "born in the radical ideologies and radical social movements of the bourgeois West, particularly those that favored the use of violent, nonparliamentary means to achieve their political goals" (20–21). The problem is that this definition is simply too rigid and too linear in its characterization of the sources of avant-garde gestures and movements. Just to cite one example, it is particularly difficult to find space for John Cage and ultimately the most prominent artists from the happenings in this definition.

37. Charlotte Canning, "Constructing Experience: Theorizing a Feminist Theatre History," *Theatre Journal* 45 (1993): 529.

38. Sell, *Avant-Garde Performance,* 5.

39. Elin Diamond, *Unmasking Mimesis* (New York: Routledge, 1999), 44.

40. It is in this latter sense that Sell's arguments about the limits of criticism, compelling though they might be, are likely to play poorly with feminist critics. This is not to discount what I take to be Sell's sincerely expressed admiration of feminist scholars like Yolanda Broyles-Gonzalez, for example. But such moments of admiration are passing references rather than anchored points of departure in Sell's project of rethinking the avant-garde.

41. Cited in Diamond, *Unmasking Mimesis,* 43.

42. Ibid.

43. Ibid., 45.

44. Canning, "Constructing Experience," 531, 529.

45. Sell, *Avant-Garde Performance,* 39. Although Sell's book includes subtle and insightful readings of the Living Theatre's *The Connection* and of the happenings, in the final analysis readers will have difficulty seeing how his provocatively contextualized case studies produce a history that, in terms of the selected avant-garde events considered, actually differs from the male-centered canonical histories offered by

Arnold Aronson's *American Avant-Garde Theatre* or Theodor Shank's *Beyond the Boundaries* (Ann Arbor: University of Michigan Press, 2002).

46. Josephine Donovan, "Toward a Women's Poetics," in *Feminist Issues in Literary Scholarship,* ed. Shari Benstock (Bloomington: Indiana University Press, 1987), 100.

47. Gayle Austin, *Feminist Theories for Dramatic Criticism* (Ann Arbor: University of Michigan Press, 1990), 17.

48. Carolee Schneemann, *More Than Meat Joy* (New York: McPherson, 1997), 53.

49. This is Margaret Croyden's phrase, cited by Canning in *Feminist Theaters,* 47.

50. The account of this performance is taken directly from the privately distributed film *Arensberg Salon at St. Duchamp* that was directed by Steven Watson and filmed by Roberto Guerra. My thanks to Steven Watson for sharing this film with me.

51. At the risk of repeating my earlier comments about Canning's *Feminist Theaters in the U.S.A.,* I want to note again that the primary concerns of her study are not with the theorizing of avant-garde theater or performance. So while Canning devotes considerable attention to feminist collectives whose blending of experimental theater and progressive politics is avant-garde, she does not consider how this blending reshapes our understanding of the avant-garde as such.

52. Gregory L. Ulmer, "The Object of Post-Criticism," in *The Anti-aesthetic: Essays on Postmodern Culture,* ed. Hal Foster (Port Townsend, WA: Bay Press, 1983), 84.

53. Marjorie Perloff, "The Invention of Collage," *New York Literary Forum* 10–11 (1983): 10.

54. In fact, one can only speak of collage as a twentieth-century innovation in the West. Joachim Fiebach reminds us, for example, that "nonnaturalism and the collage format have been dominant characteristics of cultural production in premodern, and in particular, African societies for ages" ("Avant-Garde and Performance Cultures in Africa," in Harding and Rouse, *Not the Other Avant-Garde,* 68).

55. Mark Fortier, *Theory/Theatre: An Introduction* (New York: Routledge, 1997), 71.

56. Elsewhere I have also explored how current usage of the term *cutting edge* has a tendency to elide its connection to colonialist enterprises. See, for example: James Harding, "From Cutting Edge to Rough Edges: On the Transnational Foundations of Avant-Garde Performance," in Harding and Rouse, *Not the Other Avant-Garde,* 18–40.

57. Rebecca Schneider, *The Explicit Body in Performance* (New York: Routledge, 1997), 8.

58. Ibid., 3.

59. Ibid.

60. Ibid.

61. Ibid.

62. Sue-Ellen Case and Jeanie K. Forte, "From Formalism to Feminism," *Theater* 16.2 (1985): 62.

63. In fact, Stanton Garner Jr. notes that rather than moving toward the social and material, Artaud's notion of the theater as plague moves in precisely the opposite direction, toward the metaphysical. In Artaud's conception, Garner argues, "The

plague functions as a metaphor both for the body's corporeal surrender to a primordial necessity and for its self-transcendence within a spiritualized corporeality" ("Artaud, Germ Theory, and the Theatre of Contagion," *Theatre Journal* 58.1 [2006]: 11).

CHAPTER TWO

1. Rudolf Kuenzli, "Baroness Elsa von Freytag-Loringhoven and New York Dada," in Sawelson-Gorse, *Women in Dada,* 442.

2. Margaret Anderson, "Baroness von Freytag," *Little Review,* May 1929, 34.

3. Kuenzli, "Elsa von Freytag-Loringhoven," 464.

4. Elsa von Freytag-Loringhoven, letter to Djuna Barnes, published in *Little Review,* May 1929, 35.

5. Djuna Barnes, "Elsa Baroness von Freytag-Loringhoven," obituary, *transition* 11 (February 1928): 19.

6. Margaret Anderson, *My Thirty Years' War* (New York: Horizon Press, 1969), 177.

7. John Rodker, "'Dada' and Else von Freytag von [*sic*] Loringhoven," *Little Review,* July–August 1920, 33.

8. Robert Reiss, "'My Baroness': Elsa von Freytag-Loringhoven," in *New York Dada,* ed. Rudolf E. Kuenzli (New York: Willis Locker and Owens, 1986), 81.

9. Michael Fried, "Art and Objecthood," in *Minimal Art: A Critical Anthology,* ed. Gregory Battcock (New York: Dutton, 1968), 117.

10. Ibid., 139.

11. Ibid., 125.

12. I do not want to single Kuenzli out too much in this regard, but I cannot help but feel the irony in his recognition that the Baroness "has at best been treated as an entertaining sideshow" in cultural histories, which have "tended to focus on male writers and artists and [which have] paid little attention to . . . women's contributions" ("Elsa von Freytag-Loringhoven," 447). For though the recognition certainly qualifies as the most direct scholarly acknowledgment of a gender bias that has consistently shortchanged an adequate appreciation of von Freytag-Loringhoven, Kuenzli's corrective to this gendered neglect is merely to add the Baroness as a chapter in a larger history of the American avant-garde without even questioning whether the aesthetic values that she brings to that history are fundamentally at odds with the underlying assumptions of its present historiography. The issue here is that of the logic governing the historiographical models that we employ in constructing the cultural narratives of American avant-garde performance. For if the attention given to male writers and artists has indeed cultivated aesthetic standards that underestimate (if not blind us to) the contributions of women, then we must assume that women artists like von Freytag-Loringhoven have been shortchanged in this process because they have employed aesthetic strategies that have not only *not* registered appreciably within existing historiographical models, but that also, if appreciated on their own terms, may very well be antagonistic and irreconcilable with those models and thus demand an entirely different historiography altogether, one that conceivably would devalue the work of their male counterparts. What I am suggesting, in short, is a conceptual model for appreciating von Freytag-Loringhoven that, in its relation to the current histories of the American avant-garde, is akin to her conceptions of transla-

tion, where the discursive structures and aesthetic forms appropriate in one culture or in this case social context are unsuitable in another.

13. Anderson, *My Thirty Years' War,* 178.

14. Paul Hjartarson and Douglas Spettigue, introduction to *Baroness Elsa* (her autobiography) (Ontario: Oberon, 1992), 16.

15. Anderson, *My Thirty Years' War,* 194.

16. Ibid.

17. Elsa von Freytag-Loringhoven, "Thee I call 'Hamlet of Wedding-Ring': Criticism of William Carlos William's 'Kora in Hell' and why . . . ," part 1 published in *Little Review* January–March, 1921: 48–60, part 2 published in *Little Review* Autumn, 1921: 108–11.

18. Ibid., part 1, 49.

19. Von Freytag-Loringhoven locates the pivotal mechanism of this opposition in an expression of male brutality that, broadly speaking, she associates with an aggressive desire "not to be sentimental" (ibid., 48). The underlying presumption of that desire, von Freytag-Loringhoven suggests, is a conventional association of women with sentimentality, and the aggressive desire "not to be sentimental" thus defines masculinity negatively: first, in contrast to the stereotypical definitions of women upon which it ultimately relies for its own definition of masculinity; and second, in contrast to the prescriptive, stereotypical role into which male brutality callously bullies women and thereby enacts the crudest form of unsentimental behavior. In mapping out this gendered dynamic, von Freytag-Loringhoven gradually departs from a long tradition of essentialism that fundamentally associates men with aggressiveness and women with sentimentality and that thereby enforces acquiescence to violence and hostility.

20. Rather than essential characteristics defining gender, male brutality and female sentimentality are, according to von Freytag-Loringhoven, defensive reactions against a much more fluid sense of identity:

> Male inexperience = brutality—
> female = sentimentality.
> Reaction to life—ununderstood.
> Baffles—troubles—unable to handle. (Ibid.)

Beneath this socially constructed binary, von Freytag-Loringhoven recognizes a moment of sameness where conventional notions of masculinity and femininity are, at their most basic level, arguably the product of inexperience, ignorance, and fear.

21. Ibid.

22. Ibid., 50.

23. Ibid., 49.

24. Ibid., 51. Her references to the circus, particularly as a site where acts are capable of having "purpose" and of carrying a "point," remind us that von Freytag-Loringhoven's notion of the *performative* always underlies the use in her poem of terms like *life, experience,* and *existence.* They allude to a sphere of activity that, like the loosely scripted improvisations of the circus, must constantly be renegotiated. They allude to a sphere, in short, where the performative acts constructing gender and sexuality are opened to self-conscious negotiation, experimentation, and innovation.

25. Marjorie Perloff, "The Invention of Collage," 14.

26. William Carlos Williams, *Autobiography* (New York: Random House, 1948), 164.

27. William Carlos Williams, "Sample Prose Piece. The Three Letters," *Contact* 4 (1921): 10.

28. Anderson, *My Thirty Years' War,* 210.

29. Williams, *Autobiography,* 165.

30. Francis Naumann, *New York Dada, 1915–23* (New York: Abrams, 1994), 173; Anderson, *My Thirty Years' War,* 179; Williams, "Sample Prose Piece," 10.

31. Williams, *Autobiography,* 168.

32. Ibid., 169.

33. Francis Naumann specifically situates the proposal within the context of Williams's love letter and von Freytag-Loringhoven's misunderstanding either of Williams's intentions or of his ability to follow through on the implications of his amorous expressions (see Naumann, *New York Dada,* 173–74).

34. Irene Gammel, *Baroness Elsa: Gender, Dada, and Everyday Modernity* (Cambridge: MIT Press, 2002), 266; see also 68–70.

35. William Carlos Williams, "The Baroness Elsa Freytag von Loringhoven," *Twentieth Century Literature* 35.3 (1989): 283. For accounts of testimony from von Freytag-Loringhoven's friends, see Gammel, *Baroness Elsa,* 266.

36. Those familiar with Williams' comments will recall that he follows his explanation of not being able to sleep with the Baroness with the assertions that sex is merely "a corridor to a clarity" and that "in those I must use[,] sex must be illuminated by what I desire beyond it" ("The Baroness," 283–84). Whatever clarity he refers to here implicitly pivots on a privileged prerogative to continue to "use" women rather than allowing his interactions with them to challenge the way he would "use" them to get what he "desire[s] beyond" his intercourse with them.

37. William Carlos Williams, "Kora in Hell," in *Imaginations,* ed. Webster Schott (New York: New Directions, 1970), 71.

38. Antonin Artaud, *The Theatre and Its Double,* trans. Mary Caroline Richards (New York: Grove Press, 1966), 26, 31.

39. Ibid., 16.

40. My overview here is deeply indebted to my colleague Marie McAlister. I am very grateful to her for her help.

41. All passages cited from Commission on Training Camp Activities, *When You Go Home—Take this Book with You* (Washington, D.C.: War Department, 1918), 13–15. This pamphlet is archived online by the National Museum of Health and Medicine, Armed Forces Institute of Pathology. See http://www.archive.org/details/WhenYouGoHome.

42. See Barbara Haskell, "The Aesthetics of Junk," in *Blam: The Explosion of Pop, Mimimalism, and Performance, 1958–1964* (New York: Norton, 1984), 17.

43. Michael Kirby, *Happenings* (New York: Dutton, 1965).

44. Together with his essay "The New Theatre," which appeared that same year in *TDR*'s special issue on the happenings, Kirby's introduction to his anthology almost singlehandedly codified what for nearly forty years has constituted the historiographical foundation the quasi-official history of American experimental performance. One might also point to the publication of Richard Kostelanetz's *Theatre of Mixed Means* (New York: Dial Press, 1968), which appeared three years after Kirby's

anthology and which offered a similar genealogy for the happenings. Indeed, the absence of Kirby's anthology in Kostelanetz's references is striking, given the similarity of their projects, and it suggests a certain degree of rivalry in staking out the territory that Kirby called "the New Theatre" and Kostelanetz called "the theatre of mixed means."

45. Motherwell's anthology, which for the first time collected and translated foundational documents from the Dadaists and early surrealists, has long deserved a recognition for having had an impact comparable to that of Mary Richards's subsequent translation of Artaud's *Theatre and Its Double* in 1958, for it arguably provided access to an (anti) aesthetic tradition that, on a scale that still has not been fully appreciated, inspired a generation of American artists, performers, and scholars. But Motherwell's anthology was primarily a text about a European tradition (which despite the antiliterary predilections of the avant-garde was far better documented than its U.S. counterpart), and although its translation of Georges Hugnet's 1932/34 essay "The Dada Spirit in Painting" included a passing comparison of Schwitters and von Freytag-Loringhoven (185–86), Motherwell's anthology as a whole gave an exceptionally high profile to the European avant-garde at the expense of the experimental artists in New York who were simultaneously engaged in comparable activities but who only subsequently were identified as "Dada." The notable exceptions here were the short essays by Arthur Cravan and Gagrielle Buffet-Picabia, the former titled "Exhibition at the Independents" (1914) and the latter titled "Arthur Cravan and American Dada," which includes a brief but marvelous account of Cravan's drunken lecture at the Exhibition of the Independents (1938). Motherwell placed both essays in an opening section entitled "Pre-Dada." See Robert Motherwell, ed., *The Dada Painters and Poets: An Anthology*, 2nd ed. (Cambridge: Harvard University Press, 1979).

46. Granted, the Baroness's influence was limited, but what is remarkable about the genealogy posited by Kirby is the extent to which, under the guise of "historical progression," that genealogy unconsciously blurs the boundaries between discussions of influence and discussions of precedent (24). Whereas discussions of influence document the manner in which an artist's work shapes the work of another artist, discussions of precedent are primarily framing devices shaping the critical reception of a work or works. The former address a productive relation passed from artists to artists. The latter contextualize a body of work within a constructed tradition and thereby establish the conceptual models and terms through which we understand that work. Far from being a neutral, academic exercise in determining who did what first, the question of precedent is ultimately a struggle to privilege one interpretive model over another. The implications of that struggle are especially important to our understanding precisely of the new theater that Kirby sought to introduce in his book.

47. Georges Hugnet, "The Dada Spirit in Painting," in Motherwell, *Dada Painters and Poets*, 163.

48. Ibid.

49. Williams, "Sample Prose Piece," 10.

50. See Allan Kaprow, *Assemblage, Environments, & Happenings* (New York: Harry Abrams, 1966), no page numbers.

51. Haskell, "The Aesthetics of Junk," 19.

52. Ibid.

53. Anderson, *My Thirty Years War,* 178.

54. This is, for example, Amelia Jones's argument: "Given the baroness's perhaps too total identification with the anti-aesthetic boundary-breaking nonsense of Dada, it is grotesquely fitting that, while Picabia, Man Ray, Crotti, and the others went on to more or less successful careers making objects (with Duchamp reserving himself for posterity), the baroness could only self-destruct—dying at the early age of fifty three after returning to Europe in the 1920s and living in abject poverty for several years" ("Eros, That's Life, or the Baroness's Penis," in *Making Mischief: Dada Invades New York,* ed. Francis Naumann [New York: Abrams, 1996], 244).

55. Peter Bürger, *Theory of the Avant-Garde,* trans. Michael Shaw (Minneapolis: University of Minnesota Press, 1984), 51.

56. As is well known, the great scandal of that exhibition was the rejection of Duchamp's *Fountain,* an inverted urinal to which Duchamp added the signature "R. Mutt." Despite the policy that any artist could exhibit any work as long as he or she paid the six-dollar submission fee, the governing board, without knowing that the piece came from Duchamp, decided not to exhibit the urinal. Duchamp, who was a member of the board, resigned in protest. For more discussion of the Independents Exhibition see Steven Watson, *Strange Bedfellows* (New York: Abbeville Press, 1991), 312–20.

57. Francis Naumann has seriously questioned the attribution of this work to Schamberg, noting first of all that the collection's official list, which was prepared under the supervision of Walter Arensberg himself, attributes the work to "both" Schamberg and von Freytag-Loringhoven (*New York Dada,* 234). Expanding on this note, Naumann argues that Schamberg was too "dandified and punctilious" and too interested in an "elegant and highly refined machinist vision" to produce "a sculptural artifact consisting only of a plumbing trap inverted in a miter box and called *God*" (127). It is far more likely, Naumann contends, that the work was largely the Baroness's idea:

> Based upon our knowledge of other works by the Baroness from this period, it is logical to conclude that she probably came up with the idea of combining the extraneous elements in this sculpture, as well as of assigning the unusual title, while Schamberg was probably responsible only for mounting the assembly and for recording the work, as he did in a small photograph of the sculpture positioned before one of his machinist paintings, a print which he carefully signed—in his ususal machinist script—and dated "1917" (128).

Naumann's argument has had a substantial impact on subsequent scholarship on the Baroness, finding its way into the work of scholars like Reiss, Kuenzli, and Watson—all of whom affirm Naumann's claim.

58. The interpretations are so varied and prevalent that it is difficult to account for them all, but they include citing R. Mutt as a reference to the manufacturer of the urinal Richard Mutt, as an allusion to the German word *Armut* (poverty), as an inversion of the syllables in the German word *Mutter,* as an allusion to the slang for penis (R. for Richard, an alternative to Dick).

59. Bürger, *Theory of the Avant-Garde,* 51.

60. At its most basic level, shuffling the names beneath the sculpture at the Philadelphia Museum of Art would provide us with some clarification of "the strange title, which," as Abraham Davidson has noted, "has never adequately been explained" (225). The title can easily been seen as a coded reference to Duchamp,

whom von Freytag-Loringhoven nicknamed Mars (i.e., the god of war). See Abraham Davidson, "The European Art Invasion," in Naumann, *Making Mischief,* 222–27.

61. Von Freytag-Loringhoven's description of the effect that American culture had on Duchamp appears in one of the unpublished letters included in the papers of the *Little Review* held at the University of Wisconsin. The specific passage that I quote was cited in Kuenzli's "Elsa von Freytag-Loringhoven," 449.

62. Naumann, *New York Dada,* 173.

63. David Hopkins, "Men before the Mirror: Duchamp, Man Ray and Masculinity," *Art History* 21.3 (1998): 306.

64. David Hopkins argues, for example, that Duchamp's *Fountain* ultimately "castrates the object [the urinal] doubly, as both male and female, and thereby succinctly thematizes the psychic quandary around the issue of the penis's presence/absence" (ibid.).

65. The reference here is to von Freytag-Loringhoven's poem "The Cast Iron Lover," published in *Little Review* 6.5 (1919): 3–11.

66. Rodker, "Dada," 33.

67. *The Letters of Hart Crane, 1916–1932* (New York: Heritage House, 1952), 52.

68. Watson, *Strange Bedfellows.*

69. I am indebted to Francis Naumann and especially to Laura Groves at the Philadelphia Museum of Art for their detailed descriptions of the physical makeup of the original versions of the journal. The interpretations of the significance of the journal's layout are mine.

70. Naumann, *New York Dada,* 202.

71. Rather than debating the actual authorship of this poem, scholars have simply attributed it to Marsden Hartley or Elsa von Freytag-Loringhoven. Whereas Francis Naumann and Steven Watson attribute the poem to Hartley, Paul Hjartarson and Douglas Spettigue (the editors of the published version of Baroness's autobiography) and Irene Divey attribute the poem to von Freytag-Loringhoven. The rationale for attributing the poem to her is as follows. The poem appears next to the Baroness's name and photo, and, as Gaby Divey has noted, it is "consistent with . . . [von Freytag-Loringhoven's] poetic style including the many dashes and the syntactic breaks." It "refers to Mary Garden ("not garden——mary")" whom the Baroness mentions in her letters, and "the reference to 'the late afternoon' is very similar to her 'Buddha' poem published in *Little Review*" (email to the author, December 4, 2001). Furthermore, the poem begins with the address "Dearest Saltimbanques," which coincides with the interest in the circus that von Freytag-Loringhoven expressed that same year in "Thee I Call Hamlet of Wedding-Ring." See also Gammel, *Baroness Elsa,* 298–300.

72. Robert Hughes, "Days of Antic Weirdness: A Look Back at Dadaism's Brief, Outrageous Assault on the New York Scene," *Time,* January 27, 1997, n.p.

73. If von Freytag-Loringhoven critically appropriated the image of the *vagina dentata,* Duchamp's whiskered *Mona Lisa* exemplified a subtly vicious perpetuation of that image, and in such portrayals he was not alone. Similar affirmations of the stereotypes associated with the *vagina dentata* can be found, for example, in the works of Picasso and de Kooning.

74. Reiss, "My Baroness," 86.

75. See *Little Review* 5.2 (1918): 58–59.

76. Kuenzli, "Elsa von Freytag-Loringhoven," 450.

77. See *Little Review,* December, 1918, 41.

78. It is worth noting that in a bizarre foreshadowing of the decisive point of contention between Valerie Solanas and Andy Warhol, von Freytag-Loringhoven sent Tzara a manuscript of some of her work that he apparently lost.

79. See "Klink—Hratzvenga (Deathwail)," *Little Review,* March, 1920, 11–12.

80. Anderson, *My Thirty Years' War,* 211.

81. See Amelia Jones, *Postmodernism and the En-gendering of Marcel Duchamp* (New York: Cambridge University Press, 1994), especially 146–90.

82. Jones, "Eros," 239.

83. Anderson, *My Thirty Years' War,* 179.

84. Jones, "Eros," 166.

CHAPTER THREE

1. Max Ernst, *Ecritures* (Paris: Gillimard, 1970), 256.

2. Indeed, according to a wide array of critical views, the anti- or transdisciplinary tendencies that, as I will be arguing, characterize Stein's libretto for *The Mother of Us All* are consistent with the practice of collage more generally. Derek Owens, to cite but one example among many critics, has argued that "a call for collage is inherently an argument against disciplinary thinking." See his article "The Aggregate Eye / A Rhetoric of College," *Readerly/Writerly Texts* 4.1 (1996): 24.

3. Obviously, this claim departs from the more traditional readings of Stein's work that characterize her experimental writings according to her close affinity with the cubist movement in painting. Probably the most influential of these readings is Richard Bridgeman's *Gertrude Stein in Pieces* (New York: Oxford University Press, 1970). Certainly, *The Mother of Us All* bears the imprint of cubism, as did the collages of Picasso and Braque. But in this her final piece of dramatic literature, Stein moved decisively toward the aesthetics of collage. To give just one example of the evidence supporting this claim, it is worth recalling that Stein's libretto is comprised not only of her own writing but of historical documents that she incorporated into her text, and, in this respect, her libretto falls in line with Aragon's earlier definition of collage: "The concept of collage is the introduction [into a painting] of an object, a substance, taken from the real world and by means of which the painting, that is to say the world that is imitated, finds itself once again completely open to question" (translated by and cited in Perloff, "The Invention of Collage," 10).

4. RoseLee Goldberg, *Performance Art: From Futurism to the Present,* 121.

5. Aronson, *American Avant-Garde Theatre,* 5.

6. Davis, "Feminist Methodology," 63.

7. There are two major important points of reference here. The first is connected with Allan Kaprow and articles like "The Legacy of Jackson Pollock" (1958) that were included in *Essays on the Blurring of Art and Life* (Berkeley and Los Angeles: University of California Press, 1993), 1–9. The second is Michael Kirby's widely influential book *Happenings,* in which his definition of the experimental performance associated with the happenings specifically privileges the action paintings of abstract expressionism over the theory and practice of collage (see pages 23–29). A further example

of this line of thought can be found in Noël Carroll's important article "Performance" in the journal *Formations* 3.1 (1986): 63–79.

8. I mention this issue in passing here, but it will be addressed more thoroughly in my discussions of Yoko Ono's use of collage aesthetics in *Cut Piece.*

9. The underlying logic here acknowledges that the tensions in the relation of text to performance run simultaneously in both directions. Not only is a literary dramatic text more than any performance can convey, but performance is also more than the dramatic text as well. Just as no text adequately achieves objective referentiality, no dramatic text subsumes the performance that creatively engages it.

10. The logic here is twofold. First of all, the idea that a performance is always more than a dramatic text parallels the libretto's suggestion that historical events are always more than the documents or narratives we create to account for them. Second, inasmuch as Stein structures the relation of text to performance so that performance is aligned with the pursuit of a voice denied to women in governing texts of American political culture, she implicitly equates performance with the unrecognized and unrecorded acts of women.

11. The very origin of opera tends to belie such an understanding of Stein's final dramatic work. Like *Four Saints in Three Acts, The Mother of Us All* originated as a collaborative piece between Virgil Thomson and Gertrude Stein. The impetus for this second collaboration came when Thomson approached Stein regarding a commission he had received in the spring of 1945 from the Alice M. Ditson Fund committee "for an opera to be produced in 1947 at Columbia University" (Kathleen Hoover and John Cage, *Virgil Thomson: His Life and Music* [New York: A. S. Barnes, 1970], 105). Although he ultimately gave Stein wide liberty regarding the particulars of the libretto, he wanted some focus on what he considered to be the profoundly rich oratory of American political history. "Surely," he argued, "somewhere in this noble history [of late nineteenth-century America] and in its oratory there must be the theme, and perhaps even the words, of a musico-dramatic spectacle that it would be a pleasure to compose" (105). Yet despite his request for "for opera about nineteenth-century America with perhaps the language of senatorial orators quoted," what Thomson received was a libretto whose "feminist approach" he immediately recognized and "could not deny" (i.e., reject) in part because in it he also recognized scenes about Anthony that in his opinion "might as well have been herself [Stein] and Alice Toklas conversing about Gertrude's career" (Virgil Thomson, *Virgil Thomson* [New York: Knopf, 1966], 366–67). With Thomson's approval of two drafted scenes, Stein moved quickly into a period of intensive writing, which proved unfortunately to be her last. She died of cancer in July 1946 after having sent Thomson the finished libretto in March. It was her last completed work.

12. Just to cite one example, Bowers notes: "In her characterization of Anthony and in her dramatization of the suffragist's career, Stein draws heavily on historical record, even quoting from or alluding to Anthony's actual speeches. For example, Susan B.'s first platform speech at the beginning of Act 2 is an excerpt from Susan B. Anthony's first public speech, delivered in 1849 at Canajoharie New York, to the Daughters of Temperance. Anthony's speech reads: 'Ladies! There is no Neutral position for us to assume. . . . If we say that we love the Cause and then sit down at our ease, surely does our action speak the lie' " (Jane Palatini Bowers, *They Watch Me as They Watch This: Gertrude Stein's Metadrama* [Philadelphia: University of Pennsylvania Press, 1991], 109).

13. The scope of this initial suggestion is much wider and segues into the more fundamental questioning of referentiality that is presumed in the practice of collage (see, for example, Perloff, "The Invention of Collage," *New York Literary Forum,* 40). Indeed, the questioning of referentiality is always prior to the grafting and pasting of collage. The challenge that Stein's libretto mounts against the presumption of objectivity in existing histories of experimental performance is thus less the product of severing collage fragments from their presumed inherent connection to a specific historical context than it is of a fundamental questioning of referentiality that is at the core of collage aesthetics, a questioning that precedes the radical recontextualization of fragments like those that Stein utilizes from the life of Susan B. Anthony and from the life of her antagonist in the libretto, the gifted orator and conservative politician Daniel Webster.

14. Hayden White, "The Historical Text as Literary Artifact," *Clio* 3.3 (1974): 277–303.

15. Hayden White, *Tropics of Discourse* (Baltimore: Johns Hopkins University Press, 1978), 89. The chapter from which this quote is taken is the reprinted version of "The Historical Text as Literary Artifact" that White included as a chapter in his book.

16. As White himself openly acknowledges, the notions of literature underlying his arguments derive from the literary theories of Northrop Frye's *Anatomy of Criticism,* and White directly links his own notion of historiographical "emplotment" to Frye's thesis that archetypical myths or "pregeneric plot structures" serve as the basis for all fiction (White, *Tropics of Discourse,* 83). While it may be a measure of White's subversion of established paradigms of scholarship in the mid-1970s that he drew upon the literary theories of a critic who consciously (though not unproblematically) sought to maintain a strict division between history and fiction, the larger significance of White's claims unfortunately do not compensate for the lingering conventional subtleties in his notion of literature. Those conventional subtleties have major implications for—in fact, they find their way into—White's reconceptualization of historiography.

17. The passage comes from the version of the essay reprinted in White, *Tropics of Discourse,* 47.

18. Susan Sontag, *Against Interpretation* (New York: Farrar, Straus and Giroux, 1966), 272. While it is true that Artaud hardly counts as the mainstream of the surrealist modes of representation to which White refers (after all, Breton purged Artaud from the surrealists), placing his embrace of performance at the center of White's call for alternative historiographies gains a certain degree of credibility from the fact that White calls for a surrealistic historiography at the same time that he entertains the prospect of "actionist modes of representation" as a model for historiography as well. As is well known, those actionist modes of representation had their seminal expression in the paintings of Jackson Pollock, which gained their critical acclaim (as well as their title) not as finished products but rather as mere traces calling attention to the actual action or performance of painting itself. Yet Pollock's works are not so much a representation of the act of painting as they are a remnants and by-products of painting. They are evidence that some act has occurred the form of which remains indeterminate.

19. Perloff, "The Invention of Collage," *New York Literary Forum,* 6.

20. Ibid., 40.

21. Christine Poggi, *In Defiance of Painting: Cubism, Futurism, and the Invention of Collage* (New Haven: Yale University Press, 1992), 17. Christine Poggi draws attention to Maurice Raynal's reaction to *La Lavabo* in the journal *La Section d'Or.* Raynal's critical assessment of the collage situated its elements with an antipictorial gesture. Speaking specifically about objects included in the collage, such as its famous piece of a mirror, Raynal argues: "To show that in his conception of pure painting there exists objects that are absolutely antipictorial, he has not hesitated to stick several real objects on the canvas" (cited in Poggi, 17).

22. In this respect, Stein arguably worked concurrently with a number of difference conceptual notions closely related to the readymades, applying them not only within the realms of performance but also in her understanding of the function of language as well. As Marjorie Perloff has argued in an exceptionally provocative article entitled "Of Objects and Readymades: Gertrude Stein and Marcel Duchamp," Stein treated the individual units of discourse with much the same indifference that Duchamp treated objects, a treatment incidentally that was pivotal to the emergence of the readymade as a mode of (anti)artistic expression. Indeed, Perloff equates Duchamp and Stein in terms of indifference, the former embracing a "visual indifference" and the latter embracing a "verbal indifference": "Like Duchamp, who claimed to be entirely without artistic taste or purpose, Stein regularly protested that 'Grammar is useless because there is nothing to say'" (Marjorie Perloff, "Of Objects and Readymades: Gertrude Stein and Marcel Duchamp," *Forum for Modern Language Studies* 32.2 [1996]: 143). The absence of grammar is, of course, the defining characteristic of parataxis, and is thus, as Perloff herself argued some thirteen years prior to her article on Stein and Duchamp, the basis of collage, and inasmuch as parataxis structures Stein's writing, her texts incline toward the aesthetics of collage. Similarly, the parallels that Perloff observes between Stein and Duchamp ultimately underscore the fundamental relation between the readymade and collage. This later connection is especially important to our understanding of the workings of collage within the notions of performance presumed by Stein's libretto.

23. In *The Mother of Us All,* this relation is further complicated by the musical dimensions of the opera as well. Virgil Thomson was especially aware that the score for the libretto functioned as a complement to rather than as an illustration of it. In his critical autobiography he explains, for example, "My theory was that if a text is set correctly for the sound of it, the meaning will take care of itself, and the Stein texts, for prosodizing in this way, were manna. With meanings already abstracted, or absent, or so multiplied that choice among them was impossible, there was no temptation toward tonal illustration, say, of birdie babbling by the brook or heavy, heavy hangs my heart. You could make a setting for sound and syntax only, then add, if needed, an accompaniment equally functional" (Thomson, *Virgil Thomson,* 90). But even in this context, Thomson's work provided a stark contrast of expressive modes. As Katherine Hoover has observed, Thomson's musical compositions clashed with the experimental aspects of Stein's work in profoundly provocative ways: "To most composers the lack of sense-meaning in Gertrude Stein's words would have posed a problem. Thomson gave them their natural speech inflection with the same meticulousness he would have applied if their meaning had been accessible, at the same time taking pains to make clear the emotional intention of his music. The inverted shock produced by this anti-modern treatment of an ultra-modern libretto precipi-

tated a reaction against the turgidity of much American music of the time" (Hoover and Cage, *Virgil Thomson,* 65).

24. Stein herself pointed toward the currents leading in this direction some ten years prior to *The Mother of Us All.* Speaking of the advent of cubism, Stein pinpointed sentiments that ultimately moved artistic expression toward collage aesthetics. In her 1938 monograph on Picasso, Stein notes: "The framing of life, the need that a picture exist in its frame, remain in its frame was over. A picture remaining in its frame was a thing that had always existed and now pictures commenced to want to leave their frames and this also created the necessity for cubism" (Gertrude Stein, *Picasso* [New York: Dover, 1984], 12).

25. Gertrude Stein, *The Mother of Us All,* included in *Last Operas and Plays,* ed. Carl Van Vechten (Baltimore: Johns Hopkins University Press, 1995), 60.

26. Dinnah Pladott, "Gertrude Stein: Exile, Feminism, Avant-Garde in the American Theater," in *Modern American Drama,* ed. June Schlueter (Rutherford, NJ: Fairleigh Dickinson University Press, 1990), 114.

27. Stein, *Mother of Us All,* 87.

28. Though not focusing on the performative aspects underlying the contrast that Anthony draws in this scene, Franziska Gygax offers a very clear sense of the disillusionment conveyed in the disembodied voice of Anthony: "At the end of Stein's opera women have the right to vote. But significantly, Susan B. Anthony's voice is only heard from behind a statue: She has the vote and voice, but her body is absent. The ambiguity inherent in this disembodiment with regard to her achievement is increased by her last words. . . . Anthony's voice behind the statue no longer expresses protest against the male oppression, but it does not convey satisfaction either. Doubts about the significance of women's vote overshadow her success" (Franziska Gygax, *Gender and Genre in Gertrude Stein* [Westport, CN: Greenwood, 1998], 56).

29. Stein, *Mother of Us All,* 88.

30. Ibid.

31. Indeed, in positing collage as an alternative mode of knowledge, Stein was asserting the broad epistemological relevance of what Gregory Ulmer has argued is "by most accounts . . . the single most revolutionary formal innovation in artistic representation to occur" in the twentieth century ("The Object of Post-Criticism," 84).

32. Thomson, *Virgil Thomson,* 366.

33. Just as in the graphic arts collage is at once a critical "extension of painting and its act . . . [that] plays with its subject, extending and complicating its rules by both mocking and respecting the boundaries of the arena—that is, by a highly self-conscious probing of the picture plane," so too is the collage technique employed by Stein throughout *The Mother of Us All* a self-conscious probing and a critique of the boundaries of the literary and performing arts (David Rosand, "Paint, Paste, and Plane," *New York Literary Forum* 10–11 [1983]: 122).

34. The reasoning behind this interest in the similarities between the family histories of Stein and Webster is largely the result of elements to be found in the opening scene of the opera. There a character identified only as G. S. makes a cameo appearance, announcing that her "father's name was Daniel he had a black beard" (Stein, *Mother of Us All,* 53). Since Gertrude Stein's father was also named Daniel and since he also had a black beard, critics have plausibly argued that the character G. S. represents Stein herself (much in the same manner that critics have argued that the

character Virgil T. represents Virgil Thomson). Critics have also argued that this information serves as a link between Stein and her protagonist Susan B. Anthony because Anthony's father was also named Daniel. The peculiarity of this line of argumentation is that, unlike her historical model, the character Susan B. Anthony flatly denies that her father's name was Daniel: "I had a father, Daniel was not his name" (Stein, *Mother of Us All,* 54). Though there are obviously many ways to read this denial, it does suggest the need to look beyond the coincidental for the link between Stein and Anthony.

35. Probably the best example of this tendency in the scholarly reception of *The Mother of Us All* is the argument formulated by Elizabeth Winston, who argues: "In *The Mother of Us All,* she [Stein] preserves her reputation as an artistic revolutionary by manipulating the public and private history of Susan B. Anthony and other historical personages to dramatize the life of Gertrude Stein. One of her techniques is to play freely with chronology, bringing together characters like Daniel Webster and her own contemporaries—Virgil T[homson] and Jo [Barry], for instance" (Elizabeth Winston, "Making History in *The Mother of Us All,*" *Mosaic* 20.4 [1987]: 118). While it is true that Stein, as a woman artist, has something personally at stake in seeing women artists receive a more equitable share of the recognition that they deserve, Winston's reduction of Stein's libretto to a dramatization of "the life of Gertrude Stein" significantly understates the scope of the libretto's implications.

36. Stein, *Mother of Us All,* 68.

37. Ibid., 81. Although Richard Bridgeman recognized that this "prediction of a compromised victory" is wrought with "irony" because the perception "fails to diminish . . . [Anthony's] determination to 'fight for the right'," he nonetheless fails to recognize the extent to which Stein distances her own project from the ironic shortcomings of her protagonist (Bridgeman, *Gertrude Stein in Pieces,* 342).

38. It is important to recognize the extent to which this strategy differs critically from that taken by her protagonist, who, as Jane Palatini Bowers has noted, concludes that she "must avail herself of the power of patriarchal language" (*They Watch Me,* 115).

39. Perloff, "The Invention of Collage," *New York Literary Forum,* 10.

40. This self-reflective tendency within the structure of Stein's text sets it directly at odds with the basic principles of literary historiography. As Peter Bürger has noted: "The discourse of traditional literary history is defined by a lack of reflection on its historicity. Because it aims at stabilizing a given tradition it is inevitable that it neglects its historical presuppositions. Spelling them out would counteract its social function" ("On Literary History," *Poetics* 14 [1985]: 201).

41. It is in fact the open heterogeneity of the collage constructions in Stein's libretto that are at odds with the humanistic idealism underlying readings of *The Mother of Us All* like Robert Martin's. Martin argues that "since Stein's presentation of time is not linear nor disjunct," she "makes regular use of a 'continuous present'. . . . that ultimately derives from Henri Bergson's *simultanéité* by way of William James" (Robert Martin, "*The Mother of Us All* and American History," in *Gertrude Stein and the Making of Literature,* ed. Shirley Neuman and Ira Nadel [Boston: Northeastern University Press, 1988], 210). Yet the critical force of Stein's libretto pivots its strategies of decomposition and its use of radical juxtapositions that disrupt rather than reinforce notions of historical continuity.

42. Bowers notes, for example, that "nine out of Daniel's fifteen speeches in this

scene [act 1, scene 3] are taken intact from Daniel Webster's most famous senatorial speech, the 1830 debate with Senator Hayne of South Carolina over the Foote resolution 'to consider limiting the sale of public lands.' The remaining speeches, save two, are also drawn from historical record" (*They Watch Me,* 114).

43. Important in this regard is the decisively feminist edge that the performative context adds to the attention that Stein gave to her readers and spectators. This edge is in my opinion far more significant than the parallel that Bonnie Marranca draws between Duchamp and Stein: "If for Duchamp it was the viewer who completed the work, Stein shifted attention from the text to the reader (or spectator)" (introduction to Stein, *Last Operas and Plays,* x).

44. Stein, *Mother of Us All,* 57.

45. Ibid.

46. Bowers, *They Watch Me,* 114. The Foote resolution considered "limiting the sale of public lands" (114). The speech from which this quote is taken was, as Irving Bartlett argues, "one of the two most important speeches . . . [Webster] ever made in the Senate and must still be ranked as one of the greatest addresses ever made before a house of Congress. The speech was given from twelve pages of notes. It took several hours spread over two days to deliver and, after extensive revision, was printed in a form that takes up seventy-five pages in the national edition of Webster's Works. The speech has been remembered mostly for the eloquent "liberty and union forever" peroration, which every northern schoolboy would soon commit to memory, and for Webster's argument for constitutional nationalism" (Irving Bartlett, *Daniel Webster* [New York: Norton, 1978], 117).

47. It is precisely an awareness of this lack of neutrality that is missing in works like Katherine Hoover's foundational study of Thomson (a study to which John Cage contributed a lengthy essay). Hoover argues that "the dialog [in *The Mother of Us All*] is a reflection of personality rather than a vehicle for advancing a plot. The people of the play neither answer one another nor even listen; they simply say what is most on their minds, turning the text into a bright contusion of insistencies, each clear and reasonable in itself." One could conceivably argue that Hoover is looking beyond the lack of neutrality were it not for the fact that she ties these comments into a more general assertion that a direct parallel unites Anthony's "career on the political plane and that of Gertrude Stein on the Literary" (Hoover and Cage, *Virgil Thomson,* 106–7). In fact, Stein is ultimately very critical of Anthony and the compromises to which she succumbed. That Stein would be personally concerned about Anthony's fate is borne out in the situation that Stein find herself in at the time she wrote *The Mother of Us All.* If as Hoover notes, Stein "had finally been rewarded by the recognition as a serious artist for which she had so long hungered," her final dramatic work suggested that she was acutely aware of the potentially dangerous compromises that could result from recognition (106).

48. I would even go so far as to say that this lack of neutrality undercuts the seemingly unbiased notion of "continuous present" that Robert Martin, drawing upon the work of Bergson and James, associates with Stein's libretto. Martin argues: "Since Stein's presentation of time is not linear nor disjunct, since she in other words makes regular use of a 'continuous present' . . . that ultimately derives from Henri Bergson's *simultanéité* by way of William James, she might be thought to have no place for an exploration of history" (*Gertrude Stein,* 210).

49. At one level, it is easy to see how the reassertion of autonomy among the in-

dividual elements of Stein's libretto substantiates claims like those made by Bettina L. Knapp regarding the position that the libretto occupies in the accepted histories of modern drama. Knapp argues: "Like her contemporaries, she [Stein] advocated anti-naturalism in the performing arts: no plot; directionless happenings; no characters; non-referential, and therefore self-contained movement; no logic in the sequence of event; no transitions; no connections; no sense of progress. Rather than espousing mimetism, she sought through devaluated word to create a fantasy world of her own—a magical realm, an atmosphere, a landscape" (*Gertrude Stein* [New York: Continuum, 1990], 137). The problem is that this argument tends to characterize Stein's "anti-naturalism" as a stylistic end in itself rather than as a structural reflection of a strategy for reconfiguring our basic understanding of history.

50. Graver, *The Aesthetics of Disturbance,* 31.

51. Stein, *Mother of Us All,* 77.

CHAPTER FOUR

Published in *Yes: Yoko Ono,* by Alexandra Munroe with Jon Hendricks et al. (New York: Japan Society and Harry Abrams, 2000), 289.

1. Cited in Jann S. Wenner, "The Ballad of John and Yoko," in Munroe, *Yes: Yoko Ono,* 58.

2. John Cage, "Interview with Michael Kirby and Richard Schechner," in *Happenings and Other Acts,* ed. Mariellen R. Sanford (New York: Routledge, 1995), 55.

3. Joan Rothfuss, "Somewhere for the Dust to Cling: Yoko Ono's Painting and Early Objects," in Munroe, *Yes: Yoko Ono,* 96.

4. For more discussion of the impact on Eastern philosophy on postwar American aesthetics, see Alexandra Munroe, "The Spirit of YES: The Art and Life of Yoko Ono," in Munroe, *Yes: Yoko Ono,* 16–22.

5. In her short biographical sketch of Ono, Munroe points out that "in 1952, Ono was accepted as the first female student to enter the philosophy course at Gakushin University" (ibid., 15).

6. Ibid., 13.

7. Kathy O'Dell, "Fluxus Feminus," *TDR* 41.1 (1997): 52.

8. Ibid., 55.

9. Kostelanetz, *Theatre of Mixed Means,* 34; emphasis added.

10. Jill Dolan, *Utopia in Performance* (Ann Arbor: University of Michigan Press, 2005), 17.

11. Kirby, *Happenings,* 17.

12. Yoko Ono, *Grapefruit* (New York: Simon and Schuster, 1964), n.p.

13. See Irving Sander, "The Duchamp-Cage Aesthetic," in *The New York School: The Painters and Sculptures of the Fifties* (New York: Harper and Row, 1978), 163–73.

14. Allan Kaprow, "Statement," in Kirby, *Happenings,* 44.

15. Allan Kaprow, "Happenings in the New York Scene," in *Blurring of Art and Life,* 17.

16. Allan Kaprow, "Pinpointing Happenings," in *Blurring of Art and Life,* 87.

17. Claus Oldenburg, *Store Days* (New York: Something Else Press, 1967), 10; emphasis added.

18. Yoko Ono, in Munroe, *Yes: Yoko Ono,* 268.

19. The specific piece to which Sell refers is Kaprow's *Eighteen Happenings in Six Parts,* and he bases his discussion of Kaprow's piece on Samuel Delaney's partial recollection of the happening as one of its participant/spectators. The above cited passages come from his article "Bad Memory: Text, Commodity, Happenings," in *Contours of the Theatrical Avant-Garde,* ed. James M. Harding (Ann Arbor: University of Michigan Press, 2000), 157, 158. Sell includes revised version of this article in his book *Avant-Garde Performance,* 146, 147.

20. This limited focus is actually one of the features that in general terms can be said to distinguish Fluxus events from the happenings. The former tend to be centered on a singular gesture and/or action, while the latter tend toward a simultaneous orchestration of a variety of activities. Interestingly, enough Ono's *Cut Piece* tends to skirt the fence of this distinction since an analysis of the piece necessitates some consideration not only of what transpired on the stage but also what took place simultaneously in the audience.

21. Ono, *Grapefruit,* n.p.

22. Quoted in Kristine Stiles, The Destruction in Art Symposium (DIAS): The Radical Cultural Porject of Event-Structured Live Art," Ph.D. diss., University of California, Berkeley, 1987, 610.

23. Cited in Martin Duberman, *Black Mountain: An Exploration in Community* (New York: Dutton, 1972), 357.

24. Interestingly enough, the moment of historical indeterminacy interjected by Nevin's account resembles the fluctuation between presence and absence that is generated by the radical juxtapositions of collage. Indeed, one of the primary effects of these gestures is the creation of overlapping yet contradictory, indeed, often mutually exclusive semiotic fields where a fluctuation between presence and absence is a central mechanism of its conceptual exploration of the production of meaning and knowledge, a mechanism that in Ono's performances of *Cut Piece* becomes a tool for an intensely self-reflective, critical examination of the unacknowledged performative traditions buried within collage aesthetics—traditions that strikingly echo the cultural imperialism or colonial underpinnings of modernism's more general fascination with primitivism. For a more detailed discussion of that fascination, see Schneider's *Explicit Body in Performance,* 126–51.

25. Shannon Jackson, *Professing Performance* (New York: Cambridge University Press, 2004), 131.

26. Ibid., 129.

27. Ibid.

28. Michael Kirby, "The New Theatre," in *Happenings and Other Acts,* ed. Mariellen Sandford (New York: Routledge, 1995), 31. Kirby's seminal essay was originally published in *Tulane Drama Review* 10.2 (1965): 23–43.

29. Shannon Jackson's careful comparison of Kirby's and Fried's fascination with "objecthood" is arguably the most interesting reading of Kirby in years, and I mention it here because the comparison leads her to the conclusion that, for Kirby, "nonmatrixed performance emphasized the performative—if not exactly theatrical—qualities of all levels of activity" (*Professing Performance,* 130). This conclusion is a necessary step in Jackson's compelling argument that Kirby's notions laid the foundation for what would ultimately become "performance studies." I am not particularly interested in challenging the disciplinary genealogy that Jackson develops—in part, because I think her argument is correct. But I do want to note that in its his-

torical context and in his book *Happenings,* this sense of the performative is not yet formulated and is certainly not emphasized. On the contrary, Kirby's agenda centers, like the agendas of many of his artistic contemporaries, on an idealized notion of the immediate, on what Jackson rightly describes as "non-matrixed literality," and on an "absolute reduction"—all of which his concept of nonmatrixed performance encourages us to believe are accessible and all of which are part of an "entire situation" that the nonmatrixed enables us to grasp (Jackson, 130, 131). If Jackson has reservations about the notion of "absolute reduction" (and she does), so too did Ono, and her performances of *Cut Piece* give a very good indication as to why.

30. James S. Moy, *Marginal Sights* (Iowa City: University of Iowa Press, 1993), 1.

31. Ibid.

32. Ibid., 8.

33. Ibid.

34. Ibid.

35. Ibid.

36. Ibid., 9.

37. Kirby, "The New Theatre," 33, 34.

38. Moy, *Marginal Sights,* 8.

39. Kirby, *Happenings,* 20.

40. Kirby, "The New Theatre," 35.

41. Moy, *Marginal Sights,* 8.

42. Marcel Duchamp, "The Creative Act," in *The Writings of Marcel Duchamp,* ed. Michael Sanouillet and Elmer Peterson (New York: Da Capo Press, 1973), 140.

43. Claus Oldenburg, "Statement," in Kirby, *Happenings,* 200.

44. Yoko Ono, "The World as Fabricator," in Munroe, *Yes: Yoko Ono,* 285.

45. Kristine Stiles, "Cut Piece," in Munroe, *Yes: Yoko Ono,* 158.

46. Indeed, Jieun Rhee has noted that at the time of her performance of *Cut Piece* in Japan, Ono already had a strained relationship with the Japanese public that was interested in the avant-garde. Rhee notes that two years prior to her performance of *Cut Piece,* when Ono traveled to Japan with her first husband Ichiyanagi, she "was treated as a rare (if not the only) 'female' member of the patriarchal world of the Japanese avant garde. As such, she was frequently the target of negative rumours—such as that she was a 'terrible wife,' or that she had a suspicious past" (Jieun Rhee, "Performing the Other: Yoko Ono's *Cut Piece,*" *Art History* 28.1 [2005]: 101).

47. Ibid.

48. Kristine Stiles, "Being Undyed," in Munroe, *Yes: Yoko Ono,* 147.

49. Moy, *Marginal Sights,* 8.

50. Kristine Stiles, "Between Water and Stone: Fluxus Performance: A Metaphysics of Acts," in *In the Spirit of Fluxus,* ed. Janet Jenkins (Minneapolis: Walker Arts Center, 1993), 77.

51. Cited in Kevin Concannon, "Yoko Ono's *Cut Piece* (1964): A Reconsideration," master's thesis, Virginia Commonwealth University, Richmond, 1998, 48. Preceding quotes from Concannon also come from page 48.

52. David Henry Hwang, *M. Butterfly* (New York: Plume, 1989), 95.

53. Oddly enough, Esther Kim Lee in *A History of Asian American Theatre* (New York: Cambridge University Press, 2006) doesn't discuss Ono either despite the fact that Lee has an entire section in her book devoted to "Avant-garde solo performance" (157–60) and despite the fact that Ono is one of the most prominent Asian Ameri-

can artists to have endured the full gamut of the female stereotypes that Lee argues were long established tropes in American theater at the time Ono was performing *Cut Piece.* Lee notes that prior to 1965 Asian women were consistently depicted in the theater as "either the innocent self-sacrificing lotus blossom or the much feared dragon lady" (13) In the 1960s, Ono had to endure being depicted as both.

54. Josephine Lee, *Performing Asian America* (Philadelphia: Temple University Press, 1997), 89.

55. Yoko Ono, "Biography/Statement," in Munroe, *Yes: Yoko Ono,* 301.

56. Ibid.

57. William Sonnega, "Beyond a Liberal Audience," in *African American Performance and Theater History,* ed. Harry J. Elam Jr. and David Krasner (New York: Oxford University Press, 2001), 87.

58. John O'Neal, "Motion in the Ocean: Some Political Dimensions of the Free Southern Theater" (1968), in *A Sourcebook of African-American Performance,* ed. Annemarie Bean (New York: Routledge, 1999), 116.

59. Ibid., 117.

60. Ono, "To the Wesleyan People," 289.

61. Ibid.

62. Ono, *Grapefruit* n.p.

63. Ibid., n.p.

64. The earliest score for *Cut Piece* reinforces this implication. In the collection of events that Ono scored for "Strip Tease Show" (1966) her instructions for *Cut Piece* refer to the performer with the then conventional usage of the masculine pronoun to signify both males and females.

CHAPTER FIVE

Cited in Schneemann, *More Than Meat Joy,* 278.

1. Schneemann, *More Than Meat Joy,* 153.

2. Briefly stated, Marcuse's theory of "repressive desublimation" characterizes an authoritarian political dymanic in which a socially cultivated desire for immediate gratification thwarts the social transformative power of sublimated desire. For Marcuse's full discussion of the concept of repressive desublimation, see his *One-Dimensional Man* (Boston: Beacon Press, 1964), 56–83.

3. Ibid., 70.

4. Ibid.

5. David Cooper, ed., *Dialectics of Liberation* (London: Penguin, 1968), 7.

6. Although there are numerous sources to back up this observation, it was initially brought to my attention by Dr. Craig Fees in an interview with him on July 21, 2004. Dr. Fees is the archivist at the Planned Environment Therapy Trust in Cheltenham where the archives for the Dialectics of Liberation Congress are held. I am extremely grateful to him not only for the generous assistance he provided me in the archives but also for the insightful conversations I had with him about the Congress, its organizers, and its participants.

7. Susan Sherman, "The Dialectics of Liberation," *Ikon* 1.4 (1967): 4.

8. Schneemann, *More Than Meat Joy,* 155.

9. Ibid., 52.

10. These descriptions are taken from the short definition of "Kinetic Theater" that Schneemann included in the one-page program that she prepared for her performance of *Round House.* The definition is included both in a draft copy of the program given to me by Schneemann and in the copy that is included in the archived papers of the Dialectics of Liberation Congress (PP/JB/IPS 5.3).

11. Again, these terms come from the definition of "Kinetic Theater" that Schneemann included in the one-page program for her performance of *Round House.*

12. Kristine Stiles, "Schlaget Auf: The Problem with Carolle Schneemann's Painting," in *Carolee Schneemann: Up to and Including Her Limits,* ed. David Cameron (New York: New Museum of Contemporary Art, 1996), 22.

13. Ibid.

14. Interview with Schneemann, New York City, April 15, 2004.

15. Marcuse, *One-Dimensional Man,* 70.

16. An anonymous account of one of the organizers's press conferences and a copy of the Congress poster were published in *Peace News,* June 16, 1967, 10.

17. *Peace News,* February 3, 1967, 4.

18. Quoted from original poster advertising the Congress, located in the Dialectics of Liberation Congress Archives (hereafter DLC Archives).

19. Quoted from original program to the Congress, copies of the program are located in the DLC Archives, and part of the program is published in Schneemann's *More Than Meat Joy,* 152.

20. Roger Barnard, "Round House Dialectics," *New Society,* August 3, 1967, 145.

21. Raymond Donovan, "The New Dialectics," unpublished manuscript (no date) located in the DLC Archives, PP/ JBS/IPS 5.25. In a letter from Donovan to Joseph Berke on *New Statesman* letterhead and dated August 4, 1967, Donovan speaks of plans to publish the aforementioned article on the Congress in the *New Statesman.* Berke sent a follow-up inquiring about the status of the piece to which Donovan responded, in a letter dated November 1, 1967, that the *New Statesman* "scrapped" the essay and "decided not to use it." Letters are also in the archive (PP/JBS/IPS).

22. Cited in Schneemann, *More Than Meat Joy,* 153.

23. The essay is included in Jacques Lacan, *The Four Fundamental Concepts of Psycho-analysis,* ed. Jacques-Alain Miller, trans. Alan Sheridan (New York: Norton, 1998).

24. Paul Goodman, "Objective Values," in Cooper, *Dialectics of Liberation,* 123.

25. Cited in Schneemann, *More Than Meat Joy,* 151. Schneemann attributed these comments to Cooper in an interview that I conducted with her on April 15, 2004.

26. This moment was documented in the Peter Davis's film *Anatomy of Violence* (Spectrum [Villion Films], 1967).

27. Quoted from original poster advertising the Congress, located in the DLC Archives.

28. Although the piece increasingly blurred the boundaries separating the participants from the audience, the performance was generally structured around two distinct groups of performers. There was a smaller group that included the principle participants and for obvious reasons was named the "core" group. This group included eight performers among whom were Schneemann, Michael Kustow, Brenda Dixon,

and Henry Martin. The second group, alternately identified as the "mass" group or chorus, had approximately twenty members. This group had a variety of roles, which Schneemann generally characterized as that of functioning "like a 'Greek chorus' enlarging aspects of movement and text" (Schneemann, *More Than Meat Joy,* 153), but they also had the particular assignment of interacting directly with the audience. In addition to these two groups, there was another visible group of around twenty members, some of whom worked as assistants and some of whom worked as the Roustabouts. Interestingly enough, the Roustabouts comprised young working-class men from the local community of Camden Town, which bordered Chalk Farm. Their participation in Schneemann's performance was one of the few instances in which the local working-class community took an active role in the Congress—a point that is not without its irony since Arnold Wesker had converted the Round House into a theater specifically so that it might cater to the working classes. Finally, of course, there was the audience itself, which was quite divided in its ongoing responses to the performance. Some were very supportive, while another large contingent repeatedly heckled the participants and inadvertently added an important layer of tension to the performance with their continual efforts to disrupt the event with catcalls.

29. Cited in Schneemann, *More Than Meat Joy,* 155.

30. Ibid.

31. Interview with Schneemann, April 15, 2004, New York City.

32. Schneemann, *More Than Meat Joy,* 156.

33. Quoted from original program to the Congress. Copies of the program are located in the DLC Archives, and part of the program is published in Schneemann's *More Than Meat Joy,* 152.

34. Ibid.

35. See Kristine Stiles's discussion of the Dialectics of Liberation Congress in "Sticks and Stones: The Destruction in Art Symposium," *Arts* 63:5 (January, 1989): 59–60; and also, her discussion of the Congress in "Survival Ethos and Destruction Art," *Discourse* 14.2 (1992): 85–86.

36. Stiles, "Survival Ethos," 83.

37. Hermann Nitsch, "Action 21, Fifth Abreaction Play: Destruction in Art Symposium," in *Writings of the Vienna Actionists,* ed. Malcolm Green (London: Atlas Press, 1999), 150.

38. Malcolm Green notes that rather than giving the police Nitsch's copy of the film *Penis Rinsings,* the Actionist Ralph Oritz actually gave them "a reel of unexposed film." This reference as well as the account of the police searching Nitsch in the toilet can both be found in Green, *Writings of Vienna Actionists,* 228.

39. I am indebted to correspondence with Kristine Stiles for this important bit of information. In email correspondence from October 5, 2004, she wrote to me: "No charges were brought against Nitsch. What could the Brits do? Hold a bunch of crazy Viennese for obscenity? No. Anyway, the law was after Metzger and Sharkey for staging DIAS."

40. Green, *Writings of Vienna Actionists,* 228.

41. Letter to Joseph Berke, June 9, 1967 (ellipses and punctuation Schneemann's) (PP/JB/IPS 10.4).

42. Kristine Stiles, email to the author, October 4, 2004.

43. http://news.bbc.co.uk/onthisday/hi/dates/stories/may/10/newsid_25220 00 /2522735.stm. Accessed October 1, 2004.

44. As Kristine Stiles notes in "Survival Ethos," the Congress "coincided precisely with the three-day trial of Metzger and the Irish poet and playwright John Sharkey, Metzger's principal assistant in the organization of DIAS" (85).

45. Kristine Stiles, "Synopsis of the Destruction in Art Symposium," *The Act* 1.2 (1987): 26.

46. Ibid.

47. Green, *Writings of Vienna Actionists,* 228.

48. Davis's film *Anatomy of Violence* provides the only available cinematic documentation of the Dialectics of Liberation Congress. Apparently, there was a second, longer documentary of the Congress made by Roy Battersby for the British Broadcasting Company. This TV feature, which was entitled *Hit Suddenly Hit,* was never shown, and for reasons that have never been clarified, it was confiscated by the BBC and placed under lock and key in a safe where not even Battersby was able to gain access to it again. Accounts of this bizarre treatment of Battersby's film were first conveyed to me in an email from Joseph Berke (dated January 27, 2004) in which he also speculated that the film "may have been destroyed." These comments are confirmed by documentation of Battersby's film and its strange history that I found in the loose papers on the Congress included in the file/folder "Seminar Proposals That People Said They Were Prepared to Give" (PP/JB/IPS 5.3) in DLC Archives. A short typewritten note provides an almost verbatim account of the history that Berke mentioned to me in his email.

49. Kristine Stiles, email to the author, October 4, 2004.

50. In 1967, James Harold Wilson was head of the Labour Party, which was then in power. He served as prime minister from 1964 to 1970 and then again from 1974 to 1976 when Great Britain was experiencing a period of economic difficulties and, for motives that remain unclear, he announced his resignation.

51. See Roger Barnard's very similar description of Carmichael in "Round House Dialectics," 145. Barnard, while supportive of Carmichael's interpretation of black power and analysis of the plight of people of color in the third world, is nonetheless intensely critical of what he perceived as Carmichael's "demagogery" (145).

52. Gajo Petrovi, "The Dialectics of Liberation," *Praxis: Revue Philosophique* 4 (1967): 610.

53. Ibid.

54. Ibid.

55. Petrovi notes in the introduction to his discussion of the Dialectics of Liberation Congress that "the critique of contemporary conservative and inhuman psychiatry and psychoanalysis" that characterized the work of Laing, Berke, Cooper, and Redler was derived largely from "humanistic philosophy and sociology" (ibid., 606).

56. Sherman, "The Dialectics of Liberation," 4.

57. While both of these papers were ultimately far too focused on issues of culture to be included in David Cooper's *Dialectics of Liberation,* a letter from Berke to Beck dated August 11 (no year listed, presumably 1967) indicates that initially there were plans to include Beck's talk in Cooper's anthology (letter included in DLC Archives, PP/JB/IPS 4.13). The reading of these two papers by Ginsberg and Beck was, however, included among twenty-seven record albums that documented the proceedings of the Congress. Cooper's anthology and the album collection of the Congress proceedings were shrewdly marketed by the organizers as a strategy for recouping the costs of the Congress itself, which received neither state support, grants,

or foundation monies and which was initially bankrolled by the organizers. Oft overlooked is a third publication associated with the Dialectics of Liberation Congress, namely Joseph Berke's *Counter-culture: The Creation of an Alternative Society* (London: Peter Owen, 1969). This anthology contained many of the talks that Cooper had decided not to include in *Dialectics of Liberation*. Among the essays included in Berke's anthology were the pieces by Ginsberg and Beck, and in fact the entire anthology was more concerned with questions of culture than Cooper's earlier book. Arguably, the disciplinary divisions that distinguish Cooper's anthology from Berke's anthology are a telling sign of the secondary status assigned to cultural concerns within the Congress itself.

58. In his letter of invitation to Paul Goodman (dated November 4, 1966), Joseph Berke also offered Goodman accommodations in a country house called Rotherfield Hall, where "the principal invitees will be able to stay," adding of course that "wives or girl-friends . . . would be very welcome at Rotherfield Hall." A copy of the letter is included in the DLC Archives, PP/JB/IPS 10.3.

59. This description of the accommodations is included in Berke's letter of invitation to Allen Ginsberg (dated November 8, 1966). A copy of the letter is included in the DLC Archives, PP/JB/IPS 10.3.

60. Sherman mentions this administrative work in a letter to Berke (dated July 1, 1967). In that same letter, Sherman is pleading for airfare. Despite the work that she did for the Congress, there is no clear indication that airfare ever came through. Her letter to Berke is included in the DLC Archives, PP/JB/IPS 10.4.

61. "The Institute of Phenomenological Studies," DLC Archives, PP/JB/IPS 5.25. This flyer, which is included among the papers for the Congress, was the programmatic statement of the Institute of Phenomenological Studies. The institute was more of a name than an actuality. As I mentioned in my introduction, the institute existed for the sole function of administering the Dialectics of Liberation Congress. It was founded in 1966 and continued to exist (on paper) only until all financial matters related to the Congress were resolved.

62. Ibid.

63. Ibid.

64. When Berke published *Counter-culture* in 1969, he had formally taken to calling the Dialectics of Liberation Congress an "(Anti) Congress." See his discussion of the Congress and the relation of *Counter-Culture* to it on page 410 of his anthology. But the tendency was already evident in letters of invitation that he sent out late in June 1967, some two weeks before the Congress began. In fact, Berke described the Congress as an anti-Congress in the official letter of invitation that he sent to Julian Beck (dated June 28, 1967), a letter that encouraged the entire Living Theatre to come and participate but offered no financial support or lodging to them. Given the late date of the letter and the lack of financial support or accommodations, it is little wonder that Beck arrived alone at the Congress (letter included in the DLC Archives, PP / JB / IPS 4.13).

65. Stiles, "Sticks and Stones," 60.

66. Ibid.

67. The reference here is obviously *De la grammatologie* (*Of Grammatology*), first published in France by Les Editions de Minuit in 1967.

68. John Gerasis, "Imperialism and Revolution in America," Cooper, *Dialectics of Liberation*, 90.

69. For Marcuse's comments on the PROVOS and the Diggers, see "Liberation from the Affluent Society," in Cooper, *Dialectics of Liberation,* 190.

70. Ibid., 185–86.

71. Marcuse's exact comment was "And now I throw in the terrible concept: it would mean an 'aesthetic' reality—society as a work of art" (ibid., 185).

72. Schneemann, *More Than Meat Joy,* 156.

73. On this point see Schneider, *Explicit Body in Performance,* 71–77.

74. Schneemann, *More Than Meat Joy,* 156.

75. The draft copy comes from Schneemann's personal files. The actual program is located in the DLC Archives, PP/JB/IPS 5.3.

76. Schneemann, *More Than Meat Joy,* 156.

77. R. D. Laing, "The Obvious," in Cooper, *Dialectics of Liberation,* 26.

78. Volkmar Sanders, *Mutter Courage und Ihre Kinder* (New York: Oxford University Press, 1964), xvii.

79. The score implies that the cocooned members of core group were rescued, first by the chorus placing them together in a pile, and second by the chorus loading them back onto the wagon and carting them away once *Viet Flakes* had ended, the lights had dimmed, and the collage of music had reverted back to unspecified songs by the Beatles. Once the performers had all left the stage, a local band called the Social Deviants, whose front man was Mick Farren, "plugged in their amplifiers and began to play" and "the audience got up and danced in the debris" (*More Than Meat Joy* 157).

80. Erika Fischer-Lichte, "The Avant-Garde and the Semiotics of the Antitextual Gesture," in Harding, *Contours,* 90.

CHAPTER SIX

1. Laura Winkiel, "The 'Sweet Assassin' and the Performative Politics of *SCUM Manifesto,*" in *The Queer Sixties,* ed. Patricia Juliana Smith (New York: Routledge, 1999), 72.

2. Victor Bockris, *The Life and Death of Andy Warhol* (New York: Bantam Books, 1989), 233. Oddly, a non sequitur characterizes the critical reception of Solanas's own explanation of her assault on Warhol, one that privileges textual authority over Solanas's politically charged act of violence. Typical in this respect is Laura Winkiel's leap from Solanas's explanation into a full-scale subordination of her act to the primacy and authority of her manifesto:

> When asked for a motive for the shooting during an impromptu press conference . . . [Solanas] said: "I have a lot of very involved reasons. Read my manifesto and it will tell you what I am." . . . Solanas thus deferred an explanation for the shooting to a reading of her manifesto, a document that performs a political identity. . . . It, in effect, creates the political actors by calling them into being, providing a script for action that is not based on a prior stable identity. ("Sweet Assassin," 62–63)

In fact, Solanas does not defer to her manifesto. Rather she sidesteps the question, leaving her "very involved reasons" vague. Reading her manifesto will not clarify why she shot Warhol. It will only clarify who she is. Rather than subordinating her act of violence to the so-called script of her manifesto, her statement tends instead to place her act and manifesto on a par.

3. Andy Warhol and Pat Hackett, *POPism: The Warhol 60s* (New York: Harcourt Brace Jovanovich, 1980), 277.

4. Bockris, *Life and Death,* 232.

5. Marcie Frank, "Popping Off Warhol: From the Gutter to the Underground and Beyond," in *Pop Out: Queer Warhol,* ed. Jennifer Doyle, Jonathan Flatley, and José Esteban Muñoz (Durham, NC: Duke University Press, 1996), 211.

6. Winkiel actually argues that the sanitary pad symbolized castration, which strikes me as being an equally plausible reading of the peculiar contents in the bag that Solanas left at Warhol's Factory. That reading, when combined with my suggestion that the napkin broke a conventional social code of silence about women's basic experiences, transforms the napkin into one of the most profoundly rich symbols at the site of Solanas's shooting of Warhol, and even this does not begin to address the streetwise revolutionary guerilla savvy evident in Solanas's decision to bring a feminine napkin with her. It is after all perhaps the most readily accessible temporary dressing in the event of a flesh wound.

7. Andy Warhol, *The Philosophy of Andy Warhol* (San Diego: Harcourt Brace, 1975), 78.

8. Oddly, this subordination of Solanas to a kind of publicity mongering is as true of those who have held her in contempt as it largely is for those who have defended her as a significant figure of militant feminism—as was the case, for example, with Florynce Kennedy and Grace Atkinson, founding members of the New York chapter of the National Organization of Women, who orchestrated both a legal and public defense of Solanas as "one of the most important spokeswomen of the feminist movement" (Frank, "Popping Off Warhol," 210). While Warhol's entourage maintained that Solanas violently exploited Warhol in a perverse shot at personal fame, feminists like Kennedy and Atkinson argued that Solanas did so in a misguided shot at publicizing an otherwise neglected and marginalized cause.

9. Mary Harron, dir., *I Shot Andy Warhol* (Los Angeles: Orion Pictures, 1996).

10. Andy Warhol, Kasper König, et al., eds., *Andy Warhol* (Stockholm: Moderna Museet, 1968), n.p.

11. Valerie Solanas, *SCUM Manifesto* (1967; San Francisco: AK Press, 1997).

12. Warhol and Hackett, *POPism,* 276.

13. Janet Lyon, *Manifestoes: Provocations of the Modern* (Ithaca, NY: Cornell University Press, 1999), 174. Even a quick perusal of Solanas's manifesto will reveal that it contains many of the characteristic stances of the historical avant-garde. The epitome of this stance is the anticultural attitudes that permeate the manifesto, and while on the one hand it is certainly true as Heckleman argues that Solanas's rejection of Great Art and Culture reaffirms her rejection of male culture and the status quo, these same rejections place her well within the boundaries of the avant-garde (Solanas, *SCUM Manifesto,* 38; Leah Hackleman, "Plastic Man versus the Sweet Assassin," in *Sexual Artifice,* ed. Ann Kibby, Kayann Short, and Abouali Farmanfarmaian [New York: New York University Press, 1994], 139).

14. Solanas. *SCUM Manifesto,* 43.

15. Ibid.

16. Arthur Danto argues that "Warhol's thought that anything could be art was a model, in a way, for the hope that human beings could be anything they chose,

once the divisions that had defined the culture were overthrown" (*Beyond the Brillo Box* [New York: Farrar, Straus and Giroux, 1992], 4), If as Danto maintains "what Warhol's dictum amounted to was that you cannot *tell* when something is a work of art just by looking at it, for there is no particular way that art has to look" (5), Solanas, as will be apparent momentarily, countered by implicitly identifying the patriarchal gaze from which even Warhol's art was viewed.

17. Stephen C. Foster, "Event Structures and Art Situations," in *"Event" Arts and Art Events,* ed. Stephen C. Foster (Ann Arbor: UMI Research Press, 1988), 5.

18. Solanas, *SCUM Manifesto,* 26.

19. Ibid., 26.

20. Cited in Bockris, *Life and Death,* 233.

21. Solanas, *SCUM Manifesto,* 43.

22. Hackleman, "Plastic Man," 130.

23. Melissa Deem, "From Bobbitt to SCUM: Re-memberment, Scatological Rhetorics, and Feminist Strategies in the Contemporary United States," *Public Culture* 8.3 (1996): 521.

24. Ibid., 524. Deem's discussion of the concept of a minor literature refers to Gilles Deleuze and Félix Guattari, *Kafka: Toward a Minor Literature* (Minneapolis: University of Minnesota Press, 1986).

25. Frank, "Popping Off Warhol," 214. At one level, Frank's article differs from Deem's in that it offers a pointed critique of the patronizing handling of Solanas that Deem's article continues. Frank is, for example, quite critical of Grace Atkinson and Florynce Kennedy (the members of NOW who publically rallied to Solanas's defense in June 1968) and especially of their attempts "to recuperate . . . [Solanas] as a feminist hero" by characterizing her as a figure comparable to Jean Genet, a characterization that Solanas herself emphatically rejected (Frank, "Popping Off Warhol," 221).

26. Martin Puchner, *Poetry of the Revolution* (Princeton: Princeton University Press, 2006), 5.

27. Ibid., 85.

28. Stephen Koch, *Stargazer* (New York: Marion Boyars, 1991), 130.

29. This aspect of Solanas's manifesto makes it a precursor to the rhetorical strategies later developed by groups like Queer Nation.

30. Lyon, *Manifestoes,* 9, 10.

31. Susan Rubin Suleiman, *Subversive Intent: Gender, Politics and the Avant-Garde* (Cambridge: Harvard University Press, 1990).14. Suleiman also argues: "In a system in which the marginal, the avant-garde, the subversive, all that disturbs and 'undoes the whole' is endowed with positive value, a woman artist who can identify those concepts with her own practice and metaphorically with her own femininity can find in them a source of strength and self-legitimation. Perhaps no one has done this more successfully than Hélène Cixous. Her famous essay, 'Le Rire de la Méduse' ('The Laugh of the Medusa', 1975) is the closest thing to an avant-garde manifesto written from an explicitly feminist perspective" (17), Obviously, Suleiman, whose book is primarily concerned with French literature, was unaware of Solanas's manifesto, which predates Cixous's "Le Rire de la Méduse" by almost a decade.

32. Lyon, *Manifestoes,* 14.

33. What is also amazing about the political agenda that Solanas pursues is its avoidance of troubling hierarchical political structures. While it is true, as Janet Lyon argues, that the manifesto "participates in an anarcho-libertarian tradition according

to which individual liberation is linked to the overthrow of capitalism," the political activism of that anarcho-libertarian tradition amounts to a radical juxtaposition of autonomous elements, coincidently working in concert—its own type of collage (Lyon, *Manifestoes,* 174). Indeed, Solanas's political conceptions echo the manner in which collage aesthetic runs counter to systematic thought:

> Like the anarchism promoted in the post-situationist strain of sixties radicalism—itself a mixture of direct action and theatrical improvisation—Solanas's salutary lawlessness bespeaks more a faith in anti-institutional spontaneous intervention than a belief in any kind of careful engagement with systematic critiques of capitalism. (174)

34. Hélène Cixous, "The Laugh of the Medusa" (1975), in *Critical Theory since 1965,* ed. Hazard Adams and Leroy Searle (Tallahassee: Florida State University Press, 1986), 316.

35. Ibid., 317.

36. Solanas, *SCUM Manifesto,* 7, 21.

37. Cited in Maud Lavin, *Cut with the Kitchen Knife* (New Haven: Yale University Press, 1993), 26. As those who are familiar with the history of Berlin Dada already know, Hausmann had trouble practicing what he preached. Despite his famous ongoing affair with Hanna Höch, he was never willing to give up his own rather bourgeois marriage. More to the point, though he and Höch both were interested in the "mechanical . . . and proletarian . . . connotations associated with photomontage," his support of Höch's participation in Berlin Dadaists' activities evaporated as soon as she no longer wanted to be his lover (Peter Boswell and Maria Makela, organizers, *The Photomontages of Hanna Höch* [Minneapolis: Walker Art Center, 1996], n.p.).

38. Sally Banes, *Greenwich Village, 1963* (Durham, NC: Duke University Press, 1993), 94–95.

39. Ibid., 219.

40. Michael Moon, "Screen Memories, or, Pop Comes from the Outside: Warhol and Queer Childhood," in Doyle, Flatley, and Muñoz, *Pop Out,* 84, 85. If, as Janet Lyon argues, "SCUM is the vengeful, victorious daughter of the avant-garde manifestoes of Apollinaire, Tzara, Mainetti, Debord," the list of patriarchal figures against whom Solanas rebels has to be extended to include Warhol, who, named the "Pope of Pop" by the mass media, was thus the quintessential father figure and ironically buried Solanas in a bit part in his 1967 film *I, a Man* (Lyon, *Manifestoes,* 175).

41. Lora Rempel, "The Anti-body in Photomontage: Hannah Höch's Woman without Wholeness," in Kibby, Short, and Farmanfarmaian, *Sexual Artifice,* 155.

42. F. T. Marinetti, "The Founding Manifesto of Futurism," in *Futurist Manifestos,* ed. Umbro Apollonio, trans. R. W. Flint (New York: Viking Press, 1973), 251.

43. André Breton, *Manifestoes of Surrealism,* trans. Richard Seaver and Helen R. Lane (Ann Arbor: University of Michigan Press, 1972), 125. As Laurence Senelick has noted, Breton was certainly not the only one to associate the use of a gun with avant-garde activity. Senelick cites two other memorable instances. "Huelsenbeck," he notes, "claimed that he and plants in the audience exchanged blank gunfire at his dada lectures" and "Jacque Vaché, one of Jarry's fondest admirers (Jarry had been notorious for random fusillades at home and in cafés), came to the opening night of Apollinaire's *Les Mamelles de Tirésias* brandishing a revolver and threatening to fire into the audience. The gunshot that had so often marked the climax of nineteenth-

century drama crossed the footlights to become part of an exchange between the public and the spectacle" (Laurence Senelick, "Text and Violence: Performance Practices of the Modernist Avant-Garde," in Harding, *Contours,* 28), As Senelick notes, these violent antics that continued to escalate as the twentieth century progressed were typical of the avant-garde: "Willed self-annihilation is built into the avant-garde program, and in the process the individual human being is first reduced to sheer body and then becomes sacrificed to the machine" (Senelick, "Text and Violence" 29).

44. Interestingly enough, Solanas's assault on Warhol's body finds as striking parallel in the attitude that the theatrical avant-garde took toward classical texts in the 1960s. Some sense of that attitude is conveyed in Erika Fischer-Lichte's article "The Avant-Garde and the Antitextual Gesture," where she characterizes the avant-garde's ambivalent relations to classical texts as a form of *Sparagmos:*

> This manner of dealing with classical text was taken up again in the sixties and seventies by Grotowski, Schechner, Zadek, Peymann, and others. What happened in each of these instances can perhaps be described as *Sparagmos:* tearing apart and incorporation of textual bodies in which we symbolize our cultural traditions, indeed in which we see our culture embodied. With *Sparagmos,* which in such productions was realized, the textual body supplanted the totem, the is, the sacrificial victim. The process unfolded exactly like a Greek sacrificial meal. . . . In the performance, the cultural tradition incorporated in and handed down by the text was thus questioned and examined for validity by the performers and audience on—or rather through—their own bodies. (90)

45. Boswell and Makela, *Photomontages of Hannah Höch,* 25.

46. Solanas, *SCUM Manifesto,* 25.

47. It is in this interview that Solanas tells Robert Marmorstein that SCUM stands for the "Society for Cutting Up Men" (Robert Marmorstein, "A Winter Memory of Valerie Solanis [*sic*], *Village Voice,* June 13, 1968, 9). Her manifesto also attracted the interest of Maurice Girodias from Olympia Press, the publisher of Nabokov's *Lolita* and Miller's *Tropic of Cancer.* Girodias even paid Solanas an advance to make a novel out of the manifesto (Freddie Baer, "About Valerie Solanas," in Solanas, *SCUM Manifesto,* 49).

48. As it turns out, the manuscript was not thrown away as many have speculated. Indeed, thirty years after the shooting the manuscript turned up in the Andy Warhol museum at a showing about Solanas and the shooting. George Coates saw the manuscript and decided to produce it. His production had its premier in San Francisco in January 2000. As Judith Coburn notes in her review of the Coates production:

> Coates discovered *Up Your Ass* in a small Solanas show Pittsburgh's Andy Warhol Museum had put up to mark the 30th anniversary of the shooting. Turns out the copy Warhol lost had been buried under lighting equipment in a silver trunk owned by photographer Billy Name, famous for covering the original Factory with aluminum foil. (Judith Coburn, "Solanas Lost and Found," *Village Voice,* January 12–18, 2000, http://www.villagevoice.com/news/0002,coburn,11718,1.html, accessed August 18, 2007)

49. Baer, "About Valerie Solanas," 48–49.

50. Solanas, *SCUM Manifesto,* 25.

51. Ibid., 43.

52. Bockris, *Life and Death,* 207.

53. Kathy O'Dell, *Contract with the Skin* (Minneapolis: University of Minnesota Press, 1998), 1.

54. Walter Benjamin, *Illuminations,* ed. Hannah Arendt, trans. Harry Zohn (New York: Schocken, 1968), 256 (translation corrected).

55. Marvin Carlson notes that in the early sixties Yves Klein attempted to blur the female body with the act of painting in his *Anthropometries of the Blue Period,* which "presented nude models covered with blue paint pressing against a canvas like living brushes. In Milan the following year, Piero Manzoni went further still, converting living bodies into 'authentic works of art' by signing them as if they were paintings" (*Performance: A Critical Introduction* [New York: Routledge, 1996], 96).

56. The interesting subtext to the exposed scars in Avedon's photographs goes well beyond an affirmation of Warhol's "resurrection" after having been pronounced clinically dead in the emergency room. Shortly before the shooting, Warhol had created a scandal and was even facing lawsuits because he had sent an imposter to a series of universities where he was paid to give lectures. Solanas's "marking" of Warhol's body immediately became a kind of signature of authenticity, identifying the "real" and "true" Warhol at a time when the authenticity of his person was a major artistic and legal issue. Avedon's photographic reproduction of Warhol as well as Alice Neel's 1970 portrait of him thus carry a historic, ironic undercurrent in that as works of art they openly play with, while simultaneously abandoning, direct claims to authenticity. At one level, they are reproductions and ultimately a subtle affirmation of Solanas's work as a work of art. At another level, they also suggest, as reproductions, that if the object of the universities in contracting Warhol to lecture on art was to convey an understanding of the mechanisms of art, then Warhol had arguably fulfilled his obligation precisely because he sent a reproduction. The imposter as imposter was a lesson in art—not to mention the fact that he was , by Warhol's own admission , more eloquent on the subject of art than Warhol himself could ever be.

57. Victor Bockris speaks about the politically polarizing effect of Solanas's assault on Warhol and specifically how the act politicized Warhol himself:

> As had happened so often in his life, the shooting polarized feelings about Andy Warhol. At one extreme were those from whom he had now attained a Christlike martyrdom. At the very least, having been attacked for "political" reasons, he must now be viewed as a political artist. At the other pole were the feminist revolutionaries. One group calling itself the "Up Against the Wall Motherfuckers" brought out a pamphlet entitled "Valerie lives," in which Solanas was described as a "chick with balls" and her victim as a "plastic fascist." (Bockris, *Life and Death,* 236)

58. See Hal Foster, *The Return of the Real* (Cambridge: MIT Press, 1996).

59. This information is based on Freddie Baer's biographical sketch. See Baer, "About Valerie Solanas," 54–56.

CONCLUSION

1. Puchner, *Poetry of the Revolution,* 214.

2. Ibid., 216.

3. Canning, *Feminist Theaters,* 64–65.

4. James Harding and Cindy Rosenthal, "Between Characteristics, Continuities and Change—Theorizing the Legacy of Radical Theaters," in *Restaging the Sixties,* ed. James Harding and Cindy Rosenthal (Ann Arbor: University of Michigan Press, 2006), 9.

5. Canning, *Feminist Theaters,* 60.

6. Ibid., 63.

7. James Harding, introduction to *Contours,* 10.

8. Bürger, *Theory of the Avant-Garde,* 51.

9. Rebecca Schneider, "Solo, Solo, Solo," in *After Criticism: New Responses to Art and Performance,* ed. Gavin Butt (Oxford: Wiley-Blackwell, 2004), 25–26.

Index